An Anthology of Ancient and Medieval Woman's Song

An Anthology of Ancient and Medieval Woman's Song

Edited by Anne L. Klinck

First published 2004 by
PALGRAVE MACMILLAN™
175 Fifth Avenue, New York, N.Y. 10010 and
Houndmills, Basingstoke, Hampshire, England RG21 6XS
Companies and representatives throughout the world

PALGRAVE MACMILLAN is the global academic imprint of the Palgrave Macmillan division of St. Martin's Press, LLC and of Palgrave Macmillan Ltd. Macmillan® is a registered trademark in the United States, United Kingdom and other countries. Palgrave is a registered trademark in the European Union and other countries.

ISBN 1–4039–6309–6 hardback
ISBN 1–4039–6310–X paperback

Library of Congress Cataloging-in-Publication Data
    An anthology of ancient and medieval woman's song / edited by
Anne L. Klinck.
       p. cm.
    Includes bibliographical references and index
    ISBN 1–4039–6309–6 (hc)—1–4039–6310–X (pbk.)
    1. Poetry, Ancient. 2. Poetry, Medieval. 3. Lyric poetry. 4. Poetry,
Ancient—History and criticism. 5. Poetry, Medieval—History and criticism.
6. Lyric poetry—History and criticism. 7. Women in literature. I. Klinck,
Anne Lingard, 1943–

  PN6101.A49 2004
    808.81'4083522—dc22   2003065607

A catalogue record for this book is available from the British Library.

Design by Newgen Imaging Systems (P) Ltd., Chennai, India.

First edition: February 2004
10 9 8 7 6 5 4 3 2 1

Printed in the United States of America.

CONTENTS

PREFACE

This book has arisen out of two long-standing interests—in early poetry, and in the representation of women. I came to "woman's song" via two Old English elegiac poems, *The Wife's Lament* and *Wulf and Eadwacer*, which had been compared with Continental poems of a somewhat similar kind. As an Anglo-Saxonist and in a secondary way a classicist, it was natural for me to make connections too with the ancient world. It struck me that this poetry in the voice of an eager, desiring woman was a noticeable phenomenon there, especially in archaic Greece. Let me emphasize, however, that I prefer to see woman's song, in all periods and whether composed in writing or orally, as a literary construct, rather than a primeval form growing out of the eternal feminine, its sincerity, and its closeness to nature.

Bringing together a diverse collection of woman's songs, united by recurrent themes, patterns, and motifs, has been a stimulating and challenging task, and many people have helped me with their expertise and generosity. Most of the translations are my own. Those from Arabic are English renditions of Teresa Garulo's Spanish in her *Dīwān de las poetisas de al-Andalus*. The translation from Irish has been taken from Ann Dooley and Harry Roe's *Tales of the Elders of Ireland*. I would like to warmly thank all the people who have contributed to this book by suggesting materials for inclusion, pointing out more accurate—or more poetic—translations, and rescuing me from blunders: Susan Boynton, Matilda Bruckner, Teresa Garulo, John Geyssen, Joan Grimbert, William Kerr, Bonnie MacLachlan, Nadia Margolis, Leslie Morgan, Ann Marie Rasmussen, Andrea Schutz, and Joseph Snow. Needless to say, they are not to blame for the defects that remain. I owe a special debt to Teresa Garulo, who contributed the poems by the Muslim princess Wallada, and patiently helped me with the transliteration of Arabic. A significant contribution has also been made by my research assistants, Allison Comeau and Alexandre Santos, who have assisted me with this project over a period of years, and enabled me to bring it to completion.

ANNE KLINCK
Fredericton, Canada, May 2003

Preparation of the Texts and Translations

I have simplified the conventional editorial marks indicating textual problems. Omission marks are employed for badly damaged or missing words and passages, as well as for skipped sections; a dagger indicates unreconstructed faulty text. Restorations and emendations are silently incorporated; if large or controversial, they are commented on in the Textual Notes. Square brackets are used for editorial insertions.

My translations aim to give a sense of the shape and tone of the original, but I have only occasionally attempted to reproduce rhyme, and never meter in any exact way. For the most part, translations are line-for-line; I have diverged slightly from this arrangement where it would have made the English awkward. On the rare occasions where my translation is very free, I supply a literal version in the Notes.

The translation from Middle Irish is by Ann Dooley and Harry Roe; that from Arabic is via the Spanish of Teresa Garulo. The Galician-Portuguese and Castilian sections have benefited from the sensitive suggestions of Joseph Snow.

Introduction

"I think he's equal to the gods, that man" (ancient Greece), "I tell this tale of my own sad self" (Anglo-Saxon England), "I am, by God, made for glory!" (Muslim Spain), "I feed on joy and youth" (Provence), "Fie, husband, on your love!" (medieval France), "Under the linden on the heath" (medieval Germany), "Hey nonny! I will love Sir John if I love anyone!" (late medieval England). These quotations are all the beginnings of "woman's songs"; that is, poems in which spirited women talk about love. Usually these poems express feelings toward men, but the first example quoted above declares a passion for another woman, and the man is just a foil. Starting with early Greece, and continuing with ancient Rome and medieval Europe, this anthology brings together a collection of women's voices as they speak and sing about love, or, less romantically, about sexual relationships.

"Woman's songs" is not a term that has been much used in writing about English literature. It translates *Frauenlieder* and *chansons de femme*, and means "songs narrated by women," not "songs composed by women"—although some of those in this collection are.[1] All the pieces here have a woman speaker and, broadly interpreted, an erotic theme or connection. I have picked poems and passages that appeal to me personally and that resonate with other poems and passages in this book. The voices in these poems, whether authored by women or by men, clearly emerge as contrastive to male voices. Again and again, in the poems that follow, we find a woman's voice protesting against a male-imposed state of affairs and elevating the private over the public, the individual over the group, personal ties over social responsibilities. We shall see these attitudes recurring, in poems widely separated in space and time.

Some, but not all, of these poems are "popular," in the sense of "belonging to ordinary people" and thus being composed in a lower rather than in a high style. The word *popularizing* is sometimes used, translating "popularisant," as opposed to *aristocratisant*, and drawing on the French medievalist Pierre Bec's view of two contrasting registers.[2] This lower-style poetry, has "a strong link with dance, with narrative and with refrain form."[3] In France and the Romance-language countries, especially, it often functions as a counter to courtly poetry in the high style. Calling such poems "popular" is a bit misleading, since songs of this type were enjoyed by all classes, and although they were sometimes contrastive to aristocratic or learned poetry, they could merge with it too—as we shall see.

A word needs to be said also about focussing on voice rather than authorship. The study of works *by* women and of works *about* women tends to be separated, but I believe it can very usefully be brought together. Doing so invites comparison between male-authored, female-authored, and anonymous works on the same subject. We can consider authorial gender when known, as well as analysing femininity within texts—and assessing the relationship between the two. That is, to use the terminology devised by Bec, we can look at *féminité textuelle*, without neglecting *féminité génétique*.[4] Also, choosing voice rather than authorship as the basis for a collection is an approach that is especially appropriate to the largely oral societies of the ancient world and the Middle Ages. The notion of a text as the property of a particular author, a thing conceived in writing, fixed on paper, and communicated by silent private reading is a relatively late development. All of the poems included here were designed to be performed aloud to an audience; many were intended to be sung, although, sadly, the music has been lost in the majority of cases. Some songs were also accompanied by dance. The modern clear distinction between composer and performer did not exist in the Middle Ages—or earlier.[5]

In selecting the poems that follow, I have tried to demonstrate a certain coherence while at the same time casting my net quite wide. The examples that I gather, rather eclectically, comprise not only monologue, but also dialogue if the woman's part dominates, and speech set in a narrative frame. I include as well poems that many scholars would reject as not "popular," notably those composed by known aristocratic women, like the trobairitz, the women troubadours of southern France.[6] In order to illustrate the connection between the ritual and the personal in early poetry, I have brought in poems with a cultic function in the section on ancient Greece. But since the focus of this book is essentially secular, I have excluded Christian devotional poetry. There are, of course, some close parallels between devotional and love poetry, Christ, Mary, and the Church often being addressed as the beloved. Conversely, the sentiment and the language of religious devotion are often incorporated into purely secular erotic verse. Nevertheless, the divide between the sacred and the profane is clear in the medieval period, whereas in archaic Greece, they are not separated in this way, but reinforce each other. For the overall arrangement I have grouped the selected pieces into a series of clusters by language and nationality in a loosely chronological sequence. Since ethnic grouping and chronological arrangement don't always coincide, there is inevitably some backtracking, for example, with Old Norse immediately following Old English and preceding Arabic and Mozarabic in Spain, and medieval Latin placed rather arbitrarily before the German poems because the two principal medieval miscellanies of Latin lyrics were compiled in Germany.

Reading and comparing the poems in this collection will show how, in addition to the general subject of love or sexuality, certain characteristic attitudes, themes, motifs, and patterns recur: absent lover remembered with pain or pleasure; appeal to mother or friends; emphasis on the physical body; rural, spring setting; singing and dancing; seduction attempted successfully or unsuccessfully; boorish husband contrasted with charming lover; symbolic objects like water, trees, birds; stanzaic structure with repetition or refrain. Whether or not these poems are popular, many of them are anonymous, and seem to be the product of oral culture. But some—the Latin ones, for instance—are highly literate. Again, woman's song is typically characterized by an *apparently* artless eroticism. But very often, perhaps usually, the artlessness is deliberately contrived, and sometimes it masks very subtle effects. Because most of the surviving examples are either anonymous or male-authored it is often inferred that this type of poetry reflects a male perspective. And, to be sure, these speakers are for the most part young, beautiful, and outspokenly in love.

The poems raise some fascinating questions about which scholars debate, and readers will have their own opinions. *Are* these poems popular? Why do they construct women as ingenuous and artless? Do male and female authors create significantly different kinds of woman's song? Is there really a continuous thread to be traced from the ancient into the medieval world? These are all questions I have attempted to answer myself—here and elsewhere.[7] But no answers can be definitive. The exploration is what matters. As readers proceed through this introduction, and as they look at the poems, they will find these questions coming to mind repeatedly, and being answered in different ways.

The earliest examples here come from the Greece of over 2,500 years ago. Choral lyric by Alcman and monody by Sappho, these are occasional poems composed for a specific event and performed within the context of a woman's group, whether a *thiasos* specifically brought together to enact religious rites, or merely a *hetairia*, an association of friends. The combination of communal piety with intense personal feeling, the religious with the erotic, reflects the linkage of the earliest recorded woman's song with ritual, and unites loyalties and sensibilities that later became separated, often conflicting. Some of these poems and fragments are notable for their expression of homoerotic love. Lesbian Sappho is well known, but the Alcman partheneia ("maidens' songs") also reflect this feeling. Fragment 26, like the better known Alcman 3, the Louvre Partheneion, is a cult song performed by a chorus of girls at a religious festival. Although its primary purpose is not erotic, even more noticeably than Fragment 3 it uses the language of sexual love as the speaker expresses her admiration for her beautiful chorus-leader.[8] In fact, it may well have been while performing women's religious rites together that women in early Greece experienced themselves most fully as sexual beings.[9]

Not much woman's song is preserved from the classical period of Greece, when non-lyric genres, notably the drama, dominate poetry. Women's laments are prominent in the tragedies, and sometimes, especially in Medea's outcry against Jason (*Medea* 465–519), have an erotic dimension. The lament of Andromache in *The Trojan Women* (657–83) has affinities with women's love-complaints, but also, in the context of a group of angry, grieving women, caught up in violence and war, with the "First Lay of Guthrun." In a lighter vein, Aristophanes parodies love-complaints in his *Ecclesiazusae* ("Women at the Assembly"). Later, Hellenistic poems like Theocritus's *Idyll* 18, the Epithalamion for Helen, imitate traditional occasional genres; the girls' attachment to and admiration for Helen resemble the feeling expressed for Astymeloisa, "the Darling of the City," in Alcman 26. The Locrian Song, quoted by Athenaeus around A.D. 200, is an unsophisticated composition, but particularly interesting because in giving voice to the woman's parting from her lover at dawn it foreshadows the medieval alba.

Most of the examples from classical Latin are decidedly literary and show a self-conscious intertextuality. Catullus, Virgil, and Ovid draw on the field of Greek myth and epic for their love-complaints by various legendary women.

In the renditions of all three, the dramatic element is strong and the declaration of love and loss is set in or implies a tragic narrative. Mannered, rhetorical, and overlaid with literary artifice, these love laments of Ariadne, Dido—as well as mythologized Sappho[10] and other legendary figures—transpose the "artless" confession of woman's song to a heroic context and a grander plane. Catullus's Ariadne draws on Euripides's Medea and in turn becomes a model for Virgil's Dido, and for Ovid's Ariadne in his *Heroides* ("Heroines"). In all three poets, the figure of the loving, lamenting woman raises significant questions about the heroic ethic and the conflicting demands of social and personal roles.[11]

Very different are the Sulpicia poems, a series of short pieces in elegiacs, the meter associated with love poetry, and recording the love affair between Sulpicia, a high-born girl in the Augustan period, and an unidentified Cerinthus. The Sulpicia series is included in the collection of poems attributed to the male poet Tibullus, the Corpus Tibullianum. There is some doubt as to which poems are the work of Sulpicia herself—or even whether a poet Sulpicia actually existed;[12] but some of the pieces in her voice are certainly simpler in syntax, less "poetic" in vocabulary, and more colloquial than the surrounding material. They make an interesting contrast with the undoubtedly male-authored Latin woman's songs.[13] Less elaborate in style and more realistic in topic, the Sulpicia poems present a speaker who, however madly in love she declares herself to be, never loses her self-possession—unlike Ariadne, Dido, and Ovidian (or Pseudo-Ovidian) Sappho. For all these reasons, I accept the attribution to a woman author, although contrary arguments continue to be put forward.

Echoes of the classical poets persist in late and medieval Latin, but there is a gap of several centuries during which oral lyric must have existed in the proto-Romance languages in an unrecorded "latent state."[14] The strictures of the Church councils, among their voluminous rulings on policy and behavior, show that a significant portion of this poetry must have consisted of erotic songs, frequently accompanied by dancing and performed especially by women. Thus, the Council of Auxerre, A.D. 561–65, forbids the performance of secular music or "girls' songs" in church ("non licet in ecclesia chorum saecularium vel puellarum cantica exercere"). The Council of Chalons, A.D. 647–53, condemns the singing of "obscene and shameful songs," with choruses of women ("obscina et turpea cantica, . . . cum choris foemineis"), at religious festivals. And the Council of Rome, in 853, complains that there are many people, especially women, who desecrate feast days by dancing and singing "dirty words" ("verba turpia") and having choruses in the manner of the pagans ("choros tenendo . . ., similitudinem paganorum peragendo").[15] In this context, "shameful" or "dirty" ("turpis") doubtless means "erotic."

The songs condemned by these councils would have been in the proto-Romance languages, but erotic songs performed by women also presumably existed in the other European vernaculars. There is little documentary evidence before the year 1000, but the existence of Germanic examples is indicated by a Carolingian capitulary of 789 forbidding nuns to compose "songs to a lover" (*winileudos*, a Germanic word).[16] Two Old English poems of this type come down to us in a late-tenth-century manuscript, as well as Irish woman's songs such as the Lament of Créde, and the Norse *Gudrúnarkvida in fyrsta* ("First Lay of Guthrun"), which along with the Irish poetry is a later redaction of earlier material. Like the Lament of Créde, Guthrun's Lay is a lament for the dead beloved, violently slain. All of these early Germanic and Celtic poems are strongly influenced by the conventions of heroic poetry and are set in a world of feud and tribal conflict. The mood is dark, and the geniality that characterizes most medieval love poetry is absent. Like the Roman love-complaints by mythological women, they have epic affinities. In fact, these poems are perhaps better characterized as heroic elegies than love lyrics,[17] but they are certainly lyrical in some respects. The Irish and Norse poetry is strophic. The Old English woman's songs are not, but *Wulf and Eadwacer* contains elements of strophic structure in its alternation of longer and shorter lines and its refrain-like repetition. All the poems are lyrical in their focus on the feelings associated with an intimate relationship and with a particular moment in time.

Beginning later than the Old English materials, but earlier than the Occitan (Provençal) verse that supposedly gave birth to European vernacular lyric, the kharjas from Spain caused a good deal of excitement when they were published by S.M. Stern in 1948. These kharjas, bits of love poetry in colloquial Arabic or a mixture of this and early Spanish, were appended as codas to long poems in literary Arabic or Hebrew. At first, the discovery of poetry in the Mozarabic dialect of Arabic-influenced proto-Spanish seemed to confirm the existence of a body of "popular" Romance poetry in which woman's song figured prominently. More recent criticism has qualified this rather Romantic and folkloric interpretation of the kharjas, and has emphasized their literary and Arabist qualities.[18] To be sure, the kharjas must in some way reflect the existence of lost Romance oral poetry, but it is hard to differentiate what they owe to this tradition and what to Arab or Jewish sources in the mixed society of early Spain.

We do know that the kharjas were intended to provide a contrast to the elaborate male-voice muwashshahas (love poems, often homosexual, or panegyrics) that preceded them, and that very frequently they purported to be the utterance of a young woman, perhaps the performer. Ibn Bassam al-Santarini, in the first half of the twelfth century, testifies that the inventor of the muwashshaha, al-Qabri, put colloquial and Romance words into the *markaz* (kharja) and constructed the muwashshaha around them.[19] The Egyptian anthologist Ibn Sana' al-Mulk (A.D. 1155–1211) also says that the poet first finds or composes the kharja, and then creates the muwashshaha for it; the kharja, which is outspoken and passionate and makes an abrupt transition from the preceding muwashshaha, is placed in the mouth of a woman, a child, or a drunk person.[20] Apart from implying a disparaging view of women, the remark shows that al-Mulk thought the language of this type of poetry should *appear* artless and unrestrained. Further, if the performer was a professional female musician, she was likely to have been a slave or prostitute and her "woman's song" would not have been an elevated form.[21]

"Romantic philologists" like Theodor Frings believed woman's song formed an ancient substratum beneath the courtly lyric born in Provence.[22] Probably this theory has some truth in it, insofar as some kinds of songs must have bridged the gap between the ancient and medieval worlds. But we don't need to trace the whole of European lyric back to simple songs performed, and originally composed, by women.[23] There is a rather complex relationship between woman's song and the poems of *fin'amor*, as it was called by the troubadours, or "courtly love" as modern critics have called it, following Gaston Paris in the late nineteenth century. Poetry in the courtly tradition is typically aristocratic in tone and directed by an aspiring poet-lover to an unattainable lady. Paris saw the epitome of this convention in Lancelot's devotion to Guinevere as portrayed by Chrétien de Troyes.[24] Scholars tend to divide the lyrics of Occitania (i.e., the area where Occitan was spoken) and Northern France into courtly and uncourtly genres, and to associate woman's song or *chanson de femme* with the latter. The courtly genre *par excellence* is the canso, the usually male-voice song of courtly love, called the *grand chant courtois* in north French contexts. In his classification of medieval French lyrics, Pierrre Bec defines the *chanson de femme* as embracing a variety of genres, especially the *chanson d'ami* (young girl's song about her feelings for a lover), *chanson de malmariée* of a dissatisfied wife, *chanson de toile* sung to accompany needlework, and the alba or dawn song, as well as, to some extent, the pastourelle with its encounter between knight and shepherd girl, and various types of songs to accompany dance.[25]

Not many *chansons de femme* as defined by Bec are preserved in Occitan, although they are common in Old French. The *chanson de toile* is exclusive to northern France, and the *malmariée* mainly attested there. But many of the genres embodying woman's song recur: in the Romance vernaculars, in German, in Middle English, and in medieval Latin. Occitan also contains the small but significant body of poetry composed by the trobairitz. Upwards of twenty love poems by these women troubadours are preserved.[26] Many are cansos, but the number includes some tensos (debates), one or two woman-to-woman, others male–female. The poems of the trobairitz, especially the cansos, stand in a peculiar relationship to the lyrics by the male troubadours. The women authors play with the same ideas as their male counterparts: loyalty and secrecy in love, moral improvement through love service, delight in noble joy (*ioi*) and youth (*ioven*), contempt for the boorish (*vilan*), the jealous (*gilos*), and the tattletales (*lauzengier*). However, the speaker in the trobairitz canso combines the positions of proud lady, *domna*, and pleading lover, rather than simply reversing them. She gives the troubadour's passive, silent lady a voice and an energetic will. In comparison with their male counterparts, the trobairitz use simpler, more direct language, focus on the love relationship rather than on their own poetic gifts, and attribute problems in the relationship to the lover, not to themselves. In fact, the trobairitz poems bring together the conventions of courtly canso and of earthy woman's song. When the Comtessa de Dia speaks of her own worth (*A chantar m'er* 5), she speaks as the *domna*, but when she declares her desire to be her lover's pillow (*Estat ai* 12), she resembles the girl in the Italian woman's song *Mamma, lo temp'è venuto* who tells her mother she wants her lover to be "closer to me than my shift"!

The rather thin representation of the genres associated with woman's song in Occitan[27] is probably attributable to the dominance and prestige of courtly or high-style forms there. Northern France provides many examples of the *chanson de malmariée*, in which a spirited young wife complains about her boorish old husband, whom she delights in cuckolding. *Quant lo gilos er fora* ("When that jealous man's away"), from the south, *Por coi me bait mes maris* ("Why does my husband beat poor wretched me?"), and *Fi, maris, de vostre amour* ("Fie, husband, on your love") from the north are typical. The lively dance-song

A l'entrade del tens clar ("At the beginning of the fair season"), one of the pieces for which the music is preserved, also contains elements of *malmariée* motifs. *A l'entrade* is probably Occitanized French. The *femna* in these poems contrasts with the courtly *domna* celebrated in troubadour lyric: she is vocal, aggressive, and available, unlike the aloof and silent lady to whom the troubadour addresses his pleas. Also, the *malmariée* often seems to be a peasant or bourgeoise. This need not mean, though, that songs of this type were not enjoyed by the aristocracy. Indeed, when the characters in these poetic dramas are presented as rather crass, they offer aristocratic audiences the opportunity to congratulate themselves on their own superior refinement.

Of the other genres, the *chanson de toile* is an archaizing, ballad-like form, which narrates a simple love story in the meter of the heroic *chanson de geste*. One of the characters is a maiden in the upper room of a castle who voices her feelings for a knight; there may be a dialogue between the girl and her mother, lover, or another person. Occasionally this genre too, though usually more dignified and more aristocratic in its *dramatis personae*, merges humorously with the *malmariée*. Thus, the girl's mother in *Bele Yolanz* "chastises" her daughter at the end of every stanza for deceiving her husband with a lover, and then finally tells her "suit yourself!"

For the most part it is useful to look at the genres of woman's song thematically, but they can be defined formally too. Many of those from France are dance songs, characterized by repetition and refrain. Songs of this type persist into Middle French (from 1300 on)—becoming more literary, and dissociated from their earlier musical and performance contexts—like Guillaume de Machaut's *rondeau Celle qui nuit et jour desire* ("She who night and day desires"), which may be composed by the poet himself or his young lady admirer; Eustache Deschamps's *virelai Il me semble a mon avis* ("In my opinion, it seems to me"), with its lively persona and its ironic undertones; and Christine de Pizan's *ballades* about her marriage and her widowhood.

Marcabru's *A la fontana del vergier* ("At the spring in the orchard") and the Northern French *Jherusalem* are both *chansons de croisade* in which the call of religious and patriotic duty forces the lovers apart. As in the classical laments of Ariadne and Dido, the conflict between personal ties and social obligations is here dramatized from the personal side and associated with woman's feeling. In both *chansons de croisade*, the young girl exclaims passionately against the forces ranged against her; in both, the poet engages the audience's sympathy for a love that defies Church and State. The theme and the sentiment find an echo in the German *Kreuzlied* ("cross-song") by Otto von Botenlauben *Waere Kristes lôn niht âlso süeze* ("Were Christ's reward not so sweet"). The man's conflicting feelings are also given voice in this poem, but a greater emphasis is placed on the woman's response, which follows, and forms the conclusion to this *Wechsel* ("exchange").

Often not considered woman's song at all because of its aristocratic milieu, the alba in its classic Occitan incarnation features three characters: the wife of a feudal lord, her illicit lover, and the friendly castle watchman, who warns them by announcing the dawn.[28] As Arthur Hatto has demonstrated in his massive essay collection *Eos*, the lovers' dawn parting is a universal theme although it developed a highly specialized form in medieval Europe. Typically the parting is presented from the woman's point of view, sometimes in dialogue with the watchman. Occasionally, the latter is the main speaker. The lover is nearly always silent. Typically, too, each stanza ends with an exclamatory refrain including "l'alba!" "the dawn!" Often allusion is made to the *gilos*, the odious husband, a detail anticipated in the contemptuous *keinon*, "that man," of the Locrian Song from ancient Greece. Occasionally, as in *En un vergier* ("In an orchard") and the Northern French *Entre moi et mon amin* ("My lover and I"), the love encounter takes place in the open air instead of inside a castle. Possibly, the medieval alba in its classic form combines the universal motif of the dawn parting with a genre of watchman's songs that originally had nothing to do with erotic love.[29]

Like the alba, the pastourelle is usually a narrative-framed or dialogic form; its subject, the encounter between a knight (or sometimes a clerk—a man in the employ of the Church) and a peasant girl, involves a social as well as a sexual clash. The poem's impact depends on the contrast in manners between the two speakers: the one sophisticated, plausible, and manipulative, the other earthy and direct. Sometimes the attitude toward the woman speaker is condescending. But often, as in Marcabru's lively *L'autrier jost' una sebissa*, she is credited with a wit and sagacity that are more than a match for her would-be lover. As William Paden's two-volume collection shows, the medieval pastourelle was a most prolific genre. French examples predominate, but poems of this type are also found in Occitan, Spanish (Castilian), German, Latin, and one or two in Welsh and English. A few of the poems are bilingual. In these cases the linguistic contrast highlights the social difference between a man who knows Latin, or another language associated with sophistication, and a woman who speaks her local vernacular.[30]

Woman's songs in medieval Latin are few, but revealing. Some of the most interesting ones come from two poetic miscellanies compiled in Germany: the eleventh-century Cambridge Songs (preserved in England) and the thirteenth-century *Carmina Burana*, colorfully, if not very authentically, set to music by Carl Orff. Both collections combine devotional poetry with lusty verse celebrating the pleasures of the world and the flesh—the kind of poetry that has been called "goliardic" and associated with a mythical loose-living cleric called Golias and others of the same ilk, the so-called "wandering scholars." The modern notion—now discredited—is based on what seems to have been a later interpolation in a Church council of 913 about ribald clerics ("clerici ribaldi") belonging to the tribe of Golias ("familia Goliae"),[31] and on the "Confession of Golias" (*Carmina Burana* 24), attributed to the twelfth-century Archpoet, about his pleasure-loving, wandering life. There is no particular evidence, though, aside from this poem, that the authors of this playful verse were loose-living vagabonds rather than typical clerics of settled life, who took time off to amuse themselves with amorous, bibulous, or parodic verse.

Medieval Latin woman's songs, then, like the more common male-voice Latin songs, reflect the clerical elite, for whom the composition of amatory verses in the learned language was a recreational pastime. Latin verse can be used to put women down, making fun of them in a language they cannot understand.[32] This mockery is felt behind the words of *Huc usque me miseram* ("Until now, poor wretched me"), the lament of a pregnant girl (Pierre Bec would classify it as a *chanson de délaissée*). But actually, the tone of this poem is rather subtle.

Sharp and cynical it certainly is; however, its vivid evocation of the girl's situation as social outcast is telling.[33] *Ich was ein chint so wolgetan* ("I was such a lovely girl"), which, like *Huc usque me miseram*, is one of the *Carmina Burana*, is a clearer example of the use of Latin, here alternating with German, as a social put-down. This poem belongs to the pastourelle genre, more or less, but instead of the usual narrative-framed dialogue the encounter between male sophisticate and female innocent is recounted entirely in the woman's words. Nevertheless, the male viewpoint is implicit throughout, as the poem describes in smug and rather brutal terms what amounts to a rape.

Another strain is heard in two lyrics from the Cambridge Songs: *Veni, dilectissime* ("Come, sweetheart") and *Nam languens* ("For longing with love of you"). The former expresses a passionate eroticism—a medieval censor attempted to erase it from the manuscript. The image of the girl opening her locked door to the lover who comes with his key, recalling the voluptuous language of the Song of Songs in the Old Testament (Song 5.4–5), is an obvious double entendre, gracefully treated here, and more peaceable than the imagery of military attack and entry in *Huc usque*. The words "nam languens" recall "quia amore langueo" ("because I am pining with love") in the Song (5.8). The speaker in this poem, who goes through the snow and cold to the shore and looks out for her lover's ship, resembles Catullus's and Ovid's Ariadne gazing out over the empty sea after Theseus, and perhaps too Sappho, preparing to cast herself into the sea out of despairing love for Phaon.

German woman's song has been regarded by Theodor Frings and others as combining native "folk" traditions with aristocratic genres imported from southern France. The earlier poetry, especially the anonymous pieces in Lachmann's *Minnesangs Frühling* collection of German lyrics from the High Middle Ages (the title means "The Spring of Love Poetry"), has often been seen as representing this indigenous tradition. In *Chume, chume, geselle min* ("Come, my love, come to me") and *Dû bist mîn, ich bin dîn* ("I am all yours, you all mine"), the speaker gives herself totally to her love. Poems like this, as well as *Waere diu werlt alle mîn* ("Were all the world mine") and others, resemble the apparently artless eroticism of the kharjas—but also that of *Veni, dilectissime*. Interestingly, the voice in *Waere diu werlt* has been changed, by altering *chunich* ("king") to *chuenegin* ("queen") in the manuscript, a reminder of the instability and adapability of medieval texts. Rather more complex, the two falcon songs, by Der von Kürenberg and Dietmar von Aist, implicitly associate the lover with a falcon, a powerful bird that can be tamed but that retains the potential and the will to fly away. The motif of lover as trained but still wild falcon, or hawk, reappears in the Italian *Tapina in me*.

As a poet of the *Minnesang*, the German poetry of courtly love, Reinmar der Alte is especially noted for his woman's songs and stanzas (*Frauenlieder and Frauenstrophen*), which explore fine shades of feeling with considerable sensitivity. Ingrid Kasten has made a revealing comparison between the songs of Reinmar and those of the Comtessa de Dia, seeing both as belonging to a distinct genre combining the traditions of "popular" *Frauenlied* with "courtly" *Frauendienst* (devoted service to a woman). Kasten notes that the Comtessa's persona is confident and aggressive, while Reinmar paints the usual picture of weak and timid womanhood, and his real interest lies in the relationship between himself and his art.[34]

Probably the most sophisticated and nuanced examples of Middle High German woman's song are those by Wolfram von Eschenbach and Walther von der Vogelweide. Wolfram's *Sîne klâwen* is a remarkable *Tagelied* (alba). It begins with the striking image of dawn as a bird of prey, and ends with a consummation that fuses sexual climax and lovers' parting. In between lies the conventional exchange between lady and watchman, but Wolfram draws with extraordinary finesse the watchman's protectiveness of his friend, the lady's tender feelings for her lover, the lover's sense of her physical and emotional being, as he is taken "from white arms but never from the heart." Walther's song, in some ways a pastourelle, is woman's monologue, but her blend of mild embarrassment and self-congratulation makes the poem something other than the simple *Mädchenlied* it used to be taken for. Is she a "liberated" high-born lady? When she says, "Let no one know but him and me—and a little bird," is she being coy or complacent, modest or arch? This is a different take on sex under a lime tree from *Ich was ein chint*, but almost certainly influenced by that poem or others like it. After Walther, Middle High German lyric tends to become less distinctive and more derivative, but Otto von Botenlauben's farewell between husband and wife, a *chanson de croisade*, is a touching evocation of the lovers' parting, and Neidhart's *Der mei der ist riche* ("May is mighty") is adroit and playful in its recreation of a rustic dialogue between a mother and her daughter who has found a lover.

Italian woman's songs first appear in the context of the poetry of the Sicilian School at the court of Frederick II, in the mid-thirteenth century. No distinctively Italian form emerges—except the use of the sonnet for this purpose, as in the anonymous *Tapina in me c'amava uno sparvero* ("Alas for me! I loved a hawk") and the poems by the Compiuta Donzella, the anonymous "Accomplished Young Lady" of Florence. But the established types are found here too, especially the young girl's song about her lover, the *chanson d'ami*. The hawk-lover motif reappears in *Tapina in me*. Perhaps the Italian corpus is most noteworthy for its spirited young women, whether committed to virginity and compelled to marry against their will like the Compiuta Donzella, or eager for sexual fulfilment, like the speaker in Rinaldo d'Aquino's *Ormai quando flore* ("Now when things are in bloom"), who is torn between desire and apprehension, and the girl in *Mamma lo temp' è venuto* ("Mother, the time has come") who vehemently demands her mother's permission to marry.

The largest group of medieval woman's songs comes from Galicia and Portugal, where a distinct genre developed, the *cantiga de amigo* ("song about a friend/lover"), a counterpart and contrast to the male-voice *cantiga de amor* ("song about love"). In the Galician-Portuguese context, especially, the popular/aristocratic antithesis often used to demarcate woman's song from the lyrics of courtly love breaks down. With the exception of a few anonymous poems, all of the *cantigas de amigo* are by named court poets, often the same ones who composed *cantigas de amor*. The atmosphere of the *cantigas de amigo* is simpler and more rustic, but they are composed within the same circle as their more courtly counterparts,[35] the difference being a matter of style, not audience or authorship. Whereas the *cantiga de amor* is more influenced by the Occitan *canso*, and its language and meter tend to be more elaborate, the *cantiga de amigo* is characterized by its simple musicality. The female voice here is innocent and virginal, unlike the sexually experienced voice of many woman's songs.

Nevertheless, there is a markedly sensual element, whereby certain characteristic objects acquire an erotic significance. In Mendinho's *Sedia-m'eu na ermida de San Simion* ("I was at the sanctuary of St. Simon"), the incremental effect of the rolling waves conveys the speaker's troubled feelings, which finally overwhelm her; the movement also has an erotic suggestion, culminating in final death.[36] In Pero Meogo's poetry, the mountain stags that trouble the water of the spring visited by the young girl imply the intrusion of a feral male element into her protected world. In Johan Zorro's *Cabelos, los meus cabelos* ("Flowing hair, my flowing hair"), the girl's long loose hair becomes a symbol for, as well as a marker of, her virginal state; it is not really her *hair* that the king desires and that her mother recommends her to yield.

Certain genres are specific to, or typical of, the Iberian Peninsula, notably the *marinha* ("sea-song") or *barcarola* ("boat-song"), here represented by Mendinho's and Martin Codax's examples, and the *romaria* ("pilgrimage-song"), in which the speaker meets her lover in the context of a visit to a saint's shrine. These forms persist in Castilian lyric, recorded mainly from the fifteenth century on, presumably because earlier Galician-Portuguese was the dialect associated with lyric, Castilian with epic.[37] Like the male-authored Galician-Portuguese *cantigas de amigo*, the anonymous Castilian woman's voice love lyrics are characterized by their parallel structure with refrain, their musicality, and their evocation of eager, youthful femininity. Other typical Iberian forms are the song of the reluctant nun, the *malmonjada*, of which *Agora que soy niña* ("Now while I'm young") is an example, and the *alborada* or dawn meeting, a variant of the alba, here illustrated by the Castilian *Al alva venid, buen amigo* ("Come at dawn, good friend"). Very often the *cantiga de amigo* or its Castilian successor is addressed to an imagined intimate female audience: daughter to mother, mother to daughter, a plea or an invitation to girl friends, which may be a private confidence or a social communication, like the invitation to join the dance.

The English woman's songs that have been preserved are for the most part later than their Romance and German analogues. The Middle English examples are remote from their Old English antecedents, and clearly influenced by Continental models. The spring setting, the chance encounter between man and young girl, the lament of the girl who has been seduced by a smooth-talking ne'er-do-well—all are conventions shared with Continental poetry. All of the Middle English poems included here are carols: in form, dance songs for leader and chorus, structurally similar to various Continental songs designed—at least originally—to accompany the dance. The chorus would have sung the burden, a kind of refrain that opens the carol and is repeated after each stanza. Sometimes a carol has a stanza-ending refrain as well. A favorite theme is the girl who has been seduced by a clerk; the topic suggests that such poems, like Latin poems of similar type, were often composed for and enjoyed by clerics. We find a similar knowing humor, and a similar blend of cynicism and pathos, so that it is sometimes hard to say which of the two predominates in a poem. These lyrics range from the cheerfully wanton in *Hey noyney! I wyll love our Ser John and I love eny*, with its refrain "I have no powre to say him nay," to the pathetic *Kyrie, so kyrie*, with its poignant conclusion, "Alas, I go with chylde."

The pieces selected in this anthology differ widely, and yet constantly call each other to mind. As a counterpart to male utterance, woman's voice poetry becomes the vehicle for alternative ways of perceiving. This observation has, of course, been made by others, from various angles. Joan Ferrante has seen in the treatment of women by medieval male poets both woman as idea, as "image," and woman as "realist, debunker of male fantasies."[38] Jean-Charles Huchet has doubted the very existence of the women troubadours and seen in their voices a male-constructed "other" that deconstructs the conventional poetic themes of *fin'amor* or courtly love (Huchet 90). Doris Earnshaw has found in the lyric female voice generally "an embodiment of cultural inferiority" (Earnshaw 121), but suggests that a more assertive and rational model of female speech arose in Occitania, pointing to poems like Marcabru's *L'autrier jost'una sebissa* ("The other day by a hedgerow"), and led to the emergence of the women troubadours. Those—like Jean-Charles Huchet and Pierre Bec—who emphasize the textuality of the female voice rather than seeking a biological femininity have come under fire for attempting to erase the contribution of women poets,[39] but in fact the uses to which Bec and Huchet find the female voice being put are rather similar to those detected in it by their critics.[40]

Repeatedly the woman's view is associated with protest against the assumptions and arrangements of men. Thus, Sappho contrasts what she thinks is the most beautiful thing—whatever you love—with what other people, evidently men, say it is—an army of horsemen, or of footsoldiers, or a fleet. Very often the love celebrated is illicit, and the woman's commitment defies the social order in some way. Dido curses Aeneas for abandoning her so that he can go off and fulfil his destiny, that is, found Rome. Using the dual pronoun "us two" the speaker in *Wulf and Eadwacer* pits the love of two individuals against the enmity of their two tribes. The Comtessa de Dia and Na Castelloza assert their right to choose a lover and voice their love rather than remain the passive objects of male manoeuvers. Ill-married women in Old French songs similarly, though more saucily, defy the restrictions of marriage. Often the woman's fidelity is contrasted with her man's fickleness, her immobility with his freedom to move. When unable to change events by physical action, she resorts to a powerful eloquence. Women left behind, seduced, or pregnant speak with pathos and defiance, asserting their personal feelings against male opportunism and self-congratulation, against political expediency and the pious platitudes of organized religion.

These voices of protest echo through both male- and female-authored poems. But is the woman's voice constructed differently by women and by men? Poems known to be by male authors, like the Galician-Portuguese group, often stress the beauty and desirability of the speaker, in an "autopanegyric" that clearly reflects the male author's point of view.[41] The Roman male poets—Catullus, Virgil, Ovid—present women completely deranged by love. The Ovidian Sappho has totally lost her self-control, in sharp contrast with the real Sappho, whose cool command of her voice detaches herself from her passions. Sulpicia, too, is much less melodramatic about her feelings. Like the Comtessa de Dia and Na Castelloza, she has a strong sense of her own value. Sweeping statements about the way male and female authors compose are dangerous, particularly in view of the vast body of anonymous poetry and the instability and transferability of texts. One or two of the poems included here show evidence of transference between male and female voice: pronouns have been altered in *Waere diu werlt alle min* and *Wolde God that hyt were so*; Kharja 14 in Josep Solá-Solé's collection ("I loved someone else's little son") is spoken in a male and a female version in different muwashshahas.[42] Nevertheless, as far as I can see poems known to be by female authors do not depict their speakers merely as saucy wantons or pathetic victims. We cannot logically infer, though, that therefore any anonymous poems which *do* depict them in such a way cannot possibly be authored by women.[43] Again, arguing for the existence of a historical Sulpicia, Holt Parker comments that when a male poet writes from a female perspective, "the feminine character is generic and non-specific" (Parker 46). Parker's comment is too sweeping, but I would agree that the tendency is there. It seems to me that in general, while male authors construct a femininity that appeals to men, female authors emphasize thought and opinion rather than the evocation of beguiling femininity.

Joan Ferrante finds some similarity between the voices of the trobairitz and the women's voices created by male troubadours: both, she believes, are more realistic and down-to-earth than their male counterparts.[44] She points out the prominence of direct address in the trobairitz poems and the interest in a real relationship with a real past ("Female Rhetoric" 64–66). Both Ferrante and Sarah Kay note that the rhyme schemes of trobairitz poetry are usually less complicated—although Kay looks at a couple of exceptions to this generalization.[45] Sophie Marnette also makes a comparison between the trobairitz and the male troubadours, and comes up with somewhat different conclusions than Ferrante. Including male–female debate poems (tensos) as well as monologic cansos, Marnette finds in poems of the former kind a greater cooperation on the part of the female speakers; in poems of the latter kind a vigorous expression of will, with commands and the verb *vouloir* ("L'expression féminine" 186–87 and 189).

Most of these poems and passages, whether composed by men or women, use a relatively simple vocabulary and syntax—in keeping with a poetic mode that presents itself as artless—and we wonder why this should be so. This "artless" quality has been accounted for in various ways: as associated with male fantasies about female innocence and availability,[46] an interpretation that fits the phenomenon of woman's song as a widespread cultural paradigm but is less adequate when applied to specific examples; as reflecting "a deeply felt traditional association between heightened colloquial diction and the female predicament"[47]—a rather Romantic view; as the vehicle of realism and the rejection of fantasy (Ferrante). Though superficially simple, the poems may be quite complex in intention and technique. Even those that appear to be very simple indeed, like the Locrian Song quoted by Athenaeus, or the kharjas, which are actually parts of longer poems, are more problematic when read in their contexts. Nor should we see these poems as evolving toward greater complexity in the course of history. Sappho, one of the earliest poets included here, is quite as sophisticated as Christine de Pizan, one of the latest. Thus, in her poem to Aphrodite, Sappho uses the conventional form of the cletic hymn (a summons to a deity) both to give vent to and to ironize an unrequited passion. And in *Seulete sui* ("Alone I am"), Christine laments her husband with a litany of bereavement that performs the paradoxical dual function of both honoring and exorcising her grief. The best of these poems work within and beyond the bounds of their traditional genres—as Wolfram's *Sîne klâwen* and Walther's *Under der linden* play with alba and pastourelle respectively in ways that transcend both.

The kind of poetry that I have been tracing does not come to an end with the close of the Middle Ages. It persists in "popular" tradition down to the present day. But other kinds of woman's voice poetry proliferate, named women poets become more common, and the confessional voice of the young woman describing her erotic involvements gradually ceases to be such an established literary convention. The separation of lyric from music, poetry from performance, private silent reading from group participation also contributes to this change. Thus, although breaking off this collection around 1500 is rather artificial—there is an impressive body of Spanish woman's song from the Renaissance and later, for example—this *terminus ad quem* is convenient, and corresponds to other major historical transitions. I leave it to others to point out connections between the poems included here and woman's songs from other parts of the world and from modern times.[48] I hope that readers will find, as they compare these selections with one another, interesting and fruitful similarities, in woman's voice as protest, eloquence as woman's weapon, and, especially, in superficial simplicity masking nuance, complexity—and sometimes subversion.

Notes

1. I prefer the singular "woman's" rather than "women's" as less likely to give the impression of female authorship. I have also taken the liberty of extending the concept of woman's song, found mainly in discussions of medieval works, to classical poetry in order to include ancient antecedents of the medieval poems. See Rosenberg's explanation of the term *chanson de femme* in *Songs of the Troubadours and Trouvères*; also Plummer's Introduction to *Vox Feminae* (5–17), a collection of English-language essays on woman's song. For a variety of interpretations of woman's songs, see the essays in Klinck and Rasmussen. The following discussion of the subject draws on my Introduction to that volume.
2. "Quelques réflexions sur la poésie lyrique médiévale," esp. 1325.
3. These are the words of Christopher Page in his work on the performance of songs in medieval France. See his *Voices and Instruments* 38. On the problematic use of the term "popular" as applied to woman's songs, see Klinck, "The Oldest Folk Poetry?" For some serious reservations about the traditional binary distinction between the popular and courtly registers, see Joan Tasker Grimbert in Doss-Quinby et al., 7–11.
4. Bec distinguishes between "une féminité génétique," in which the author is known to be a woman, and "une féminité textuelle," in which the lyric "I" is a woman ("*Trobairitz* et chansons de femme" 235–36).
5. The actual performance of songs is an important subject, which, however, lies outside the scope of the present book. See Boynton, "Women's Performance of the Lyric before 1500," in Klinck and Rasmussen, and her discography there; also the discussions by Le Vot and Switten in Rosenberg et al., eds., *Songs of the Troubadours and Trouvères* (7–13, and 14–28, resp.), and the musical editions and commentary by Aubrey in Doss-Quinby et al., eds., *Songs of the Women Trouvères*, 44–56, 188–251, and passim. The CD-Rom by Margaret Switten et al., *Teaching Medieval Lyric with Modern Technology*, includes music, as well as facsimiles, editions, and translations.
6. Plummer, in the Preface to his *Vox Feminae*, specifically excludes poems by aristocratic authors like the trobairitz (*Vox Feminae* v). Similarly, Bec comments in his edition of the trobairitz that the *chansons de femme* shouldn't be grouped with them, because the "*cansós* troubadouresques à auteur féminin . . . ne sont pas pour nous des 'chansons de femme' au sens strict . . ." (*Chants d'amour* 47), although he does include some of the latter in his collection—in a separate section.

7. See Klinck, "The Oldest Folk Poetry?", "Sappho and Her Daughters," and "Poetic Markers of Gender."

8. The existence of homoerotic feeling is unmistakable in Fragment 26; in Fragment 3 it is accepted by Calame in his study of girl choruses, but rejected by some recent critics. See Ingalls 10–12, esp. n. 41. (Alcman 26 and 3 numbered 3 and 1, resp., in other editions.)

9. See Williamson 108–09.

10. The lament of Sappho, *Heroides* 15, is attributed to Ovid, but may be by an imitator.

11. Cf. Pavlock, who, commenting on Ovid's Ariadne, notes that he "does not use the female to express male values but rather explores the problems of passion . . ." 145.

12. See Holzberg, who finds no historical Sulpicia, but "a fictional autobiography in elegiac form," "Four Poets and a Poetess?" 189.

13. Parker finds no logical basis for inferring female authorship from a supposedly feminine diction, and argues for the attribution of two more elaborate poems to Sulpicia, as well as the shorter and simpler pieces in her voice. See "Sulpicia" 51–52.

14. "Estado latente," the term used by Menéndez Pidal, "Cantos románicos" 266–67.

15. Quoted from Synodus Diocesana Autissiodorensis, canon 9, in de Clercq 266; Concilium Cabilonense, canon 19, in de Clercq 307; Concilium Romanum, canon 35, in Wilfried Hartmann 328.

16. Text of this capitulary contained in Pertz, MGH *Leges* 1.68.

17. Cf. Bray 152.

18. See, e.g., the work of Hitchcock and Jones, and the article by Kelley.

19. See Galmés de Fuentes 32.

20. I am referring here to the German translation of Ibn Sana' al-Mulk included in Heger's collection of kharjas and related materials (Heger 187). For an English account, see Linda Fish Compton's summary of al-Mulk's pronouncements about the muwashshaha (*Andalusian Lyrical Poetry* 3–7).

21. Cf. Judith Cohen's comment on the attitude reflected in two medieval romances, where an aristocratic woman makes a point of dissociating herself from the profession of the *joglaresa*, the paid performer who is likely also to be a prostitute. Cohen titles her essay "Ca no soe joglaresa," "because I am not a *joglaresa*," a quotation from the *Libro de Alexandre* (line 1723), and refers to a similar passage in the *Libro de Apolonio* (line 490). See "Women and Music in Medieval Spain's Three Cultures," Klinck and Rasmussen 68.

22. Frings set out his views in a number of publications, especially in his 1949 *Minnesinger und Troubadours*. The term "Romantic philologists" is used by Auerbach in a review of Frings's book (Auerbach 66).

23. As was done by Jeanroy in his *Origines de la poésie lyrique*, first published 1889; see p. 445, and passim.

24. Paris coined the phrase "amour courtois" in his study of Chrétien de Troyes's romance of Lancelot, "Études sur la Table Ronde" 519. For the problems with the term "courtly love," see Wendy Pfeffer in Doss-Quinby et al., 35–37.

25. *Lyrique française* 1.60 ff. But see Christopher Page, p. 38, and n. 3, in the present introduction. Cf. also Zumthor, who contrasts "le registre de la requête d'amour, spécifique du grand chant courtois," with "le registre de la bonne vie," associated with game, dance, "repas champêtre," and love (*Essai* 251–52).

26. The figure is uncertain because sometimes female authorship is questionable, especially when the author is anonymous. There are twenty-two extant poems, and parts of poems, attributed to named women; one of these, the sirventes by Gormonda de Monpeslier, is a political–religious polemic. The others relate to the subject of love, although not all of them are love songs in a narrow sense.

27. Except for the alba, which Bec does include among the *chansons de femme*, but which some scholars do not, at least when its setting is aristocratic.

28. Gail Sigal, though she dissociates the alba from "women's oral folk poetry" (8), sees it as the lyric genre that develops the female perspective: the alba lady is "more

responsive than the canso *domna* and more dignified than the pastourelle shepherdess" (75).

29. An example of the latter, with Christian overtones, would be the tenth-century Latin *Phoebi claro* ("When bright Phoebus has not yet risen"), with a refrain in early Occitan. For a translation of *Phoebi claro*, see Wilhelm 8–9; Latin text, Wilhelm 299–301.

30. Deyermond analyzes male–female dialogues in several languages, and suggests the form was an adaptation of the pastourelle initiated by the troubadour Raimbaut de Vaqueiras's debate between an Occitan-speaking man and a Genoese woman. See "Lust in Babel" 200–02, and 217–18.

31. For a discussion of Golias and the goliards, see the Introduction to Blodgett and Swanson, ix–xiii.

32. See Schotter 21–24.

33. Neil Cartlidge finds that "her complaint is given a genuinely tragic resonance" ("Alas, I Go with Chylde" 400).

34. See "The Conception of Female Roles," Klinck and Rasmussen 152–67.

35. See Ashley 39.

36. Cf. the use of the word "die" for sexual climax, a common poetic metaphor in English literature of the late sixteenth and seventeenth centuries, as the *Oxford English Dictionary*'s examples show (see definition 7d, *OED*, under the verb "die").

37. See Jensen, *The Earliest Portuguese Lyrics* 266–68; *Medieval Galician-Portuguese Poetry* cxiv–cxv.

38. See, respectively, her book *Woman as Image* and her article "Male Fantasy and Female Reality"; here, 67.

39. See, e.g., Joan Grimbert in Doss-Quinby et al., 3–4, and 67, n. 8.

40. Bruckner believes it is important not to deny the existence of women poets, but agrees with Huchet that the woman's voice can be used as a vehicle for alternative opinion. See "Fictions of the Female Voice" 128–29. Tilde Sankovitch characterizes the poems of the women troubadours as ludic and subversive, and, following Irigary, associates the feminine with catachresis; see "Trobairitz" 116–20, and 126, n. 10.

41. See Corral, "Feminine Voices in the Galician-Portuguese *Cantigas de Amigo*" 83.

42. Two Arabic and one Hebrew, all of them expressing love for a boy. Solá-Solé sees the kharja as uttered by the poet in the Arabic muwashshahas, by a young girl in the Hebrew. And cf. Heale's comments on the changing of the pronoun "she" to "they," in a sixteenth-century English love complaint ("Women and the Courtly Love Lyric" 309–12).

43. As, e.g., Faral did with poems he regarded as too lascivious to have been composed or performed by women. See "Les chansons de toile ou chansons d'histoire." And note Bruckner's warning about "subjective and culturally determined assumptions" ("Fictions of the Female Voice" 132). Also Heale's analysis of the comments and interventions by women copying the poems in the Devonshire ms.; she observes that they could respond to misogynist poems with wit (see esp. 313).

44. "Female Rhetoric" 69–71.

45. Ferrante, "Female Rhetoric" 66–67; Kay, "Derived Rhyme," esp. 165.

46. "Thus woman has in primitive literature a role imposed upon her by man, answering him with the very words of longing he has suggested to her"—Spitzer's dated but still thought-provoking reaction to the kharjas in the light of Frings's theories about woman's song (Spitzer 22).

47. Whetnall, "Lírica Feminina" 147.

48. For comparisons between medieval Hispanic poetry featuring women or composed by women and similar modern songs from the oral traditions of the Middle East, see Cohen.

CHAPTER 1
ANCIENT GREECE

Most of the poetry in this collection reflects heterosexual love, but in some of the earliest pieces, by Alcman and Sappho, the feeling is homoerotic. That Sappho was a "lesbian" is well known, but just what that means continues to be debated. Some, but not all, scholars relate her milieu to that evoked by the ancient girl-choruses, such as the one that speaks in Alcman 26. This poem, like those of Sappho, is in a fragmentary state. Many of the very short fragments, like Sappho 47–140 here, are preserved as quotations from the writers of later antiquity.

Not much independent lyric survives from classical Greece, and it is to the drama that we must turn for women's voices. The passage included here from Aristophanes's *Ecclesiazusae* spoofs love poetry in a hilarious exchange between a sex-crazed couple. On a very different plane, Euripides, in *Medea*, gives us one of drama's great tragic characters, both terrible and compelling. *The Trojan Women* shows us the consequences of war for women—here, for Andromache. Although they could hardly be more different, both Medea and Andromache, in their outpouring of grief, anger, and despair, convey a devastating criticism of male brutality and folly.

Theocritus's Epithalamion for Helen looks back to the choral poetry of an earlier age, and also, through its characters and meter, to epic. As a wedding song, this poem claims to be created for a specific occasion, but is occasional only as a literary artifice. The much simpler Locrian Song seems to be an isolated representative of a vast body of lost popular poetry.

On women in relation to Greek literature and society, see Gail Holst-Warhaft, *Dangerous Voices* (1992). On Alcman, see Claude Calame, *Choruses of Young Women* (English translation 1997), and, for a different view, Wayne Ingalls, "Ritual Performance" (2000). For Sappho, see Margaret Reynolds, *The Sappho Companion* (2001), and Anne Carson's poetic rendering, *If Not, Winter* (2002). Further, L.K. Taaffe, *Aristophanes and Women* (1993); *Euripides, Women, and Sexuality*, ed. Anton Powell (1990); Emily McDermott, *Euripides' Medea* (1989); J.J. Clauss and S.I. Johnston, *Medea: Essays on Medea in Myth, Literature, Philosophy, and Art* (1997); N.T. Croally, *Euripidean Polemic: The Trojan Women and the Function of Tragedy* (1994). On Theocritus's Epithalamion for Helen, see Maria Pantelia, "Theocritus at Sparta," *Hermes* 123 (1995): 76–81. And on women and cult in Locri, Bonnie MacLachlan, "Love, War, and the Goddess in Fifth-Century Locri," *The Ancient World* 26 (1995): 203–23—a possible background to the Locrian Song.

The Archaic Period

Alcman

26—A Partheneion or Maidens' Song

Fragment of a choral poem to be sung and danced by young women at a religious festival. The speaker, a generic chorus-member, expresses passionate attachment to her beautiful chorus-leader Astymeloisa, whose name means "A Care to the City," that is, "Darling of the City."

Ὀλυμπιάδες περί με φρένας	Around me the Olympian Muses [inspire?] my heart
. . . -ς ἀοιδας	. . . songs
. . . -ωδ' ἀκούσαι	. . . to listen to
. . . -ας ὀπός	. . . voice
5 . . . -ρα καλὸν ὑμνιοισᾶν μέλος	. . . singing the lovely melody
. . . -οι	
ὕπνον ἀπὸ γλεφάρων σκεδασεῖ γλυκύν	[She] will scatter sweet sleep from my eyelids,
. . . -ς δέ μ' ἄγει πεδ' ἀγὼν' ἴμεν	and leads me to go to the contest-place
μάλιστα κόμαν ξανθὰν τινάξω·	[where] eagerly I'll toss my yellow hair.
10 . . . σχ- . . . ἁπαλοὶ πόδες	. . . tender feet
. . .	. . .

lines 11–60 missing

λυσιμελεῖ τε πόσῳ, τακερώτερα	with limb-loosening desire, more meltingly
δ' ὕπνω καὶ σανάτω ποτιδέρκεται·	than sleep and death she looks at [me].
οὐδέ τι μαψιδίως γλυκ- . . . -ήνα·	Not in vain is she sweet.
Ἀστυμέλοισα δέ μ' οὐδὲν ἀμείβεται	Yet Astymeloisa answers me nothing.
65 τὸν πυλεών' ἔχοισα . . .	Holding the garland,
ὤ τις αἰγλάεντος ἀστήρ . . .	like some falling star
ὠρανῶ διαιπετής	that darts through the radiant heaven,
ἢ χρύσιον ἔρνος ἢ ἁπαλὸν ψίλον	or like a golden sapling, or a soft feather,
. . . -ν	. . .
70 . . . διέβα ταναοῖς ποσί	she has passed along, with light, pointed feet.
. . . -κομος νοτία Κινύρα χάρις	The scent of Cyprian perfume
ἐπὶ παρσενικᾶν χαίταισιν ἴσδει·	lies moist on her youthful hair.
Ἀστυμέλοισα κατὰ στρατόν	All along the host, Astymeloisa,
. . . μέλημα δάμῳ	the darling of the people,
75 . . . -μαν ἐλοῖσα	. . . taking
. . . -λέγω·	. . .
. . . εναβαλ' αἴ γὰρ ἄργυριν	for if . . . throw silver.
. . . -ία	. . .
. . . -α ἴδοιμ' αἴ πως με . . . -ο φίλοι	I would see if somehow she might love me,
80 ἆσσον ἰοῖσ' ἁπαλᾶς χηρὸς λάβοι,	if coming close to me she'd take my tender hand;
αἶψά κ'ἐγὼν ἱκέτις κήνας γενοίμαν	I'd be her suppliant straightaway.
νῦν δ' . . . -δα παῖδα βαθύφρονα	But as it is [she loves?] a deep-counselled girl,
παιδι . . . μ' ἔχοισαν	having . . . [compared?] to a girl [like?] me.
. . . -ν ἁ παίς	. . . This girl
85 . . . χάριν·	. . . grace
. . .	. . .

remaining lines missing

Provenance: Sparta, middle to late seventh century B.C.
Meter: Nine-line stanza. Lines 1, 7, 8 dactylic; 2, 3, 4 trochaic; 5, 9 aeolic (choriambic).

Sappho

1—*Hymn to Aphrodite*

In Poem 1, Sappho adapts the ritual prayer formula as she begs Aphrodite to assist her in winning over a reluctant girl: she addresses the goddess by a traditional epithet, locates her in her habitual home, reminds her of past favors, and requests "whatever my heart desires to be accomplished, accomplish it." The poem evokes the epiphany of the goddess, who materializes, smiles, and speaks words of power.

Ποικιλόθρον' ἀθανάτ' Ἀφρόδιτα,
παῖ Δίος δολόπλοκε, λίσσομαί σε,
μή μ' ἄσαισι μηδ' ὀνίαισι δάμνα,
πότνια, θῦμον,

Immortal Aphrodite of the exquisite throne,
wile-weaving child of Zeus, to you I pray.
Don't subdue with pains and torments,
lady, my heart.

5 ἀλλὰ τυίδ' ἔλθ', αἴ ποτα κἀτέρωτα
τὰς ἔμας αὔδας ἀίοισα πήλοι
ἔκλυες, πάτρος δὲ δόμον λίποισα
χρύσιον ἦλθες

But come hither, if ever also in the past,
catching my voice from afar,
you listened, left your father's home
of gold, and came,

ἄρμ' ὑπασδεύξαισα· κάλοι δέ σ' ἆγον
10 ὤκεες στροῦθοι περὶ γᾶς μελαίνας
πύκνα δίννεντες πτέρ' ἀπ' ὠράνωἴθε-
ρος διὰ μέσσω·

yoking your car. Beautifully you were drawn,
swiftly, over the dark earth, by sparrows
whirring a cloud of wings, from heaven
through the mid air.

αἶψα δ' ἐξίκοντο· σὺ δ', ὦ μάκαιρα,
μειδιαίσαισ' ἀθανάτῳ προσώπῳ
15 ἤρε' ὅττι δηὖτε πέπονθα κὦττι
δηὖτε κάλημμι

Instantly they arrived. And you, oh blessed one,
smiling with immortal face,
asked what it was I'd suffered again, and why
again I called,

κὦττι μοι μάλιστα θέλω γένεσθαι

and what it was I most longed to be done
 for me,

μαινόλαι θύμῳ· τίνα δηὖτε πείθω

in my maddened heart. Whom again shall
 I persuade

. . . σάγην ἐς σὰν φιλότατα; τίς σ', ὦ
20 Ψάπφ', ἀδίκησι;

and bring to know your love? Who,
Sappho, is wronging you?

καὶ γὰρ αἰ φεύγει, ταχέως διώξει,
αἰ δὲ δῶρα μὴ δέκετ', ἀλλὰ δώσει,
αἰ δὲ μὴ φίλει, ταχέως φιλήσει
κωὐκ ἐθέλοισα.

For if she flees, soon she'll pursue;
if she takes not your gifts, others she'll give;
if she loves not, soon she'll love,
even unwillingly.

25 ἔλθε μοι καὶ νῦν, χαλέπαν δὲ λῦσον
ἐκ μερίμναν, ὄσσα δέ μοι τέλεσσαι
θῦμος ἰμέρρει, τέλεσον, σὺ δ' αὔτα
σύμμαχος ἔσσο.

Come to me now too, and set me free
from grievous cares; fulfil for me
those things my heart desires. It's you I need.
Fight on my side!

Provenance: Lesbos, turn of the seventh and sixth century B.C.
Meter: Sappho's most characteristic meter, the Sapphic stanza: three 11-syllable lines followed by one 5-syllable line, all based on the choriamb (a long syllable, two short, and another long).

16—"Some say an army of horse, some of foot"

Sappho rejects the brilliant military display celebrated by epic verse in favor of a personal admiration for a young woman. The poem begins with a "priamel" offering inadequate examples of the most beautiful thing, only to climax them with "it's whatever you love." Helen of Troy is selected both as the most beautiful of women, and as someone who gives up everything in order to follow what she loves.

Οἰ μὲν ἰππήων στρότον οἰ δὲ πέσδων
οἰ δὲ νάων φαῖσ' ἐπὶ γᾶν μέλαιναν
ἔμμεναι κάλλιστον, ἔγω δὲ κῆν' ὄτ-
τω τις ἔραται·

Some say an army of horse, some of foot,
some of ships, on the dark earth
is the loveliest thing, but *I* say it's what-
ever you love.

5 πάγχυ δ' εὔμαρες σύνετον πόησαι
πάντι τοῦτ', ἀ γὰρ πόλυ περσκέθοισα
κάλλος ἀνθρώπων Ἐλένα τὸν ἄνδρα
τὸν . . . ἄριστον

It's perfectly easy to make everyone
understand this, for she who far exceeded
all mortals in beauty, Helen, left
the noblest man,

καλλίποισ' ἔβα 'ς Τροίαν πλέοισα
10 κωὐδὲ παῖδος οὐδὲ φίλων τοκήων
πάμπαν ἐμνάσθη, ἀλλὰ παράγαγ' αὔταν

. . . -σαν

and went sailing off to Troy.
Her child and her own parents
she remembered not a whit, but [Paris?]
carried her
away . . .

. . .

. . .

15 . . . -με νῦν Ἀνακτορίας ὀνέμναι-
σ' οὐ παρεοίσας,

. . .
. . .
And now I remember Anactoria,
who's gone.

τᾶς κε βολλοίμαν ἔρατόν τε βᾶμα
κἀμάρυχμα λάμπρον ἴδην προσώπω
ἢ τὰ Λύδων ἄρματα κἀν ὄπλοισι
20 πεσδομάχεντας.

I'd rather have her lovely step,
her face so full of brightness to look upon,
than Lydian chariots, and a host all armed
of foot-soldiers.

. . . -μεν οὐ δύνατον γένεσθαι
. . . -ν ἀνθρωπ- . . . πεδέχην δ' ἄρασθαι
. . .
. . .

But it's not possible for it to be
. . . mortals . . . to share in and to pray for
. . .
. . .

25 . . .

. . .

remaining lines missing

Meter: Sapphic stanza.

31—"I think he's equal to the gods"

The sight of a beloved girl sitting opposite a young man who is enjoying her attention fills Sappho with a crippling sense of her own passion. The poem has sometimes been read as a wedding song, but the overwhelming physical effect of the speaker's passionate love and not the heterosexual relationship between girl and man are its main focus. Translated, with reference to his affair with "Lesbia," in Poem 51 of Catullus.

Φαίνεταί μοι κῆνος ἴσος θέοισιν
ἔμμεν' ὤνηρ, ὄττις ἐνάντιός τοι
ἰσδάνει καὶ πλάσιον ἆδυ φωνεί-
σας ὐπακούει

5   καὶ γελαίσας ἰμέροεν, τό μ' ἦ μὰν
καρδίαν ἐν στήθεσιν ἐπτόαισεν·
ὡς γὰρ ἔς σ' ἴδω βρόχε' ὤς με φώνη-
σ' οὐδὲν ἔτ' εἴκει,

ἀλλ' ἄκαν μὲν γλῶσσα †ἔαγε†, λέπτον
10   δ' αὔτικα χρῷ πῦρ ὐπαδεδρόμακεν,
ὀππάτεσσι δ' οὐδὲν ὄρημμ', ἐπιβρό-
μεισι δ' ἄκουαι,

†ἔκαδε† μ' ἴδρως κακχέεται, τρόμος δὲ
παῖσαν ἄγρει, χλωροτέρα δὲ ποίας
15   ἔμμι, τεθνάκην δ' ὀλίγω 'πιδεύης
φαίνομ' ἔμ' αὔτα.

ἀλλὰ πὰν τόλματον, ἐπεὶ †καὶ πένητα†

Meter: Sapphic stanza.

I think he's equal to the gods,
that man—whoever he is—across from you
who sits, and close by, while you're talking
sweetly, listens,

while you laugh charmingly. But for me,
it sets my heart pounding in my breast,
the moment I look at you; I can't
speak any more.

But my tongue is broken and silent,
   a delicate fire
suddenly runs under my skin,
my eyes see nothing, and there's a humming
in my ears,

sweat pours down me, trembling
grips my whole body; I'm paler than parched
grass. I'm almost going to die,
it seems to me.

But everything must be borne, for even
   a poor man

Sappho 47, 102, 105c, 111, 130, 140

In archaic Greek poetry, Eros (both the god and "desire") is by no means a gentle and amiable power. It is a mysterious and invincible external force, attacking and overwhelming the lover—in 47 with the violence of a storm. In 130, Eros is serpent-sly ("orpeton" means "creeping thing"), and bitter-sweet, or more accurately "sweet-bitter" ("glukupikron"), as well as invincible ("amachanon"). The innocent girl in love confiding in her mother, in 102, resembles a persona common in medieval Hispanic poetry. 105c, with its pathetic image of bloom and beauty heedlessly destroyed, is often interpreted as a symbol of defloration. 111 is from a wedding song, performed by a chorus of maidens—possibly antiphonally by choruses of girls and youths. 140 is part of a ritual lament in honor of Adonis, the second line in the persona of Aphrodite (Cytherea) bewailing her youthful lover, the first line spoken by her attendants.

47—"Eros has shattered my heart"

῎Ερος δ' ἐτίναξέ μοι
φρένας, ὠς ἄνεμος κὰτ ὄρος δρύσιν ἐμπέτων.

Eros has shattered my heart,
like a mountain wind falling upon the
   oak-trees.

Meter: Glyconic with two internal dactyls. The glyconic is an 8-syllable sequence: two syllables, long or short; then long–short–short–long–short–long.

102—"Sweet mother, I cannot ply the loom"

Γλύκηα μᾶτερ, οὔ τοι δύναμαι κρέκην τὸν
   ἴστον
πόθῳ δάμεισα παῖδος βραδίναν δι' 'Αφροδίταν

Sweet mother, I cannot ply the loom.
I'm overcome
with desire for a boy, because of slender
   Aphrodite.

Meter: Tetrameters; 1st measure iambic; 2nd–3rd glyconic; 4th baccheus. Baccheus: short–long–long.

105c—"Just as in the mountains the shepherd men trample a hyacinth"

οἴαν τάν ὑάκινθον ἐν ὤρεσι ποίμενες ἄνδρες

πόσσι καταστείβοισι, χάμαι δέ τε πόρφυρον
  ἄνθος . . .

Just as in the mountains the shepherd men
  trample a hyacinth
with their feet, and the purple flower lies on
  the ground.

Meter: Dactylic hexameters.

111—"Raise high the roof-beam"

῍Ιψοι δὴ τὸ μέλαθρον,
ὑμήναον,
ἀέρρετε, τέκτονες ἄνδρες·
ὑμήναον.
γάμβρος †εἰσέρχεται ἶσος ῎Αρευι†,
ἄνδρος μεγάλω πόλυ μέσδων.
ὑμήναον.

Raise high the roof-beam!
Hymen!
Raise it, you carpenters!
Hymen!
The bridegroom is coming like Ares—
much bigger than a big man.
Hymen!

Meter: Uncertain.

130—"Once again limb-loosening Eros shakes me"

῎Ερος δηῦτέ μ' ὁ λυσιμέλης δόνει,
γλυκύπικρον ἀμάχανον ὄρπετον

Once again limb-loosening Eros shakes me,
insinuating, irresistible, bitter though sweet.

Meter: Glyconic with internal dactyl.

140—"He is dying, Cytherea, graceful Adonis. What shall we do?"

Κατθνάσκει, Κυθέρη', ἄβρος ῎Αδωνις· τί κε
  θεῖμεν;
καττύπτεσθε, κόραι, καὶ κατερείκεσθε κίθωνας

He is dying, Cytherea, graceful Adonis.
  What shall we do?
Beat your breasts, maidens, and tear your
  garments.

Meter: Pherecratic (two syllables, long or short; then long–short–short–long–long) with two internal choriambs.

The Classical Period

Aristophanes

Ecclesiazusae ("Women at the Assembly") 952a–68b

In this farcical comedy, women take over the Athenian Assembly (the Ecclesia) and vote that everything, including sex, is to be shared in common, with the older and uglier having precedence over the younger and more attractive in the choice of partners. The following extract is part of a love duet between two young people. Immediately afterward, an old woman claims the young man, only to be challenged by an older, and then a still older and more hideous crone—to the horror of the hapless youth. The passage seems to parody a type of love-song very like some of the medieval examples included here, especially *Chume, chume, geselle min*, later. Compare also the unbridled passion of this pair of lovers with the tragic, destructive passion of Euripides's Medea.

952a Δεῦρο δή, δεῦρο δή,	Hither, hither,
952b φίλον ἐμόν, δεῦρό μοι	my love! Come hither to me.
πρόσελθε καὶ ξύνευνέ μοι	Come and lie with me,
954a τὴν εὐφρόνην ὅπως ἔσει.	and stay the whole night.
954b πάνυ γάρ τις ἔρως με δονεῖ	I'm completely overwhelmed with desire
955 τῶνδε τῶν σῶν βοστρύχων.	for your curling hair.
ἄτοπος δ' ἔγκειταί μοί τις πόθος,	An extraordinary longing possesses me;
ὅς με διακναίσας ἔχει.	it's worn me to a shred.
μέθες, ἱκνοῦμαί σ', Ἔρως,	Give me relief, I beg you, Eros,
959a καὶ ποίησον τόνδ' ἐς εὐνὴν	and make him come
959b τὴν ἐμὴν ἱκέσθαι.	to my chamber.
960 δεῦρο δή, δεῦρο δή,	Hither, hither,
φίλον ἐμόν, καὶ σύ μοι	my love! Come to me too.
καταδραμοῦσα τὴν θύραν	Come running and open the door.
ἄνοιξον τήνδ'· εἰ δὲ μή, καταπεσὼν κείσομαι.	If you don't, I'll fall down and lie here.
ἀλλ' ἐν τῷ σῷ βούλομαι κόλπῳ	But I want to be in your bosom
965 πληκτίζεσθαι μετὰ τῆς σῆς πυγῆς.	exchanging thrusts with your rear.
Κύπρι, τί μ' ἐκμαίνεις ἐπὶ ταύτῃ;	Cypris, why are you making me mad for her?
μέθες, ἱκνοῦμαί σ', Ἔρως,	Give me relief, I beg you, Eros,
968a καὶ ποίησον τήνδ' ἐς εὐνὴν	and make her come
968b τὴν ἐμὴν ἱκέσθαι.	to my chamber.

Provenance: Aristophanes lived ca. 450–ca. 388 B.C. *Ecclesiazusae* was produced in Athens, around 391 B.C.
Meter: One of the sung sections of the play, this passage uses cretic (long-short-long), iambic, possibly anapaestic (short–short–long), and trochaic meters. All of these are common in comedy; the iambic is associated with invective and burlesque, the cretic and trochaic with vigorous movement.

Euripides

Medea 465–519

When Jason went to Colchis to bring back the Golden Fleece, Medea, the king's daughter, helped him with her magic, and then fled with him, murdering and dismembering her brother to distract her father from his pursuit. Subsequently, she tricked the daughters of Pelias into killing their father by a grisly death, thinking they were going to make him young again. The action of Euripides's play takes place years later. Now Jason has abandoned Medea, and married the daughter of the king of Corinth. Medea will take a terrible vengeance, burning both princess and king to death by sending her a poisoned dress and crown. Nevertheless, the powerful speech that follows excites our sympathy. Euripides's Medea is no mere monster or oriental witch. She is indeed a sensationally bad woman, but also a heroic and tragic one. When, later in the play, she resolves to murder her children to punish her faithless husband, we see her torn between the tenderness of a mother and the fury of a woman scorned. With the following speech of Medea, and her condemnation of Jason, compare the words of Ovid's Ariadne, who condemns Theseus in very similar terms.

465 ὦ παγκάκιστε, τοῦτο γάρ σ᾽ εἰπεῖν ἔχω,

Oh, dregs of humanity! This is the greatest abuse

γλώσσῃ μέγιστον εἰς ἀνανδρίαν κακόν,

my tongue could contrive for your baseness!

ἦλθες πρὸς ἡμᾶς, ἦλθες ἔχθιστος γεγώς;

Have you actually come to me, you who are my direst enemy?

. . .

. . .

οὗτοι θράσος τόδ᾽ ἐστὶν οὐδ᾽ εὐτολμία,

This is not boldness; this is not courage—

470 φίλους κακῶς δράσαντ᾽ ἐναντίον βλέπειν,

to look your dear ones in the eye when you have wronged them.

ἀλλ᾽ ἡ μεγίστη τῶν ἐν ἀνθρώποις νόσων

but the greatest sickness that afflicts mankind,

πασῶν, ἀναίδει᾽. εὖ δ᾽ ἐποίησας μολών

the greatest of all, lack of shame. Yet, you have done some good,

ἐγώ τε γάρ λέξασα κουφισθήσομαι

for when I've said my say I will feel better,

ψυχὴν κακῶς σὲ καὶ σὺ λυπήσῃ κλύων.

and you will suffer hearing it.

475 ἐκ τῶν δὲ πρώτων πρῶτον ἄρξομαι λέγειν·

I'll begin at the beginning.

ἔσωσά σ᾽, ὡς ἴσασιν Ἑλλήνων ὅσοι

I saved you. The Greeks know it,

ταὐτὸν συνεισέβησαν Ἀργῷον σκάφος,

all those who embarked on that ship, the Argo,

πεμφθέντα ταύρων πυρπνόων ἐπιστάτην

when you were sent to subdue the fire-breathing bulls to the yoke

ζεύγλαισι καὶ σπεροῦντα θανάσιμον γύην·

and sow the deadly field.

480 δράκοντά θ᾽, ὃς πάγχρυσον ἀμπέχων δέρος

The dragon which surrounded the Golden Fleece,

σπείραις ἔσῳζε πολυπλόκοις ἄυπνος ὤν,

sleeplessly guarding it with his many-folded coils,

κτείνασ᾽ ἀνέσχον σοι φάος σωτήριον.

I killed—I held up for you the light of safety.

αὐτὴ δὲ πατέρα καὶ δόμους προδοῦσ᾽ ἐμοὺς

I personally betrayed my father and my house,

τὴν Πηλιῶτιν εἰς Ἰωλκὸν ἱκόμην

when I came to Iolchos and the foot of Mount Pelion

485 σὺν σοί, πρόθυμος μᾶλλον ἢ σοφωτέρα·

with you; I was more eager than wise.

Πελίαν τ᾽ ἀπέκτειν᾽, ὥσπερ ἄλγιστον θανεῖν,

I killed Pelias; he died a most dreadful death,

παίδων ὕπ᾽ αὐτοῦ, πάντα τ᾽ ἐξεῖλον δόμον.

at the hands of his own daughters; I brought ruin on the whole house.

καὶ ταῦθ᾽ ὑφ᾽ ἡμῶν, ὦ κάκιστ᾽ ἀνδρῶν, παθὼν

And when I had done all this for you, vilest of men,

προύδωκας ἡμᾶς, καινὰ δ᾽ ἐκτήσω λέχη,

you betrayed me: you got yourself a new marriage bed,

490 παίδων γεγώτων· εἰ γὰρ ἦσθ᾽ ἄπαις ἔτι,

though I had borne your children. If you had been still childless

συγγνώστ' ἂν ἦν σοι τοῦδ' ἐρασθῆναι λέχους.

it would have been pardonable to lust after another.

ὅρκων δὲ φρούδη πίστις, οὐδ' ἔχω μαθεῖν

Fidelity to oaths has vanished. I can't discover

εἰ θεοὺς νομίζεις τοὺς τότ' οὐκ ἄρχειν ἔτι

whether you think the gods who ruled no longer do,

ἢ καινὰ κεῖσθαι θέσμι' ἀνθρώποις τὰ νῦν,

or believe there are new divine decrees for modern men,

495 ἐπεὶ σύνοισθά γ' εἰς ἔμ' οὐκ εὔορκος ὤν.

since you well know you have broken your vow to me.

φεῦ δεξιὰ χείρ, ἧς σὺ πόλλ' ἐλαμβάνου

Alas, my right hand, which you often used to clasp,

καὶ τῶνδε γονάτων, ὡς μάτην κεχρώσμεθα

and my knees—how idly I have been touched in appeal

κακοῦ πρὸς ἀνδρός, ἐλπίδων δ' ἡμάρτομεν.

by an evil man. I have been disappointed in my hopes.

ἄγ', ὡς φίλῳ γὰρ ὄντι σοι κοινώσομαι

Come now. Shall I speak to you as if you were still dear to me?

500 (δοκοῦσα μὲν τί πρός γε σοῦ πράξειν καλῶς;

What benefit could I think to get from a man like you?

ὅμως δ', ἐρωτηθεὶς γὰρ αἰσχίων φανῇ)·

Yet I will appeal, for then you will be revealed as even more shameless.

νῦν ποῖ τράπωμαι; πότερα πρὸς πατρὸς δόμους,

Now where am I to turn? To my father's halls?

οὓς σοὶ προδοῦσα καὶ πάτραν ἀφικόμην;

I betrayed them and my country to you when I came here.

ἢ πρὸς ταλαίνας Πελιάδας; καλῶς γ' ἂν οὖν

Or to the wretched daughters of Pelias? They would welcome me

505 δέξαιντό μ' οἴκοις ὧν πατέρα κατέκτανον.

into the household whose father I had killed!

ἔχει γὰρ οὕτω· τοῖς μὲν οἴκοθεν φίλοις

This is how it is. To my dear family at home

ἐχθρὰ καθέστηχ', οὓς δέ μ' οὐκ ἐχρῆν κακῶς

I have become an enemy. Those whom I should not have ill-treated

δρᾶν, σοὶ χάριν φέρουσα πολεμίους ἔχω.

I have made my foes—to do a favor to you.

τοιγάρ με πολλαῖς μακαρίαν Ἑλληνίδων

You have made many Grecian women bless me

510 ἔθηκας ἀντὶ τῶνδε· θαυμαστὸν δέ σε

for these things. What a fine trustworthy

ἔχω πόσιν καὶ πιστὸν ἡ τάλαιν' ἐγώ,

husband I have in you, wretched me,

εἰ φεύξομαί γε γαῖαν ἐκβεβλημένη,

if I am cast out of the country and must flee,

φίλων ἔρημος, σὺν τέκνοις μόνη μόνοις·

bereft of friends, alone with my orphaned children:

καλόν γ' ὄνειδος τῷ νεωστὶ νυμφίῳ,

a nice reproach to a new husband,

515 πτωχοὺς ἀλᾶσθαι παῖδας ἥ τ' ἔσωσά σε.

that your children wander as beggars, with the woman who rescued you.

ὦ Ζεῦ, τί δὴ χρυσοῦ μὲν ὃς κίβδηλος ᾖ

Oh, Zeus, why, when you gave people

τεκμήρι' ἀνθρώποισιν ὤπασας σαφῆ,

clear proofs of gold that was counterfeit,

ἀνδρῶν δ' ὅτῳ χρὴ τὸν κακὸν διειδέναι

did you not set a mark on the bodies of men,

οὐδεὶς χαρακτὴρ ἐμπέφυκε σώματι;

by which to know the evil from the good!

Provenance: Euripides lived ca. 485–406 B.C. *Medea* was produced at Athens in 431.
Meter: Iambic trimeters, the usual meter for dramatic dialogue.

The Trojan Women 657–83

Troy has fallen. All the men are dead, the women and children captive. In this play, the women of Troy lament their fate. Prominent among them are Hecuba and Andromache, the widows of Priam and Hector, respectively. Here, Andromache tells Hecuba that the recent killing of her daughter Polyxena as a sacrifice to the slain Achilles is less tragic than Andromache's own fate. Her misery springs not only from the loss of her husband but also from the loss of her own status, and the prospect of enslavement to the son of the man who killed Hector. Even more intense than the present speech are her later words spoken over Astyanax, their little son, about to be flung to his death from the walls of Troy. Andromache's grief and humiliation in *The Trojan Women* invite comparison with Guthrun and her circle of women, similarly grieving—but also furiously angry, in the Norse "First Lay of Guthrun."

καὶ τῶνδε κληδὼν ἐς στράτευμ' Ἀχαιικὸν	It was my praise coming to the Achaean army
ἐλθοῦσ' ἀπώλεσέν μ'· ἐπεὶ γὰρ ᾑρέθην,	that destroyed me, for when I was captured
Ἀχιλλέως με παῖς ἐβουλήθη λαβεῖν	Achilles' son wished to take me
660 δάμαρτα· δουλεύσω δ' ἐν αὐθεντῶν δόμοις.	as his wife. So I shall be a slave in the house of murderers.
κεἰ μὲν παρώσασ' Ἕκτορος φίλον κάρα	If I put my beloved Hector aside
πρὸς τὸν παρόντα πόσιν ἀναπτύξω φρένα,	and welcome my present husband into my heart,
κακὴ φανοῦμαι τῷ θανόντι· τόνδε δ' αὖ	I shall seem to do the dead man wrong. But if
στυγοῦσ' ἐμαυτῆς δεσπόταις μισήσομαι.	I spurn this new husband, I shall be hated by my own master.
665 καίτοι λέγουσιν ὡς μί' εὐφρόνη χαλᾷ	Yet they say that a single night dissolves
τὸ δυσμενὲς γυναικὸς εἰς ἀνδρὸς λέχος·	the loathing a woman feels for a man's bed.
ἀπέπτυσ' αὐτὴν ἥτις ἄνδρα τὸν πάρος	I spit on anyone who casts her first husband aside,
καινοῖσι λέκτροις ἀποβαλοῦσ' ἄλλον φιλεῖ.	takes a new bed, and loves another.
ἀλλ' οὐδὲ πῶλος ἥτις ἂν διαζυγῇ	No filly separated from the filly with whom she has been reared
670 τῆς συντραφείσης ῥᾳδίως ἕλκει ζυγόν.	finds it easy to bear the yoke.
καίτοι τὸ θηριῶδες ἄφθογγόν τ' ἔφυ	Yet a beast is dumb and without intellect,
ξυνέσει τ' ἄχρηστον τῇ φύσει τε λείπεται.	and of a lower order.
σὲ δ', ὦ φίλ' Ἕκτορ, εἶχον ἄνδρ' ἀρκοῦντά μοι,	In you, dear Hector, I had a man who was all I wanted:
ξυνέσει γένει πλούτῳ τε κἀνδρείᾳ μέγαν,	great in intellect, in birth, in wealth, and in valor.

675 ἀκήρατον δέ μ' ἐκ πατρὸς λαβὼν δόμων | You took me intact from my father's house.

πρῶτος τὸ παρθένειον ἐζεύξω λέχος. | You were the first to yoke my virginity in the marriage bed.

καὶ νῦν ὄλωλας μὲν σύ, ναυσθλοῦμαι δ' ἐγὼ | And now you are gone, and I must sail

πρὸς Ἑλλάδ' αἰχμάλωτος ἐς δοῦλον ζυγόν. | to Greece, a captive, to the yoke of slavery.

ἆρ' οὐκ ἐλάσσω τῶν ἐμῶν ἔχει κακῶν | Is not Polyxena's violent death, which you bewail,

680 Πολυξένης ὄλεθρος, ἥν καταστένεις; | less dreadful than my woes?

ἐμοὶ γὰρ οὐδ' ὃ πᾶσι λείπεται βροτοῖς | For me not even the last thing left for all mortals remains—

ξύνεστιν ἐλπίς, οὐδὲ κλέπτομαι φρένας | hope. I cannot deceive my heart

πράξειν τι κεδνόν· ἡδὺ δ' ἐστὶ καὶ δοκεῖν. | that I will receive any comfort—but fantasy is sweet.

Provenance: Athens, 415 B.C.
Meter: Iambic trimeters.

The Hellenistic and Roman Periods

Theocritus

Idyll 18 (The Epithalamion for Helen) 9–58

Whereas Sappho's epithalamia were composed for performance at real weddings, Theocritus's is a literary fiction that evokes the mythical past. Here Helen is a young girl, and the Trojan War not yet dreamed of. Helen's playmates sing in praise of their idol, celebrating her somewhat in the way Alcman's girl-chorus celebrate Astymeloisa. The 8-line introductory passage is omitted.

Οὕτω δὴ πρῳζὰ κατέδραθες, ὦ φίλε γαμβρέ; | Are you abed so early, dear bridegroom?

10 ἦ ῥα' τις ἐσσὶ λίαν βαρυγούνατος; ἦ ῥα φίλυπνος; | Were you heavy-kneed and anxious for sleep?

ἦ ῥα πολύν τιν' ἔπινες, ὅκ' εἰς εὐνὰν κατεβάλλευ; | Had you drunk rather well when you came to your bed?

εὕδειν μὰν σπεύδοντα καθ' ὥραν αὐτὸν ἐχρῆν τυ, | If you were eager to sleep, you should have slept alone!

παῖδα δ' ἐᾶν σὺν παισὶ φιλοστόργῳ παρὰ ματρί | And left that young girl with her friends at her kind mother's house,

παίσδειν ἐς βαθὺν ὄρθρον, ἐπεὶ καὶ ἔνας καὶ ἐς ἀῶ | playing till late in the morn. For until tomorrow's dawn,

15 κῆς ἔτος ἐξ ἔτεος, Μενέλαε, τεὰ νυὸς ἅδε. | and through all the years to come, this bride, Menelaus, will be your own.

ὄλβιε γάμβρ', ἀγαθός τις ἐπέπταρεν ἐρχομένῳ τοι | Favored bridegroom, some good soul sneezed auspiciously

ἐς Σπάρταν ἄπερ ὦλλοι ἀριστέες, ὡς ἀνύσαιο· | so you would win, when you came to Sparta with the other fine men.

μῶνος ἐν ἡμιθέοις Κρονίδαν Δία πενθερὸν ἑξεῖς. | You alone of those heroes shall call Zeus son of Cronos your father-in-law.

Ζανός τοι θυγάτηρ ὑπὸ τὰν μίαν ἵκετο χλαῖναν,
For Zeus's daughter has come beneath the same coverlet as you.

20 οἷα 'Αχαιιάδων γαῖαν πατεῖ οὐδεμί' ἄλλα·
No other like her treads the earth of Greece.

ἦ μέγα κά τι τέκοιτ' εἰ ματέρι τίκτοι ὁμοῖον.
Wondrous will be her offspring if her child is like its mother.

ἄμμες δ' αἱ πᾶσαι συνομάλικες, αἷς δρόμος ωὑτός
All we girls of the same age ran races together,

χρισαμέναις ἀνδριστὶ παρ' Εὐρώταο λοετροῖς,
oiling our bodies like men, by the Eurotas where we bathed,

τετράκις ἑξήκοντα κόραι, θῆλυς νεολαία,
four time sixty maidens, a band of young girls,

25 τᾶν οὐδ' ἅτις ἄμωμος ἐπεί χ' Ἑλένᾳ παρισωθῇ.
but not one would be perfect compared to Helen.

'Αὼς ἀντέλλοισα καλὸν διέφανε πρόσωπον,
The rising dawn has shown her lovely face,

πότνια Νύξ, τό τε λευκὸν ἔαρ χειμῶνος ἀνέντος·
Lady Night, like shining spring when winter passes away.

ὧδε καὶ ἁ χρυσέα Ἑλένα διεφαίνετ' ἐν ἁμῖν.
Thus golden Helen showed herself among us.

πιείρα μεγάλα ἅτ' ἀνέδραμε κόσμος ἀρούρᾳ
As thick grain standing high gives splendor to a fertile field,

30 καὶ κάπῳ κυπάρισσος, ἢ ἅρματι Θεσσαλὸς ἵππος,
a cypress-tree to a garden, and a Thessalian horse to a chariot,

ὧδε καὶ ἁ ῥοδόχρως Ἑλένα Λακεδαίμονι κόσμος·
just so rose-soft Helen gives splendor to Lacedaemonian Sparta.

οὐδέ τις ἐκ ταλάρω πανίσδεται ἔργα τοιαῦτα,
No woman draws out the thread from the basket as well-spun as she,

οὐδ' ἐνὶ δαιδαλέῳ πυκινώτερον ἄτριον ἱστῷ
nor at the cunning loom weaves a closer web,

κερκίδι συμπλέξαισα μακρῶν ἔταμ' ἐκ κελεόντων.
stamping it with the rod between the mighty beams.

35 οὐ μὰν οὐδὲ λύραν τις ἐπίσταται ὧδε κροτῆσαι
No one knows how to sound the lyre,

'Άρτεμιν ἀείδοισα καὶ εὐρύστερνον 'Αθάναν
hymning Artemis and broad-breasted Athene,

ὡς Ἑλένα, τᾶς πάντες ἐπ' ὄμμασιν ἵμεροι ἐντί.
like Helen, in whose eyes all love-desires are born.

ὦ καλά, ὦ χαρίεσσα κόρα, τὺ μὲν οἰκέτις ἤδη.
Oh fair, oh grace-endowed maiden, you have your own household now.

ἄμμες δ' ἐς Δρόμον ἦρι καὶ ἐς λειμώνια φύλλα
But we shall slip away early to the race-course and the flowery meadows,

40 ἑρψεῦμες στεφάνως δρεψεύμεναι ἁδὺ πνέοντας,
to pluck garlands breathing sweet fragrance—

πολλὰ τεοῦς, Ἑλένα, μεμναμέναι ὡς γαλαθηναί
thinking of you, Helen, just as the lambs

ἄρνες γειναμένας ὄιος μαστὸν ποθέοισαι.
long to draw milk from the teat of their mother ewe.

πρᾶταί τοι στέφανον λωτῶ χαμαὶ αὐξομένοιο
We shall be the first to weave a garland of clover that spreads

πλέξαισαι σκιαρὰν καταθήσομεν ἐς πλατάνιστον·
over the ground, and hang it on a shady plane-tree.

45 πρᾶται δ' ἀργυρέας ἐξ ὄλπιδος ὑγρὸν ἄλειφαρ
We shall be the first to take moist oil in a silver flask

λαζύμεναι σταξεῦμες ὑπὸ σκιαρὰν πλατάνιστον·
to drip under that shady plane-tree.

γράμματα δ' ἐν φλοιῷ γεγράψεται, ὡς παριών τις
And letters shall be written in the bark for the passer-by to read

ἀννείμη Δωριστί· "σέβευ μ'· Ἑλένας φυτόν εἰμι."	this message in Doric style: "Hold me sacred; I am Helen's tree."
Χαίροις, ὦ νύμφα· χαίροις, εὐπένθερε γαμβρέ.	Farewell, bride; farewell bridegroom and favored son-in-law.

50

Λατὼ μὲν δοίη, Λατὼ κουροτρόφος, ὕμμιν	May Leto, nurse of the young, grant to you
εὐτεκνίαν, Κύπρις δέ, θεὰ Κύπρις, ἶσον ἔρασθαι	fine children, and Aphrodite of Cyprus reciprocated love,
ἀλλάλων, Ζεὺς δέ, Κρονίδας Ζεύς, ἄφθιτον ὄλβον,	and Zeus son of Cronos unfading prosperity,
ὡς ἐξ εὐπατριδᾶν εἰς εὐπατρίδας πάλιν ἔνθῃ.	that will pass from noble parents to noble children.
εὕδετ' ἐς ἀλλάλων στέρνον φιλότατα πνέοντες	Sleep on each other's breast, breathing love

55

καὶ πόθον· ἐγρέσθαι δὲ πρὸς ἀῶ μὴ 'πιλάθησθε.	and desire. But remember to wake at dawn.
νεύμεθα κάμμες ἐς ὄρθρον, ἐπεί κα πρᾶτος ἀοιδός	We too shall come at daybreak, when the first songster
ἐξ εὐνᾶς κελαδήσῃ ἀνασχὼν εὔτριχα δειράν.	summons us from bed, as he lifts his feathery neck to crow.
Ὑμὴν ὦ Ὑμέναιε, γάμῳ ἐπὶ τῷδε χαρείης.	Oh Hymen, Wedding God, may you rejoice in this wedding.

Provenance: Theocritus lived ca. 300–ca. 260 B.C. Born in Syracuse, Sicily, he seems to have been active on the island of Cos and in Alexandria.
Meter: Dactylic hexameters.

Anonymous

The Locrian Song

The following fragment is quoted by Athenaeus around the turn of the second to third century A.D. as an example of adulterous ("moichikai") songs. He also mentions Locrian songs earlier, noting that Clearchus [who wrote in the fourth century B.C.] said they were no different from the poems of Sappho and Anacreon (Athenaeus 15.639a and 697b–c), presumably meaning that they were similarly erotic. Though undistinguished poetically, the Locrian Song is an interesting early example of the song of dawn parting, the alba. The illicit love and the jealous husband, familiar in medieval albas, also appear here.

ὦ τί πάσχεις; μὴ προδῷς ἄμμ', ἱκετεύω·	Oh, what is the matter with you? Don't betray us, I beg;
πρὶν καὶ μολεῖν κεῖνον, ἀνίστω,	get up before "he" comes.
μὴ κακόν σε μέγα ποιήσῃ	Lest he do violence to you
κἀμὲ τὰν δειλάκραν.	and poor me.
ἀμέρα καὶ ἤδη τὸ φῶς	It is already day. Don't you see the light
διὰ τᾶς θυρίδος οὐκ εἰσορῇς;	coming in through the window?

Provenance: Locri Epizephyrii in southern Italy, ca. A.D. 200. This is very late, but songs of this type go back a long way, probably well beyond Clearchus's fourth-century reference to them.
Meter: Uncertain; apparently a stanza from a song. The term "Locrian" may refer to music and meter as well as content.

CHAPTER 2
ANCIENT ROME

Nearly all extant classical Latin poetry is male authored. The composers of personal love poems—Catullus, Propertius, Tibullus, and Ovid—write almost exclusively from the man's point of view in this supposedly confessional poetry, for which they use elegiac couplets. Latin love elegy is a well-developed genre, but very little of it is woman's song. Propertius 4.3 is composed in the persona of a woman writing to her lover. Horace, *Odes* 3.12 *may* be a dramatic monologue on the subject of love in the persona of a woman. However, if we turn to epic poetry, we find women's voices echoing themes of anger and betrayal that resonate with other voices throughout this book, and that recall especially the women's voices of Greek tragedy. Epic lends itself to dramatic speeches, and provides Catullus and Virgil with a framework within which to breathe life into women from the mythic past. In the *Heroides*, Ovid adapts love elegy to a mythological setting. The epistolary voices of his "heroines" can be rather stilted; Ariadne's is one of the more dynamic. Ovidian, or pseudo-Ovidian, Sappho is titillatingly scandalous. Roman Ariadne, Dido, and Sappho speak in the grand style, and are very much the products of a learned, intertextual literary culture.

The poems of Sulpicia stand apart from all these, and closer to most of the other woman's songs in this collection. Composed in elegiacs, they lay claim to the same territory as the male love-elegists, but their voice is very different. Sulpicia's more unassuming style, coupled with her strong sense of personal worth, invites comparison with the real Sappho before her, and with the women troubadours after.

See Julia Haig Gaissner, "Threads in the Labyrinth: Competing Views and Voices in Catullus 64," *American Journal of Philology* 116 (1995): 579–616; Judith Hallett, "Women's Voices and Catullus' Poetry," *Classical World* 95 (2002): 421–24; Francis Cairns, *Virgil's Augustan Epic* (contains chapters on Dido) (1989); S. Georgia Nugent, "The Women of the Aeneid: Vanishing Bodies, Lingering Voices," *Reading Vergil's Aeneid*, ed. Christine Perkell (1999); Mathilde Skoie, *Reading Sulpicia* (2002); Alison Keith, *Tandem venit amor* (on Sulpicia), and Pam Gordon, "The Lover's Voice in *Heroides* 15," both in *Roman Sexualities*, ed. Judith Hallett and Marilyn Skinner (1997); Florence Verducci, *Ovid's Toyshop of the Heart: Epistulae Heroidum* (1985); Marilynn Desmond, "When Dido Reads Virgil: Gender and Intertextuality in Ovid's *Heroides* 7," *Helios* 20 (1993): 56–68, and, by the same author, *Reading Dido: Gender, Textuality, and the Medieval Aeneid* (1994).

Catullus

Carmina 64.124–201—*Lament of Ariadne*

Poem 64, an epyllion, or mini-epic, on the marriage of Peleus and Thetis, contains a long description of the splendid coverlet for the marriage bed, embroidered with the story of Ariadne and Theseus. The centrepiece of this account is the soliloquy of Ariadne when she finds herself abandoned on the island of Naxos, after she helped Theseus escape from the labyrinth of the Minotaur. Ariadne's lament combines the desperation of her own plight with a passionate outcry against her seducer, culminating in a final curse.

saepe illam perhibent ardenti corde furentem	They say that in her frenzy, with burning heart and deep-drawn breath,
125 clarisonas imo fudisse e pectore voces,	repeatedly she cried aloud,
ac tum praeruptos tristem conscendere montes,	then sadly climbed the steep hills
unde aciem in pelagi vastos protenderet aestus,	to fix her gaze on the ocean's restless expanse,
tum tremuli salis adversas procurrere in undas	then ran out to meet the waves of the shifting sea,
mollia nudatae tollentem tegmina surae,	lifting her light robe from her bare limbs,
130 atque haec extremis maestam dixisse querellis,	and mournfully uttered her final lament,
frigidulos udo singultus ore cientem:	with tear-soaked face and trembling sobs:
"sicine me patriis avectam, perfide, ab aris,	"Have you left me like this, the girl whom you carried off from her father's hearth,
perfide, deserto liquisti in litore, Theseu?	abandoned on a desolate shore, false, false Theseus?
sicine discedens neglecto numine divum,	Are you departing like this, ignoring the power of the gods,
135 immemor a! devota domum periuria portas?	unmindful of me—oh!—taking your cursed perjuries home with you?
nullane res potuit crudelis flectere mentis	Could nothing change your cruel plans?
consilium? tibi nulla fuit clementia praesto,	Was there no kindness in you
immite ut nostri vellet miserescere pectus?	to prompt your ruthless heart to pity me?
at non haec quondam blanda promissa dedisti	These are not the smooth promises your voice once made me;
140 voce mihi, non haec miserae sperare iubebas,	this is not what you bade me hope for— wretched me,
sed conubia laeta, sed optatos hymenaeos,	but a joyful union, a happy wedding—
quae cuncta aerii discerpunt irrita venti.	all empty words to scatter to the airy winds.
nunc iam nulla viro iuranti femina credat,	But now let no woman have faith in a man,
nulla viri speret sermones esse fideles;	let no woman hope a man's words will be trustworthy;
145 quis dum aliquid cupiens animus praegestit apisci,	as long as their minds are set on getting what they crave,

nihil metuunt iurare, nihil promittere parcunt:

they shrink from no oaths, spare no promises:

sed simul ac cupidae mentis satiata libido est,

but as soon as they've satisfied the desire of their lustful hearts,

dicta nihil meminere, nihil periuria curant.

they remember nothing of their words, care nothing for their broken vows.

certe ego te in medio versantem turbine leti

It was I, in truth, who saved you whirling in the labyrinth

150 eripui, et potius germanum amittere crevi,

of death, and I thought it better to lose my brother,

quam tibi fallaci supremo in tempore dessem.

than fail you at that desperate time—you who have deceived me.

pro quo dilaceranda feris dabor alitibusque

For this I'll be given to the beasts and birds to tear apart

praeda, neque iniacta tumulabor mortua terra.

as prey. I'll lie unburied, when I'm dead; no earth will be piled over me.

quaenam te genuit sola sub rupe leaena,

What lioness bore you beneath a solitary rock?

155 quod mare conceptum spumantibus exspuit undis,

What sea conceived you and spewed you from its foaming waves?

quae Syrtis, quae Scylla rapax, quae vasta Carybdis,

What Syrtis, what greedy Scylla, what vast Charybdis?

talia qui reddis pro dulci praemia vita?

—you who return this thanks for sweet life preserved.

si tibi non cordi fuerant conubia nostra,

If our marriage was not what you had at heart—

saeva quod horrebas prisci praecepta parentis,

because you feared the cruel commands of your strict father,

160 attamen in vestras potuisti ducere sedes,

yet you could have brought me to your home

quae tibi iucundo famularer serva labore,

to serve you as your slave with cheerful labor,

candida permulcens liquidis vestigia lymphis,

washing your white feet with clear water,

purpureave tuum consternens veste cubile.

or laying purple spreads over your bed.

sed quid ego ignaris nequiquam conquerar auris,

But why do I lament in vain to the heedless winds,

165 externata malo, quae nullis sensibus auctae

crazed at my evil fate? They possess no senses;

nec missas audire queunt nec reddere voces?

they can neither hear words spoken nor utter them in reply.

ille autem prope iam mediis versatur in undis,

For by this time he's tossing on the high sea,

nec quisquam apparet vacua mortalis in alga.

and there's no mortal in sight on this empty, weed-strewn shore.

sic nimis insultans extremo tempore saeva

Mocking me thus in my extremity, a savage fate

170 fors etiam nostris invidit questibus auris.

denies even an ear to my laments.

Iuppiter omnipotens, utinam ne tempore primo

Great Jupiter, if only the ships of Cecrops' race

Cnosia Cecropiae tetigissent litora puppes,

had never touched Cnossos' shore.

indomito nec dira ferens stipendia tauro

If only that traitor, with his dreadful wages for the untamed bull

perfidus in Creta religasset navita funem,

had never moored his ship's cable in Crete,

175 nec malus hic celans dulci crudelia forma	nor, evil guest, hiding cruel plans under winning looks,
consilia in nostris requiesset sedibus hospes!	ever sojourned in my home!
nam quo me referam? quali spe perdita nitor?	For where shall I turn? I am lost—what hope is there in my struggle?
Idaeosne petam montes? at gurgite lato	Shall I seek the mountain of Ida? But the dividing expanse
discernens ponti truculentum dividit aequor.	of the turbulent sea and its mighty surge lie between.
180 an patris auxilium sperem? quemne ipsa reliqui	Shall I hope for help from my father whom I left behind
respersum iuvenem fraterna caede secuta?	to follow a young man stained with my brother's blood?
coniugis an fido consoler memet amore?	Shall I console myself with a husband's faithful love—
quine fugit lentos incurvans gurgite remos?	the husband who is hastening across the sea, bending to the resisting oars?
praeterea nullo litus, sola insula, tecto,	Besides, the shore is shelterless, the island solitary.
185 nec patet egressus pelagi cingentibus undis.	The waves encircle it; there's no way out—
nulla fugae ratio, nulla spes: omnia muta,	no means of flight, no hope; all is dumb,
omnia sunt deserta, ostentant omnia letum.	all deserted; all points to the fatal end.
non tamen ante mihi languescent lumina morte,	But let not my eyes grow dim in death,
nec prius a fesso secedent corpore sensus,	nor the senses leave my exhausted body
190 quam iustam a divis exposcam prodita multam	until I demand the gods' just punishment for my betrayal,
caelestumque fidem postrema comprecer hora.	and plead to faithful heaven in my final hour.
quare facta virum multantes vindice poena	Therefore, you who punish with avenging pains the deeds of men,
Eumenides, quibus anguino redimita capillo	Eumenides, heads framed with snaky hair
frons exspirantis praeportat pectoris iras,	that hisses out the rage within your breasts,
195 huc huc adventate, meas audite querellas,	come, come hither, and hear my lamentations,
quas ego, vae misera, extremis proferre medullis	which I, poor wretch, wring from my very vitals,
cogor inops, ardens, amenti caeca furore.	forced to this point, helpless, burning, blinded by love's madness.
quae quoniam verae nascuntur pectore ab imo,	Because my laments are true, because they spring from my inmost heart,
vos nolite pati nostrum vanescere luctum,	don't let my sorrows be in vain,
200 sed quali solam Theseus me mente reliquit,	but, as unconcerned as when he abandoned me,
tali mente, deae, funestet seque suosque!"	just so, goddesses, let Theseus defile with death his loved ones and himself."

Provenance: Gaius Valerius Catullus, 84–54 B.C. From Verona; active in Rome.
Meter: Dactylic hexameters.

Virgil

Aeneid 4.305–30, 365–87—Two Laments of Dido

Dido, queen of Carthage, has befriended Aeneas, shipwrecked on her shore, and taken him as her lover. Now summoned by Mercury to set off on his way for Italy again and fulfill his mission, Aeneas is abandoning her. Dido first pleads eloquently, and then rails with savage bitterness. Like Ariadne's, her words culminate in a chilling curse.

305 "dissimulare etiam sperasti, perfide, tantum	"Did you even think, traitor, you could hide
posse nefas tacitusque mea decedere terra?	such a crime, and sneak away from my country?
nec te noster amor nec te data dextera quondam	Doesn't our love hold you back, our hands once joined,
nec moritura tenet crudeli funere Dido?	the cruel death awaiting Dido?
quin etiam hiberno moliris sidere classem	Why are you launching your ships under wintry skies,
310 et mediis properas Aquilonibus ire per altum,	hurrying to sea in the midst of north winds?
crudelis? quid, si non arva aliena domosque	Cruel! If you weren't aiming at foreign fields
ignotas peteres, et Troia antiqua maneret,	and homes unknown, if old Troy were still standing,
Troia per undosum peteretur classibus aequor?	would you head for Troy with your ships across the swelling sea?
mene fugis? per ego has lacrimas dextramque tuam te	Are you running away from me? By these tears, by your right hand
315 (quando aliud mihi iam miserae nihil ipsa reliqui),	(since by my own actions I have deprived myself of everything else, poor wretch),
per conubia nostra, per inceptos hymenaeos,	by our wedded life together, by our marriage begun,
si bene quid de te merui, fuit aut tibi quicquam	if I have deserved anything from you, if you have found anything in me
dulce meum, miserere domus labentis et istam,	sweet, have pity on a falling house and on your Dido,
oro, si quis adhuc precibus locus, exue mentem.	I beg you, if there is any place left for my appeals, change your mind.
320 te propter Libycae gentes Nomadumque tyranni	Because of you the Libyan tribes, the Nomad chieftains,
odere, infensi Tyrii; te propter eundem	and the fierce Tyrians hate me; because of you too
exstinctus pudor et, qua sola sidera adibam,	I put aside my modesty and that by which alone I aspired to the stars,
fama prior. cui me moribundam deseris,— hospes	my former good name. To what are you abandoning me, my guest
(hoc solum nomen quoniam de coniuge restat)?	(since only that name is left of 'husband')?
325 quid moror? an mea Pygmalion dum moenia frater	For what should I wait? Until my brother Pygmalion
destruat aut captam ducat Gaetulus Iarbas?	tears down my walls, or Gaetulian Iarbas leads me captive?
saltem si qua mihi de te suscepta fuisset	At least if there perhaps had been a child of mine

ante fugam suboles, si quis mihi parvulus
   aula
luderet Aeneas, qui te tamen ore referret,

330   non equidem omnino capta ac deserta viderer.

. . .

365   nec tibi diva parens generis nec Dardanus
    auctor,
perfide, sed duris genuit te cautibus horrens

Caucasus Hyrcanaeque admorunt ubera
   tigres.
nam quid dissimulo aut quae me ad maiora
   reservo?
num fletu ingemuit nostro? num lumina
   flexit?
370   num lacrimas victus dedit aut miseratus
   amantem est?
quae quibus anteferam? iam iam nec maxima
   Iuno
nec Saturnius haec oculis pater aspicit aequis.

nusquam tuta fides. eiectum litore, egentem

excepi et regni demens in parte locavi.

375   amissam classem, socios a morte reduxi

(heu furiis incensa feror!): nunc augur Apollo,

nunc Lyciae sortes, nunc et Iove missus ab
   ipso
interpres divum fert horrida iussa per auras.

scilicet is superis labor est, ea cura quietos

380   sollicitat. neque te teneo neque dicta refello:

i, sequere Italiam ventis, pete regna per
   undas.
spero equidem mediis, si quid pia numina
   possunt,
supplicia hausurum scopulis et nomine Dido

saepe vocaturum. sequar atris ignibus absens

385   et, cum frigida mors anima seduxerit artus,

omnibus umbra locis adero. dabis, improbe,
   poenas.
audiam et haec manis veniet mihi fama sub
   imos."

conceived by you before your flight, if some
little Aeneas
played in my courtyard, who would in spite
of things bring back your face,
then I would not seem so wholly vanquished
and deserted.

. . .

No goddess was your mother, nor Dardanus
the founder of your race,
traitor, but the savage Caucasus with its
hard rocks
engendered you, and Hyrcanean tigresses
gave you their teats.
What am I hiding, what greater occasion
saving myself for?
Has he groaned at my weeping? Has he
turned his eyes?
Has he been moved to tears, or taken pity on
his lover?
What complaints should I make, to whom?
Now, now neither great Juno
nor Saturnian Jupiter looks on these events
with impartial eyes.
Nowhere can good faith be counted on.
When he was cast destitute upon the shore,
I took him in, settled him in part of my
kingdom—I was mad!
I brought back his lost fleet, restored his
companions from death
(oh, I must be carried away, inflamed by the
Furies!): now Apollo prophesies
and the Lycian oracle; now, sent by high
Jupiter himself,
even the Messenger of the Gods brings
dreadful commands through the air.
This business, to be sure, makes work for
those above, this care disturbs their rest.
I will not detain you nor challenge your
words:
go, head for Italy with the winds, seek your
kingdom across the waves.
Indeed, I hope—if righteous gods have any
power—
you'll drain the cup of agonies, surrounded
by sharp rocks, and call repeatedly
on Dido's name. Far away, in smoky funeral
flames, I'll follow you,
and when icy death has parted soul and
limbs,
my shade will be present everywhere. Wicked
man! You'll be punished,
and I'll hear; the news of it will come to me
deep among the dead below."

Provenance: Publius Vergilius Maro, 70–19 B.C. From Mantua; active there and in Rome. Began work on the *Aeneid* ca. 27 B.C.
Meter: Dactylic hexameters.

Sulpicia

Carmina Tibulli *3.13–18—Six Love Poems*

These poems depict the course of a love affair between Sulpicia and "Cerinthus." In the manuscript tradition, they are included in the collected works of the male poet Tibullus, though stylistically different and probably by another author, Sulpicia herself, who seems to have been an aristocratic young woman, the ward of Messala, at the beginning of the Empire. It has been argued, though, that the poems show the influence of Ovid, and therefore must have been written somewhat later. The almost colloquial evocation of daily life contrasts sharply with the mannered, self-consciously literary construction of the female voice in Catullus, Virgil, and Ovid.

Carmina Tibulli *3.13*

Tandem venit amor, qualem texisse pudori

    quam nudasse alicui sit mihi fama magis.

exorata meis illum Cytherea Camenis

    attulit in nostrum deposuitque sinum.

5 exsolvit promissa Venus: mea gaudia narret,

    dicetur si quis non habuisse sua.

non ego signatis quicquam mandare tabellis,

    ne legat id nemo quam meus ante, velim,

sed peccasse iuvat, vultus componere famae

10 taedet: cum digno digna fuisse ferar.

Finally love has come. The rumour that I had covered it would be
a greater shame than laying it bare.
Cytherea, won over by my Muse,
has brought him and placed him in my bosom.
Venus has kept her promises: let them narrate my joys;
let people who have never had such tell about mine.
I wouldn't want to entrust anything to writing tablets
lest someone read it before my love.
It's sweet to have sinned; keeping up appearances for reputation's sake
is a bore: let people say I'm worthy and I've been with a worthy man.

Carmina Tibulli *3.14*

Invisus natalis adest, qui rure molesto

    et sine Cerintho tristis agendus erit.

dulcius urbe quid est? an villa sit apta puellae

    atque Arretino frigidus amnis agro?

5 iam, nimium Messalla mei studiose, quiescas,

    non tempestivae saepe, propinque, viae.

hic animum sensusque meos abducta relinquo,

    arbitrio quamvis non sinis esse meo.

It's my hateful birthday, which I must spend in the tiresome country.
Without Cerinthus it will be sad.
What's more pleasant than the city? Is a country house right for a girl
and the chilly river on the plain of Arretium?
Now, Messalla, far too concerned about me, stop worrying.
Often, uncle, journeys are inopportune.
Carried away, I leave my mind and senses behind,
though you won't let them be at my disposal.

Carmina Tibulli *3.15*

Scis iter ex animo sublatum triste puellae?	Do you know that miserable journey has been lifted off your girl's mind?
natali Romae iam licet esse meo.	Now I'm allowed to stay in Rome for my birthday.
omnibus ille dies nobis natalis agatur,	Let's all celebrate that birthday,
qui nec opinanti nunc tibi forte venit.	which now comes by luck to you when you didn't expect it.

Carmina Tibulli *3.16*

Gratum est, securus multum quod iam tibi de me	It's fortunate, since you serenely allow yourself so much liberty with me
permittis, subito ne male inepta cadam.	that I haven't, like a fool, slipped into a sudden disaster.
sit tibi cura togae potior pressumque quasillo	Trouble yourself about a toga-wearing tart, and some piece of tail smuggled
scortum quam Servi filia Sulpicia.	in a basket, rather than about Sulpicia daughter of Servius.
5 solliciti sunt pro nobis, quibus illa dolori est	People are anxious about me; it's a great issue, causing them distress
ne cedam ignoto, maxima causa, toro.	that I shouldn't give myself to the bed of a nobody.

Carmina Tibulli *3.17*

Estne tibi, Cerinthe, tuae pia cura puellae,	Don't you feel a devoted concern about your girl, Cerinthus,
quod mea nunc vexat corpora fessa calor?	because now a fever is plaguing my exhausted body?
a ego non aliter tristes evincere morbos	Oh, I wouldn't want to overcome this wretched illness at all,
optarim, quam te si quoque velle putem.	unless I thought you wanted it too.
5 at mihi quid prosit morbos evincere, si tu	What use is it to me to overcome my illness, if you
nostra potes lento pectore ferre mala?	can bear my sufferings with an unmoved heart?

Carmina Tibulli *3.18*

Ne tibi sim, mea lux, aeque iam fervida cura	My light! let me no longer be the burning obsession to you
ac videor paucos ante fuisse dies,	I seemed to be a few days ago,
si quicquam tota commisi stulta iuventa	if in all the follies of my youth
cuius me fatear paenituisse magis,	there's anything I regret confessing more
5 hesterna quam te solum quod nocte reliqui,	than leaving you alone last night
ardorem cupiens dissimulare meum.	because I wanted to hide my passion.

Provenance: Rome, ca. 20 B.C.—or possibly a generation later. The identity and even the existence of a woman poet Sulpicia are not universally accepted.
Meter: Elegiac couplets (hexameter followed by pentameter).

Ovid

Heroides *10.1–36, 59–74, 145–50—Lament of Ariadne*

The *Heroides* ("Heroines") are a collection of twenty-five poems, purporting to be letters composed by their narrators. Nos. 1–15 are spoken by various legendary women. Nos. 16–21 are pairs, letters from heroes with the heroine's reply. As the following excerpts show, Ovid's Ariadne, who engineered the escape of the lover now rejecting her, is obviously indebted to Catullus's, and also to Euripides's *Medea*. *Heroides* 7 (Dido to Aeneas) and 12 (Medea to Jason) are not included here.

Mitius inveni quam te genus omne ferarum;	I have found every kind of wild beast gentler than you.
credita non ulli quam tibi peius eram.	I could better have trusted myself to any of them than to you.
quae legis, ex illo, Theseu, tibi litore mitto	I am sending you the letter you are reading, Theseus, from that shore
unde tuam sine me vela tulere ratem,	whence the sails carried your ship away without me,
5 in quo me somnusque meus male prodidit et tu,	where you and my sleep tricked me,
per facinus somnis insidiate meis.	you who criminally plotted against me while I was asleep.
tempus, erat, vitrea quo primum terra pruina	It was that time, early, when the earth is scattered with crystals of frost,
spargitur et tectae fronde queruntur aves.	and the birds housed in the leaves twitter plaintively.
incertum vigilans a somno languida movi	Vaguely waking, and languid from sleep, I raised myself,
10 Thesea prensuras semisupina manus—	and stirred my hands to take hold of Theseus—
nullus erat! referoque manus iterumque retempto,	no one was there! I drew back my hands and tried again,
perque torum moveo bracchia—nullus erat!	and stretched my arms over the bed—no one was there!
excussere metus somnum; conterrita surgo,	Fear banished sleep; terrified, I sprang up,
membraque sunt viduo praecipitata toro.	and flung my limbs from the empty bed.
15 protinus adductis sonuerunt pectora palmis,	At once I beat my breast with loud blows,
utque erat e somno turbida, rupta coma est.	and tore my hair, just as it was, dishevelled with sleep.
luna fuit; specto, siquid nisi litora cernam.	The moon was up. I look to see if there is anything but the shore.
quod videant oculi, nil nisi litus habent.	Nothing but that shore can my eyes see.
nunc huc, nunc illuc, et utroque sine ordine, curro;	I run hither and thither, in any direction, randomly.
20 alta puellares tardat harena pedes.	The deep sand slows down my girlish feet,
interea toto clamanti litore "Theseu!"	while from the whole shore, as I cried "Theseus!"
reddebant nomen concava saxa tuum,	the hollow rocks echoed back your name.

et quotiens ego te, totiens locus ipse vocabat.

    ipse locus miserae ferre volebat opem.

25   mons fuit—apparent frutices in vertice rari;

    hinc scopulus raucis pendet adesus aquis.

adscendo—vires animus dabat—atque ita late

    aequora prospectu metior alta meo.

inde ego—nam ventis quoque sum crudelibus usa—

30   vidi praecipiti carbasa tenta Noto.

ut vidi haut dignam quae me vidisse putarem,

    frigidior glacie semianimisque fui.

nec languere diu patitur dolor; excitor illo,

    excitor et summa Thesea voce voco.

35   "quo fugis?" exclamo; "scelerate revertere Theseu!
    flecte ratem! numerum non habet illa suum!"

. . .

Quid faciam? quo sola ferar? vacat insula cultu.

60   non hominum video, non ego facta boum.

omne latus terrae cingit mare; navita nusquam,
    nulla per ambiguas puppis itura vias.

finge dari comitesque mihi ventosque ratemque—
    quid sequar? accessus terra paterna negat.

65   ut rate felici pacata per aequora labar,

    temperet ut ventos Aeolus—exul ero

non ego te, Crete centum digesta per urbes,

    adscipiam, puero cognita terra Iovi!

at pater et tellus iusto regnata parenti

70   prodita sunt facto, nomina cara, meo,

cum tibi, ne victor tecto morerere recurvo,

    quae regerent passus, pro duce fila dedi,

And every time I called you, the place itself called too.

The place itself wished to help me in my misery.

There was a mountain—with scattered bushes at its summit—

from which hangs a cliff, eaten away by the sounding waves.

I climbed it—my determination gave me strength—

and so I scanned the vast ocean from my vantage point.

From there—for the winds have treated me cruelly too—

I saw your sails spread to the driving wind.

When I saw that—not a sight, I thought, that I deserved to see—

I felt half-dead, and colder than ice.

But my misery won't let me languish long. I'm roused by it,

roused to call Theseus at the top of my voice.

"Where are you fleeing to?" I cry. "Come back, wicked Theseus!
Turn your ship around. She is missing her crew."

. . .

What am I to do? Where go, alone? The island's empty and uncultivated.

I see no evidence of men or cattle.

The sea encircles the land on every side. No sailor is to be seen,

no ship about to set off over the uncertain paths of the sea.

Imagine if I had companions, favoring winds, and a ship.

What direction am I to follow? My father's country is barred to me.

Even if I glide over a calm sea in a fortunate vessel,

and Aeolus restrains the winds—I shall be an exile.

I shall not look upon you, Crete, spread over a hundred cities,

land known to Jupiter when he was a child.

But my father and the land ruled by a just parent,

both things dear to me, were betrayed by my action,

when I gave you the thread to steer your steps instead of a human guide,

lest you should die within those winding halls despite your victory,

cum mihi dicebas: "per ego ipsa pericula iuro,
　te fore, dum nostrum vivet uterque, meam."

when you were saying to me, "By these perils I swear
　that as long as both of us live you shall be mine."

. . .

. . .

5　Has tibi plangendo lugubria pectora lassas
　　infelix tendo trans freta longa manus;
　hos tibi—qui superant—ostendo maesta capillos!
　　per lacrimas oro, quas tua facta movent—
　flecte ratem, Theseu, versoque relabere vento
50　　si prius occidero, tu tamen ossa feres.

These hands, weary with beating my sad breast,
　in my misfortune I stretch out to you over the wide sea.
This unbound hair—what is left of it—in my grief I show to you.
By these tears, which your actions prompted, I pray to you.
Turn your ship, Theseus; glide back to me with a changed wind.
Even if I die first, still, you will carry away my bones.

Provenance: Publius Ovidius Naso was born in 43 B.C., in Pelignia, a hundred miles or so east of Rome, and died at Tomi on the Black Sea in A.D. 17 or 18. His earlier poetry, including the *Heroides*, was composed in Rome. The dates of the *Heroides* are uncertain, nos. 1–14 between 20 and 2 B.C.
Meter: Elegiac couplets.

Ovid?

Heroides 15 (Epistula Sapphus) 1–20, 123–34, 157–72, 195–220—Lament of Sappho

Heroides 15 is thought by many not to be the work of Ovid, because of its different manuscript history, and its rather salacious, voyeuristic content. This Sappho, besotted with the beautiful youth Phaon, is not remotely like the persona that emerges from her own poems, but seems to come from burlesques of Sappho in the comic drama of classical and postclassical Greece.

Ecquid, ut adspecta est studiose littera dextrae,
　protinus est oculis cognita nostra tuis—
an, nisi legisses auctoris nomina Sapphus,
　hoc breve nescires unde movetur opus?
5　forsitan et quare mea sint alterna requiras
　　carmina, cum lyricis sim magis apta modis.
flendus amor meus est—elegiae flebile carmen;
　non facit ad lacrimas barbitos ulla meas.
uror, ut indomitis ignem exercentibus Euris

Now, when you looked at the letter from my eager hand,
did your eyes see at once that it was mine?
Or, if you hadn't read the writer's name, Sappho,
would you not have known whence this little opus came?
Perhaps you're asking why my lines are alternating,
since I'm more inclined to lyric meters.
My love makes me lament, and elegiacs are for lamenting songs.
No lyre fits my tears.
I am burning, as, when the wild east winds fan the flame,

10   fertilis accensis messibus ardet ager.

the rich grain-field burns, with its blazing
        harvest.

arva, Phaon, celebras diversa Typhoidos
    Aetnae;
    me calor Aetnaeo non minor igne tenet.

But you, Phaon, haunt the far-off fields by
        Typhoean Etna.
A heat as great as Etna's fire
        grips me.

nec mihi, dispositis quae iungam carmina
    nervis,
    proveniunt; vacuae carmina mentis opus!

Nor do songs that I can set to steady
        music
come to me; lyric songs are a task for an
        unburdened mind.

15   nec me Pyrrhiades Methymniadesve puellae,

The girls of Pyrrha and Methymna give me
        no pleasure

nec me Lesbiadum cetera turba iuvant.

nor a host of other Lesbian
        girls.

vilis Anactorie, vilis mihi candida Cydro;

Anactoria means nothing to me; fair Cydro
        nothing;

non oculis grata est Atthis, ut ante, meis,

Atthis delights not my eyes, as she did
        before,

atque aliae centum, quas non sine crimine
    amavi;

and a hundred others whom I have loved, not
        without blame.

20   inprobe, multarum quod fuit, unus habes.

Wicked one, to possess all alone what once
        belonged to many.

. . .   . . .

Tu mihi cura, Phaon; te somnia nostra
    reducunt—
    somnia formoso candidiora die.

You're my obsession, Phaon. My dreams
        bring you back,
dreams brighter than the lovely
        day.

125 illic te invenio, quamvis regionibus absis;

There I find you, though you're in regions far
        away.

sed non longa satis gaudia somnus habet

But the joys sleep holds aren't long
        enough.

saepe tuos nostra cervice onerare lacertos,

I've often seemed to lean my head upon your
        shoulder,

saepe tuae videor supposuisse meos;

and often to put my arms around your
        neck.

oscula cognosco, quae tu committere linguae

I know the kisses you used to give with your
        tongue,

130 aptaque consueras accipere, apta dare.

close kisses, for giving and
        receiving.

blandior interdum verisque simillima verba

Sometimes I caress you, and say words just
        like the real ones;

eloquor, et vigilant sensibus ora meis.

my lips are awake although my senses
        sleep.

ulteriora pudet narrare, sed omnia fiunt,

I am ashamed to say the rest, but everything
        happens.

et iuvat, et siccae non licet esse mihi.

It pleases me, and I can't hold
        back.

. . .   . . .

Est nitidus vitroque magis perlucidus omni

There is a sacred spring, bright and clearer
        than any crystal—

fons sacer—hunc multi numen habere
    putant—
quem supra ramos expandit aquatica lotos,

many believe a divine presence
        haunts it.
Over it the water-lotus spreads its
        stems,

160 una nemus; tenero caespite terra viret.

like the trees of a wood. The ground is green with tender turf.

hic ego cum lassos posuissem flebilis artus,

When, weeping, I had laid my weary limbs down in this spot,

constitit ante oculos Naias una meos.

a Naiad stood before my eyes.

constitit et dixit: "quoniam non ignibus aequis
ureris, Ambracia est terra petenda tibi.

She stood there, and said, "Since you are burning with the fires
of unrequited love, Ambracia is the land you must seek.

165 Phoebus ab excelso, quantum patet, adspicit aequor—
Actiacum populi Leucadiumque vocant.

There, from the height, Phoebus looks down on the vast expanse
of ocean; people call it the Leucadian promontory of Actium.

hinc se Deucalion Pyrrhae succensus amore

From this, Deucalion, inflamed with love for Pyrrha,

misit, et inlaeso corpore pressit aquas.

flung himself, and struck the waves all unharmed.

nec mora, versus amor fugit lentissima Pyrrhae
170 pectora, Deucalion igne levatus erat.

Immediately his love for Pyrrha was dispelled, and fled
the breast where it had lingered; Deucalion was free of his passion.

hanc legem locus ille tenet. pete protinus altam
Leucada nec saxo desiluisse time!"

This is the law of the place. Make straightaway for that high spot,
and do not fear to leap from the Leucadian Rock."

. . .   . . .

195 nunc vellem facunda forem! dolor artibus obstat,
ingeniumque meis substitit omne malis.

Now I could wish to be eloquent, but my pain hampers my skill,
and my sufferings have halted all my poetic gift.

non mihi respondent veteres in carmina vires;

My former powers will no longer respond in verse.

plectra dolore tacent, muta dolore lyra est.

My plectrum is silent for grief; for grief my lyre is dumb.

Lesbides aequoreae, nupturaque nuptaque proles,
200 Lesbides, Aeolia nomina dicta lyra,

Women of sea-girt Lesbos, young marriageable women and brides,
girls of Lesbos, whose names I have uttered to the Aeolian lyre,

Lesbides, infamen quae me fecistis amatae,

Lesbian girls, you lovers who have made me infamous,

desinite ad citharas turba venire meas!

stop coming in your throngs to hear my cithara.

abstulit omne Phaon, quod vobis ante placebat,
me miseram, dixi quam modo paene "meus!"

Phaon has taken away all my gifts that once delighted you.
Poor me! How nearly I said "My Phaon" then.

205 efficite ut redeat; vates quoque vestra redibit.

Make him come back, and your poet will come back too.

ingenio vires ille dat, ille rapit.

He gives me my creative power, and he takes it away.

ecquid ago precibus, pectusve agreste movetur?
an riget, et Zephyri verba caduca ferunt?

But what do my prayers achieve? Do I move his savage breast?
Or is he impervious, and do the winds bear my perishable words away?

qui mea verba ferunt, vellem tua vela referrent;	Since they sweep away my words, I might wish they'd bring back your sails
210 hoc te, si saperes, lente, decebat opus.	This would be fitting for you if you were wise, you unyielding one.
sive redis, puppique tuae votiva parantur	If you're coming back, and preparing votive offerings for your ship,
munera, quid laceras pectora nostra mora?	why do you tear my heart with your delay?
solve ratem! Venus orta mari mare praestat amanti.	Weigh anchor! Seaborn Venus stands by a lover on the sea.
aura dabit cursum; tu modo solve ratem!	The wind will send you on your way. You need only weigh anchor!
215 ipse gubernabit residens in puppe Cupido;	Cupid himself will steer, sitting on the stern.
ipse dabit tenera vela legetque manu.	With his soft hand he himself will unfurl and furl the sails.
sive iuvat longe fugisse Pelasgida Sapphon—	But if it pleases you to flee far away from Pelasgian Sappho—
non tamen invenies, cur ego digna fugi—	yet you will find no reason to flee from me—
hoc saltem, miserae crudelis epistula dicat,	at least let a harsh letter from you tell me so in my misery,
220 ut mihi Leucadiae fata petantur aquae!	so I will seek my fate in the Leucadian waves.

Provenance: Uncertain. As for *Heroides* 10–14, or by an early imitator of Ovid.
Meter: Elegiac couplets.

CHAPTER 3
IRELAND

Old Irish poems and tales, rooted in the pagan past, before the conversion of Ireland to Christianity by Saint Patrick in the fifth century, survive in Middle Irish manuscripts. The following poem is drawn from the *Acallam na Senórach* (*Tales of the Elders of Ireland*—also known as *The Colloquy of the Ancients*), which purports to be a collection of stories told to Saint Patrick by the two last survivors of the warband (Fían) of Finn Mac Cumhal. Cáel is a Fenian—a member of the Fían, and Créde is a Sidhé woman, both of them semi-supernatural. In spite of Finn's warning, Cáel seeks and wins Créde's hand. In the great Battle of Ventry, Créde helps the Fenians, but near the end Cáel is drowned chasing his opponent into the sea. Set in the context of this heroic, warrior society, Créde's Lament for Cáel is at the same time noteworthy for its sympathetic awareness of the natural world, a characteristic feature of early Irish poetry.

For a collection of early Irish and Welsh literature in English translation, see *The Celtic Heroic Age*, ed. John Koch and John Carey (2000); for the literary and social background to the *Acallamh*, see the Introduction to *Tales of the Elders of Ireland*, trans. Ann Dooley and Harry Roe (1999). For further reading, see Kim McCone, *Pagan Past and Christian Present in Early Irish Literature* (1990); Joseph Nagy, *The Wisdom of the Outlaw* (1985); and Dáithi Ó Hógáin, *Fionn Mac Cumhall: Images of a Gaelic Hero* (1988).

The Irish section of this book has been prepared with the assistance of Andrea Schutz. Extract from Gerard Murphy's *Early Irish Lyrics* printed with the kind permission of Four Courts Press, Dublin. Translation reprinted by permission of Oxford University Press from Ann Dooley and Harry Roe, *Tales of the Elders of Ireland*.

Anonymous

Créde's Lament for Cáel

One of the poems incorporated in the prose *Acallam na Senórach*. Caílte, the fleetest of the Fían, tells the story of Créde and Cáel to Patrick. At this point, Créde has just found the body of her drowned husband.

"Táinic an ingen 7 do sín re 'tháebh hí 7 do-rinne núalghubha 7 toirrsi mhór. 'Cidh dhamsa,' ol sí, 'gan bás d'fagháil do chumhaid mu chéle in tan a-tát na fíadhmhíla folúaimnecha ac fagháil bháis dá chumhaid?' 7 at-bert Crédhe:

"Créde came and lay down beside him with great mourning and lamentation. 'Why should I not die here,' she said, 'mourning for my husband, when wild creatures recklessly die in sorrow?' She then recited the following poem:

I	Géisid cúan	A roar rises
	ós buinne rúad Rinn Dá Bhárc:	from the great flood of Reenverc.
	bádud laích Locha Dá Chonn	The youth from Two Hound Lake has drowned,
	is ed chaínes tonn re trácht.	the waves along the shore lament.

II 5	Luinchech corr	The crane's clear song
	i seiscenn Droma Dá Thrén:	from the marsh of Druimm nDá Thrén,
	sisi ní aincenn a bí—	she who cannot save her young
	coinfíad dá lí for tí a hén.	from the jaws of the two-coloured fox.

III	Trúag in faíd	Sad as well is the cry
10	do-ní in smólach in nDruim Chaín;	of the thrush on Druimm Caín,
	ocus ní nemthrúaige in scol	and no less sad the strains
	do-ní in lon i Leitir Laíg.	of the blackbird of Leittir Láeig.

IV	Trúag int séis	Sorrowful the sound
	do-ní in dam i nDruim Dá Léis:	of the stag on Druimm nDá Leis,
15	marb eilit Droma Sílenn;	a mighty lament for the death
	géisid dam dílenn dá héis.	of the doe of Druimm Silenn.

V	Ba sáeth lim	I grieve for the warrior's death,
	bás in laích ro laiged lim:	for the one who lay with me,
	mac na mná a Daire Dá Dos,	the son of the woman of Daire Dá Doss.
20	a beith is cros úasa chinn.	A cross above his head.

VI	Sáeth lim Cáel	I grieve for the death of Cáel,
	do beith i richt mairb rem tháeb,	now lifeless by my side.
	tonn do thecht tar a tháeb ngel:	The tide flows over his pale side,
	is ed rom-mer mét a áeb.	its beauty still affects me.

VII	Trúag in gáir	Sad is the cry
25	do-ní tonn tráchtare tráig;	of the wave, striking against the shore.
	ó ro báid fer ségda sáer	I weep that the noble youth
	sáeth lim Cáel do dul 'na dáil.	ever encountered the sea.

VIII	Trúag in fúaimm	Sad is the sound
30	do-ní in tonn risin trácht túaid,	of the wave against the northern shore,
	ac cenngail im charraic caín,	encircling the glistening rocks,
	ac caíned Chaíl ó do-chúaid.	lamenting the death of Cáel.

IX	Trúag in tres	Sad is the crash
	do-ní in tonn risin trácht tes;	of the wave against the southern coast,
35	mise do-dechaid mo ré:	and I, whose time has come,
	messaite mo gné (ro-fes).	am now destroyed by grief.

X	Caínce corr	Swelling is the song
	do-ní tonn trom Tulcha Léis;	of the wave of Druimm nDá Leis.
	mise nochan fuil mo maín	My treasure is no more
40	ó rom-maíd in scél rom-géis.	since I heard its roaring boast.

XI	Ó ro báided mac Crimthain	Since the son of Crimthann died,
	nochan fuil m'inmain dá éis;	no love remains for me.
	is mór tríath ro thuit le a láim;	Many a chieftain he killed.
	a scíath i ló gáid nír géis.	His shield in battle screamed.

7 do sín an ingen re táebh Cháeil 7 fúair bás dá chumhaid; 7 do hadlacad íat ar-áen a n-áeinfert ann sin; 7 as misi féin," ar Caílte, "ro tocuibh in lía fil ósa lighi, conidh Feart Cáeil 7 Créidhe a-derur ris." "Ad-ráe búaid 7 bennacht a Chaílte," ar Pádraic: "as maith in scél do innisis; 7 caidhi Brócán scribhnid?" "Sunna," ar Brócán. "Scribhar lat gach ar chan Caílte." 7 do scríbadh.

Créde then lay down beside Cáel and died of sorrow. They were buried together in a single grave," said Caílte, "and it was I who raised the stone above their grave, still called the Grave of Cáel and Créde." "May you have victory, Caílte, and blessing," said Patrick. "The story you have told is a good one. Where is Broccán, our scribe?" "Here," said Broccán. "Then write down everything that Caílte recited." And he did.

Provenance: The *Acallam na Senórach* is dated ca. 1200 but contains earlier material.
Meter: Rhyming quatrains.

CHAPTER 4

ANGLO-SAXON ENGLAND

Very little that we would regard as lyric poetry has been preserved from the Old English period, though it is inconceivable that songs did not exist. Some of the poetry that comes closest to lyric is found in the group of poems that modern scholars have called the "elegies." These are fairly short reflective pieces that treat themes of loss, absence, and transience, usually in the male voice and with reference to the communal life of a warrior society. But two of the poems in this group are spoken by women; what these speakers miss is not the *comitatus*, the band of warriors around a warlord, but the man they love. In these poems, the traditional language of Old English heroic poetry is adapted to a more personal situation. Very likely, too, these two poems, especially *Wulf and Eadwacer*, are influenced by the language and meter of other, more lyrical, kinds of poetry, now lost. It is not universally accepted that *Wulf and Eadwacer* and *The Wife's Lament* are love poems, although that is the usual interpretation.

See Lois Bragg, *The Lyric Speakers of Old English Poetry* (1991), Helen Bennett, "Exile and Semiosis of Gender in Old English Elegies," in *Class and Gender in Early English Literature*, ed. Britton Harwood and Gillian Overing (1994); on these two poems in particular, see Pat Belanoff, "Women's Songs, Women's Language," in *New Readings in Old English Literature*, ed. Helen Damico and Alexandra Olsen (1990), and, by the same author, "*Ides geomrode giddum*," in *Medieval Woman's Song*, ed. Klinck and Rasmussen (2002).

Anonymous

Wulf and Eadwacer

The speaker laments her separation from her lover, "Wolf"; they are on different islands surrounded by marsh, and "bloodthirsty men" await him. Eadwacer, "Guardian of Property," seems to be another man, who has some position of power over the speaker, perhaps her husband. Their "whelp" will be carried off to the forest by Wolf—or a wolf. The poem is truly enigmatic, but its power and anguish are unmistakable.

Leodum is minum swylce him mon lac gife.	It is to my people as if one gave them a gift.
Willað hy hine aþecgan gif he on þreat cymeđ.	They will take him if he comes into their troop.
Ungelic is us.	Unalike are our lots.
Wulf is on iege, ic on oþerre.	Wolf is on one island, I on another.

5   Fæst is þæt eglond,   fenne beworpen.
Sindon wælreowe   weras þær on ige.

Willað hy hine aþecgan   gif he on þreat
  cymeð.
Ungelice is us.
Wulfes ic mines widlastum   wenum
  dogode,
10   þonne hit wæs renig weder   ond ic reotugu
  sæt,
þonne mec se beaducafa   bogum bilegde—

wæs me wyn to þon;   wæs me hwæþre eac
  lað.
Wulf, min Wulf,   wena me þine
seoce gedydon,   þine seldcymas,
15   murnende mod,   nales meteliste.
Gehyrest þu, Eadwacer?   Uncerne earmne
  hwelp
bireð wulf to wuda.
Þæt mon eaþe toslited   þætte næfre
  gesomnad wæs,
uncer giedd geador.

Fast is that island, surrounded by fen.
They're bloodthirsty, the men there on that
  island.
They will take him if he comes into their
  troop.
Unalike are our lots.
I dogged my Wolf's wide wanderings with my
  hopes,
when it was rainy weather, and I sat
  weeping,
when the man keen in battle laid his arms
  about me—
there was joy for me in that, but there was
  pain too.
Wolf, my Wolf, my hoping for you
has made me sick, your seldom coming,
my mourning heart, not lack of food.
Do you hear, Eadwacer? Our wretched
  cub
the wolf will carry to the forest.
It's easy to tear apart what was never
  together—
the story of us two.

Provenance: Tenth century or earlier.
Meter: The alliterative long line of early Germanic verse: four principal stresses, one or both of the first two alliterating with the third but not the fourth. This poem is metrically unusual, with some short lines and a tendency toward stanzaic structure.

Anonymous

The Wife's Lament

Another poignant and enigmatic poem. The banished wife has been cast off by her husband, apparently as a result of the machinations of his kinsmen. He has become alienated from her, but she still loves him. It seems that he went overseas and she subsequently went to look for him. Now she is condemned to live alone in a cave under an oak tree in the wilderness, a place that may have pagan, supernatural implications. At the end of the poem she exclaims against a young one (her husband? herself? a hypothetical person?) who must have a hard and sad heart whether he fares well or ill, and she ends with a cry of woe for herself and the man from whom she is parted.

Ic þis giedd wrece   bi me ful
  geomorre,
minre sylfre sið.   Ic þæt secgan mæg
hwæt ic yrmþa gebad   siþþan ic up
  weox,
niwes oþþe ealdes,   no ma þonne nu.
5   A ic wite wonn   minra wræcsiþa.

Ærest min hlaford gewat   heonan
  of leodum
ofer yþa gelac.   Hæfde ic uhtceare

I tell this tale of my own sad self,

my own life's journey. I can say
what miseries I have endured, since
  I grew up,
new and old, none more than now.
Constantly I have endured the pain of my
  exile journeys.
First, my lord departed hence from his
  people,
over the tossing waves. At night I wondered
  anxiously

	Old English	Translation
	hwær min leodfruma londes wære.	where, in what land, my lord might be.
	Đa ic me feran gewat folgað secan,	Then I left to go seek service,
10	wineleas wræcca for minre weaþearfe.	a friendless exile, in my wretched need.
	Ongunnon þæt þæs monnes magas hycgan	The man's kinsmen began to take thought
	þurh dyrne geþoht þæt hy todælden unc,	with secret scheming, that they would separate us,
	þæt wit gewidost in woruldrice	keep us far apart in the world,
	lifdon laðlicost, ond mec longade.	living most hatefully, and I pined.
15	Het mec hlaford min her heard niman.	In his cruelty, my lord bade me to be seized here.
	Ahte ic leofra lyt on þissum londstede,	I possessed few dear ones in this country,
	holdra freonda; forþon is min hyge geomor,	loyal friends; and so my heart is sad,
	ða ic me ful gemæcne monnan funde	because I have found a well-matched man
	heardsæligne, hygegeomorne,	ill-starred, heavy-hearted,
20	mod miþendne, morþor hygcende	concealing his purpose, plotting a crime,
	bliþe gebæro. Ful oft wit beotedan	with cheerful looks. Full often we vowed
	þæt unc ne gedælde nemne deað ana,	that nought would part us save death alone,
	owiht elles. Eft is þaet onhworfen.	nothing else. But that has changed.
	Is nu swa hit no wære	now it is as if it had never been,
25	freondscipe uncer. Sceal ic feor ge neah	our love. Far and near I must
	mines felaleofan fæhðu dreogan.	bear the enmity of my beloved.
	Heht mec mon wunian on wuda bearwe,	I was bidden to dwell in a grove of the forest,
	under actreo in þam eorðscræfe.	under an oak-tree, in the earth-cave.
	Eald is þes eorðsele; eal ic eom oflongad.	Old is this earth-hall; I am pining away.
30	Sindon dena dimme, duna uphea,	Dim are the valleys, high the hills,
	bitre burgtunas brerum beweaxne,	bitter the enclosures overgrown with briars,
	wic wynna leas. Ful oft mec her wraþe begeat	joyless dwellings. Full often here came harshly upon me
	fromsiþ frean. Frynd sind on eorþan,	the thought of my lord's departure. There are lovers on earth,
	leofe lifgende leger weardiað,	dear ones living, keeping their bed,
35	þonne ic on uhtan ana gonge	while I at dawn pace alone
	under actreo geond þas eorðscrafu,	through these earth-caves under the oak-tree,
	þær ic sittan mot sumorlangne dæg,	where I must sit the summer-long day,
	þær ic wepan mæg mine wræcsiþas,	where I have to weep my exile wanderings,
	earfoþa fela, forþon ic æfre ne mæg	my many hardships, for I can never
40	þære modceare minre gerestan,	rest from my suffering,
	ne ealles þæs longaþes þe mec on þissum life begeat.	nor from all the sadness that's befallen me in this life.
	A scyle geong mon wesan geomormod,	Ever must that young one be sad of mind,
	heard heortan geþoht swylce habban sceal	hard the heart's thought, and must have too,
	bliþe gebæro eac þon breostceare,	with cheerful looks, care in the breast,
45	sinsorgna gedreag, sy æt him sylfum gelong	a host of endless troubles, whether he have at his own command
	eal his worulde wyn, sy ful wide fah	all his happiness in the world, or whether it be that outlawed far off,
	feorres folclondes þæt min freond siteð,	in a distant country my beloved sits
	under stanhliþe, storme behrimed,	under a rock-cliff, whitened with the storm,
	wine werigmod wætre beflowen,	my sad-hearted friend, water washing around,
50	on dreorsele; dreogeð se min wine	in a dreary hall. My friend endures
	micle modceare; he gemon to oft	great suffering of mind; too often he remembers
	wynlicran wic. Wa bið þam þe sceal	a happier home. Woe to the one who must
	of langoþe leofes abidan!	with pining heart await a beloved!

Provenance: Tenth century or earlier.
Meter: Alliterative long line.

CHAPTER 5

SCANDINAVIA OR ICELAND

Anonymous

Guðrúnarkviða in fyrsta *("The First Lay of Guthrun")*

This lament of Guthrun is found in the collection of mythological and heroic poems called the *Poetic* or *Elder Edda*. Most of the heroic poems, in the second half of the manuscript, are connected with Sigurd the dragon-slayer; several are uttered by his widow, Guthrun. The story of Sigurd/Siegfried, comparable to Greek myth and tragedy in its passion and horror, is also found in the *Saga of the Volsungs* and in the Middle High German *Nibelungenlied*, with significant differences in character and plot. The main characters in the Norse versions are Sigurd, Guthrun, her brothers Gunnar and Hogni, Brynhild, and her brother Atli (Attila). Sigurd married Guthrun, but when he went to woo Brynhild the valkyrie for Gunnar he captured her love. Nevertheless, she married Gunnar, thinking he was the man who had wooed her. In fury at the deception, she persuaded Gunnar and Hogni to treacherously kill Sigurd, and committed suicide herself. Later, Guthrun married Atli, who enticed her brothers to his court and had them killed to obtain the dragon's treasure. Hogni laughed while his heart was being cut out; thrown in a snake pit, Gunnar played his harp until he was bitten to death. Guthrun punished Atli by serving him the bodies of their two sons, before killing him and burning his hall to the ground. *Guðrúnarkviða in fyrsta* focusses on Guthrun's grief and Brynhild's jealousy after the death of Sigurd. The poem's turning point is the poignant moment when the uncovering of Sigurd's body unleashes Guthrun's pent-up tears.

For an English translation of the *Poetic Edda*, see Carolyne Larrington (1996). Ursula Dronke's definitive edition of the *Edda* (1969–) has not reached *Guðrunarkviða in fyrsta*. For the treatment of women, see the essays in *Cold Counsel*, ed. Sarah Anderson and Karen Swenson (2002); also Jenny Jochens, *Old Norse Images of Women* (1996), especially 135–55 on Guthrun as avenger.

My translation of *Guðrúnarkviða in fyrsta* is based on that in the Appendix to *The Old English Elegies*, ed. Anne Klinck.

Guðrún sat yfir Sigurði dauðom. Hon grét eigi sem aðrar konor, enn hon var búin til at springa af harmi. Til gengo bæði konor ok karlar at hugga hana; enn þat var eigi auðvelt. Þat er sögn manna, at Guðrún hefði etið af Fáfnis hjarta ok hon skildi því fugls rödd. Þetta er enn kveðit um Guðrúno:

Guthrun sat over the dead Sigurd. She did not weep like other women, but she was ready to burst with grief. Both women and men went to her to cheer her, but it was not easy. They say that Guthrun had eaten [the dragon] Fafnir's heart and that she understood the speech of birds. This is a lay about Guthrun.

I   Ár var þatz Guðrún   gorðiz at deyja
er hon sat sorgfull   yfir Sigurði.
Gerðit hon hiúfra   né höndom slá,
ne kveina um   sem konor aðrar.

Once, Guthrun was ready to die,
as she sat grieving over Sigurd.
She did not lament, nor wring her hands,
nor wail like other women.

II 5   Gengo jarlar   alsnotrir fram,
þeir er harðz hugar   hána lötto.
Þeygi Guðrún   gráta mátti,
svá var hon móðug,   mundi hon springa.

Wise earls went to her
to relieve her hard heart.
But Guthrun could not weep.
She was so angry she could have burst.

III   Sáto ítrar   jarla brúðir
10   gulli búnar,   fyr Guðrúno.
Hver sagði þeira   sinn oftrega
þann er bitrastan   um beðit hafði.

The earls' lovely wives sat,
adorned with gold, beside Guthrun.
Each told her own woe,
the bitterest she had endured.

IV   Þa kvað Gjaflaug, Gjúka systir:
"Mik veit ek á moldo   munar lausasta.
15   Hefi ek fimm vera   forspell beðit,
þriggja dœtra,   þriggja systra,
átta brœðra,   þó ek ein lifi."

Then said Gjaflaug, Gjuki's sister,
"I know I am the most joyless one on earth.
I have suffered the loss of five husbands,
three daughters, three sisters,
eight brothers, but I still live, alone."

V   Þeygi Guðrún   gráta mátti;
svá var hon móðug   at mög dauðan
20   ok harðhuguð   um hrer fylkis.

Yet Guthrun could not weep,
so angry was she at her husband's death,
and hard of heart over the prince's body.

VI   Þá kvað þat Herborg, Húnalanz drótning:
"Hefi ek harðara harm   at segja.
Mínir sjau synir   sunnan lanz,
verr inn átti,   í val fello;

Then said Herborg, Lady of the Huns,
"I have a harsher grief to tell.
My seven sons fell in a southern land,
in battle, and my husband the eighth;

VII 25   faðir ok móðir,   fjórir brœðr,

þau á vági   vindr of lék,
barði bára   við borðþili.

my father and mother too, and my four
   brothers,
whom the storm sported with at sea,
when the swelling wave beat against the
   ship's bulwarks.

VIII   Sjálf skylda ek göfga,   sjálf skylda ek götva,

sjálf skylda ek höndla   helfor þeira.

It was I who must prepare them, I who must
   bury them,
I who must lay them out for their
   Hel-journey.

30   Þat ek alt um beið   ein misseri,
svá at mér maðr engi   munar leitaði.

All that I endured in six months,
and no one comforted me.

IX   Þá varð ek hapta   ok hernuma
sams misseris   síðan verða.
Skylda ek skreyta   ok skúa binda

Then I became a captive and bond-woman,
after that, in the same six months.
I must dress the chieftain's wife and tie
   her shoes

35   hersis kván   hverjan morgin.

every morning.

X   Hon œgði mér   af afbrýði,
ok hörðom mik höggom keyrði.
Fann ek húsguma   hvergi in betra,
enn húsfreyjo   hvergi verri."

She threatened me out of jealousy,
and beat me with hard blows.
Never did I find a better master,
nor a worse mistress."

XI 40	Þeygi Guðrún gráta mátti, svá var hon móðug at mög dauðan ok harðhugud um hrer fylkis.	Yet Guthrun could not weep, so angry was she at her husband's death, and hard of heart over the prince's body.
XII 45	Þá kvað þat Gullrönd, Gjúka dóttir. "Fá kanntu, fóstra, þótt þú fróð sér, ungo vífi annspjöll bera."	Then said Gullrond, Gjuki's daughter, "Though you are wise, foster-mother, you can give few answers to the young woman."
	Varaði hon at hylja um hrør fylkis.	She urged them to uncover the prince's body.
XIII 50	Svipti hon blæjo af Sigurði ok vatt vengi fyr vífs knjám: "Líttu á liúfan, legðu munn við grön, sem þú hálsaðir heilan stilli."	She swept back the sheet from Sigurd, and put his cheek at his wife's knees: "Look on your beloved. Lay your mouth to his lips, as you embraced him when he was still unwounded."
XIV	Á leit Guðrún eino sinni; sá hon döglings skör dreyra runna, fránar sjónir fylkis liðnar, hugborg jöfurs hjörfi skorna.	Once only did Guthrun look. She saw the lord's hair run with blood, the bright eyes of the people's prince, the warrior's breast pierced by the sword.
XV 55	Þá hné Guðrún höll við bólstri; haddr losnaði, hlýr roðnaði, enn regns dropi rann niðr um kné.	Then Guthrun bent down, leaned on the pillow. Her hair came loose, her cheek grew red, and a rain of tears ran down to her knee.
XVI 60	Þá grét Guðrún, Gjúka dóttir, svá at tár flugo tresc í gognom, ok gullo við gæss í túni, mœrir fuglar, er mær átti.	Guthrun, Gjuki's daughter wept, so that the tears flowed through her hair, and the geese in the yard called out in reply, the beautiful birds that the maiden owned.
XVII 65	Þá kvað þat Gullrönd, Gjúka dóttir: "Ykrar vissa ek ástir mestar manna allra fyr mold ofan; undir þú hvárki úti né inni, systir mín, nema hjá Sigurði."	Then said Gullrond, Gjuki's daughter, "I know of no greater love all over the world than yours. You were not happy, outdoors or within, my sister, except with Sigurd."
XVIII 70	"Svá var minn Sigurðr hjá sonom Gjúka, sem væri geirlaukr ór grasi vaxinn, eða væri bjartr steinn á band dreginn, jarknasteinn yfir öðlingom.	"My Sigurd beside the sons of Gjuki was like the garlic over the grass, or a bright stone set in a ring, a precious stone. Thus he stood out over the princes.
XIX	Ek þóttak ok þjóðans rekkom hverri hærri Herjans dísi. Nú em ek svá lítil, sem lauf sé opt í jölstrom, at jöfur dauðan.	And I seemed to the king's men higher than any of Herjan's maids. Now I am as slight as a little leaf on a laurel tree, now my lord is dead.
XX 75	Sakna ek í sessi ok í sæingo míns málvinar, valda megir Gjúka. Valda megir Gjúka míno bölvi ok systr sinnar sárom gráti.	At bed and board I miss my husband. The sons of Gjuki caused that. The sons of Gjuki caused my sorrow, their sister's sore grief.
XXI 80	Svá ér um lýða landi eyðit, sem ér um unnoð eiða svarða. Mana þú, Gunnarr, gullz um njóta,	So may your land lose its people as you broke the oaths you had sworn. You will have no joy of the gold, Gunnar,

þeir muno þér baugar   at bana verða,
er þú Sigurði   svarðir eiða.

but the rings shall become your bane,
because you swore false oaths to Sigurd.

XXII
85
Opt var í túni   teiti meiri,
þá er minn Sigurðr   söðlaði Grana,
ok þeir Brynhildar   biðja fóro,
armrar vættar,   illo heilli."

There was greater joy in the courtyard
when my Sigurd saddled Grani,
and they went out to ask for Brynhild,
wretched woman—ill came of that!"

XXIII
90
Þá kvað þat Brynhildr,   Buðla dóttir:
"Vön sé sú vættr   vers ok barna,
er þik, Guðrún,   gráz um beiddi
ok þér í morgon   málrúnar gaf."

Then said Brynhild, Buthli's daughter,
"May she be husbandless and childless,
that woman who let you weep
and gave you speech runes this morning!"

XXIV
Þá kvað þat Gullrönd,   Gjúka dóttir:
"Þegi þú, þjóðleið,   þeira orða!

Urðr öðlinga   hefir þú æ verið.
95
Rekr þik alda hverr   illrar skepno,
sorg sára   sjau konunga,
ok vinspell   vífa mest."

Gullrond, Gjuki's daughter said,
"Be silent! Keep from such words, vile
woman.
You have always been the bane of princes.
Every ill wave drives you on,
a bitter sorrow to seven kings,
and deadliest to your lover of all women."

XXV
100
Þá kvað þat Brynhildr,   Buðla dóttir:
"Veldr einn Atli   öllo bölvi,
of borinn Buðla,   bróðir minn;

Then said Brynhild, Buthli's daughter,
"Atli alone caused all this ill,
my brother born of Buthli,

XXVI
Þá er við í höll   húnskrar þjóðar

eld á jöfri   ormbeðs litom,
þess hefi ek gangs   goldit síðan
þeirar sýnar,   sámk ey."

when we saw around the prince in the hall of
the Huns
the fiery gold taken from the dragon's lair.
I have paid for that visit ever since;
I shall forever see that sight."

XXVII
106
Stóð hon und stoð,   strengði hon elvi;

brann Brynhildi,   Buðla dóttur,

eldr ór augom,   eitri fnæsti,
er hon sár um leit   á Sigurði.

She stood by the pillar and gathered her
strength.
A fire burned from the eyes of Brynhild,
Buthli's daughter;
she breathed venom
when she saw the wounds on Sigurd.

Guðrún gekk þaðan á braut til skógar á eyðimerkr ok fór alt til Danmarkar ok var þar með Þóro, Hákonar dóttur, sjau misseri.
    Brynhildr vildi eigi lifa eptir Sigurð. Hon lét drepa þræla sína átta ok fimm ambóttir. Þá lagði hon sik sverði til bana, svá sem segir í Sigurðarkviðo inni skömmo.

Guthrun went away from there to the wild woods, and travelled all the way to Denmark, and stayed there with Thora, Hakon's daughter, for three and a half years.
    Brynhild did not want to live after Sigurd. She had her eight male and five female slaves put to death. Then she killed herself with a sword, as is told in the Short Lay of Sigurd.

Provenance: Iceland, twelfth century, incorporating earlier material.
Meter: Alliterative long line (essentially the same as in *Wulf and Eadwacer*, earlier); called *fornyrðislag*, "old story," that is, "epic meter," in Old Norse contexts.

CHAPTER 6
EARLY MEDIEVAL SPAIN

After the conquest of Andalusia (Southern Spain) by the Moors in the eighth century, the three communities of Christians, Muslims, and Jews coexisted for several centuries, each with its own traditions. In the Muslim community, women poets are found at all levels of society, from slaves to aristocrats. The most famous of them is Wallada, a princess of the Umayyad dynasty, and evidently a woman of independent mind, who participated in the circle of male poets of the time, and was for a while the lover of one of them, Ibn Zaydun. A different kind of woman's voice poetry developed in the context of the Andalusian muwashshaha, an Arabic genre that was also practised by Hebrew poets, and that treated amatory and panegyric themes in terms of hyperbolic admiration. The beloved breathes perfume, shoots wounding arrows from his or her eyes, seems to be made of precious stones, is like the full moon, and so on. These muwashshahas are written in literary Arabic or Hebrew, but often their kharjas (codas, literally "exits") are composed in the Mozarabic dialect, based on the colloquial Romance speech of the Christians. In fact, some, perhaps most, of the kharjas must have had a previous independent existence. They are introduced as quotations; sometimes the same kharja is found attached to more than one muwashshaha, and occasionally a muwashshaha has more than one kharja. Frequently, too, the kharja doesn't really "fit." Typically, the Romance kharjas are uttered in the persona of a young woman expressing passionate feelings for her lover. Whereas these little pieces in some ways anticipate the Galician-Portuguese *cantigas de amigo*, also male-authored, in their construction of an ingenuous, ardent femininity, Wallada's spirited verses have more in common with the woman-authored poetry of Provence; compare the Comtessa de Dia, later.

For further reading, see James T. Monroe, *Hispano-Arabic Poetry: A Student Anthology* (1974); also the essays in *Studies on the Muwaššaḥ and the Kharja*, ed. Alan Jones and Richard Hitchcock (1991); and, on women poets, Judith Cohen, "Women and Music in Medieval Spain's Three Cultures," *Medieval Woman's Song*, ed. Klinck and Rasmussen (2002). The Andalusian women poets of the eighth to fourteenth centuries are presented in Spanish translation in Teresa Garulo's *Dīwān de las poetisas de al-Andalus* (1986).

The following section on Wallada has been compiled with the assistance of Teresa Garulo.

Arabic

Wallada

Ana wa-l-Lahi asluhu li-l-ma'ali—*"I am, by God, made for glory"*

Wallada, who was criticized by some of her contemporaries for not behaving with appropriate decorum, wore these provocative lines embroidered on her sleeves. She seems to have enjoyed an unusual freedom, perhaps because, as well as belonging to the highest rank of society, she also lived at a time of political upheaval.

Ana wa-l-Lahi asluhu li-l-ma'ali	I am, by God, made for glory,
wa-amshi mishyati wa-atihu tiha	and I go my own way with pride.
wa-umkinu 'ashiqi min sahni khaddi	I give my lover power over my cheek,
wa-u'ti qublati man yashtahi-ha,	and I offer my kisses to him who desires them.

Provenance: Cordoba, first half of the eleventh century. Wallada was the daughter of Muhammad III al-Mustakfi, Caliph of Cordoba for six months, 1024–25.
Meter: Since the Arabic lines are very long, they are printed by hemistich (half-line). Like ancient Greek and Latin meters, Arabic meters are quantitative, and take account of syllable length. Here, *wafir*: hemistich of 2 longer and 1 shorter foot, with the underlying syllable pattern short–long–short–short–long (first two feet); short–long–long (final foot); the two adjacent short syllables can be replaced by a long. Lines rhyme in -*ha*.

Taraqqab idha janna l-zalamu ziyarati—*"When night falls, plan to visit me"*

For Ibn Zaydun.

Taraqqab idha janna l-zalamu ziyarati	When night falls, plan to visit me.
fa-inni ra'aytu l-layla aktama li-l-sirri	For I believe night is the time that keeps secrets best.
wa-bi min-ka ma law kana bi-l-shamsi lam taluh	I feel a love for you that if the lights of heaven felt, the sun would not shine,
wa-bi-l-badri lam yatlu' wa-bi-l-najmi lam yusri.	nor the moon rise, nor the stars begin their nightly journey.

Meter: *Tawil*: hemistich of 14 syllables with an underlying pattern of alternating 3-syllable and 4-syllable feet; short syllable followed by 2 long or 3 long. Rhyme in -*ri*.

A-la hal la-na min ba'di hadha l-tafarruqi—*"Is there no way for us to meet again after our parting?"*

A poem of poignant longing. The wish for rain at the end embodies an outpouring of generosity, and also implies the relief of tears, and, perhaps, a release from the shackles of self-involvement.

A-la hal la-na min ba'di hadha l-tafarruqi	Is there no way for us to meet again after our parting?
sabilu^n fa-yashku kullu sabbi^n bi-ma laqi	Alas, all lovers voice their love-complaints.
wa-qad kuntu awqata l-tazawuri fi l-shita	In winter I spent the times of our assignations

abitu ʿala jamriⁿ mina l-shawqi muhraqi	burning with the brands of desire.
fa-kayfa wa-qad amsaytu fi hali qitʿati	How can it be otherwise when we are separated?
la-qad ʿajila l-maqduru ma kuntu attaqi	How soon has my destiny brought me what I feared.
tamurru l-layali la ara l-bayna yanqadi	Night after night passes, and our separation never ends,
wa-la l-sabru min riqqi l-tashawwuqi muʿtaqi	nor does patience free me from the shackles of yearning.
saqa l-Lahu ardaⁿ qad gadat la-ka manzila	May God water the ground where you dwell
bi-kulli sakubiⁿ hatili l-wabli mugdaqi	with rains abundant and plenteous!

Meter: *Tawil*. Rhyme in -*qi*.

Law kunta tunsifu fi l-hawa ma bayna-na—*"If you had been true to the love between us"*

A poem expressing Wallada's anger and wounded pride at being rejected in favor of her own slave. The comparison to the full moon is highly conventional, but acquires a distinctive bitter edge here.

Law kunta tunsifu fi l-hawa ma bayna-na	If you had been true to the love between us,
lam tahwa jariyati wa-lam tatakhayyari	you would not have picked my slave-girl and loved her.
wa-tarakta gusnaⁿ muthmiraⁿ bi-jamali-hi	You have left a branch that flourishes in beauty
wa-janahta li-l-gusni l-ladhi lam yuthmiri	and turned towards a barren bough.
wa-la-qad ʿalimta bi-anna-ni badru l-sama	You know I am the full moon of the heavens,
lakin dahayta li-shaqwati bi-l-mushtari	but, to my sorrow, you have fallen in love with an inferior planet.

Meter: *Kamil*: hemistich with an underlying pattern of 3 alternating feet; 2 short (1st and 3rd feet) or 1 long (2nd foot) syllable followed by long-short-long. Rhyme in -*ri*.

Mozarabic

Abu ʿIsa ibn Labbun, Abu al-Walid Yunus ibn ʿIsa al-Khabbaz al-Mursi

Ya mamma, mio al-habibi—*"Oh mother, my lover is going"*

In two muwashshahas expressing love for a young girl. The Ibn Labbun version introduces the kharja via the poet's sympathy for a girl who has been badly treated by her lover. The al-Khabbaz says the kharja is uttered by a "girl of thirteen"; she resembles, but is perhaps not to be identified with, the "slave gazelle" whose charms have overwhelmed the poet.

Ya mamma, mio al-habibi bay-she e no me tornade.	Oh mother, my lover is going and won't come back.
Gar ke fareyo ya mamma in no mio ʿina' leshade.	Tell me what to do, mother, if my suffering won't abate.

Provenance: Ibn Labbun lived in the eleventh century. Nothing is known of al-Khabbaz.
Meter: Rhyming distich of 8 + 8-syllable lines.

Moshe ibn 'Ezra, Abu Bakr Yahya al-Saraqusti al-Jazzar, Abu Bakr Yahya ibn Baqi

Adamey filiolo alieno e el a mibi—*"I loved someone else's little son"*

Appended to one Hebrew and two Arabic muwashshahas, all poems expressing love for a boy. In the Arabic poems the kharja is uttered in the persona of the poet. But in the Ibn 'Ezra version the kharja is sung by a "gazelle" and introduced by the words "weeping she sang in front of me a song of gazelles."

Adamey filiolo alieno, e el a mibi.   I loved someone else's little son and he me.
Kered-lo de mib katare shuo al-raqibi.   His guardian wishes to take him from me.

Provenance: The earliest version is probably that of al-Saraqusti, who stopped writing at the end of the eleventh century. Ibn Baqi died in 1145. Ibn 'Ezra was a Jewish scholar who died in 1139.
Meter: Rhyming distich of 3 + 5 + 5-syllable lines (with vowel elisions).

Muhammad al-Kumayt al-Garbi

No she kedadh—*"He's not staying"*

In a love poem which is also preserved with a different kharja. The poet rapturously praises the wonders of the girl he has fallen in love with. The kharja is introduced with the words "I would say, while sleep fills your eyes . . . ."

No she kedadh ni me keredh gaire kilma.   He's not staying, nor will he speak to me
                                 one word.
Non ayo kon sheno eshushto dormire,   I cannot sleep my breast is burning so,
  mamma.   mother.

Provenance: Al-Kumayt was attached to the court of Al-Musta'in, king of Saragossa 1085–1110.
Meter: Rhyming distich of 11 + 2-syllable lines.

Yehuda Halevi, Abu Bakr Muhammad ibn Ahmad ibn Ruhaym, Abu Bakr Yahya ibn Baqi

Non me tanqesh, ya habibi—*"Don't touch me, oh my lover"*

The rabbi Yehuda Halevi is one of the best known Hebrew poets of medieval Andalusia. This kharja is appended to three muwashshahas, Halevi's, and two by Arabic poets, all love poems describing the speaker's attraction to a marvellously beautiful girl, and, finally, an encounter in which she objects to his behavior.

Non me tanqesh, ya habibi; fa-encara   Don't touch me, oh my lover; it still
  dannosho.   hurts me.
Al-gilala raksa a toto ¡bashta! me refusho.   My bodice is fragile. Enough! I say no to this.

Provenance: Yehuda Halevi lived ca. 1075–1141; Ibn Ruhaym was alive in 1120; Ibn Baqi died in 1145.
Meter: Rhyming distich of 8 + 6-syllable lines.

Yehuda Halevi

Garid bosh, ay yermanellash—*"Tell me, oh my sisters"*

In a muwashshaha of praise for Rabbi Ishaq ibn Qrispin. Much of the language is indistinguishable from that of erotic poetry; the kharja is presented as the words of a girl in love with Ibn Qrispin.

Garid bosh, ay yermanellash, kom kontenir el mio male. Shin al-habib non bibreyo; ed bolarey demandare.	Tell me, oh my sisters, how to contain my suffering. I can't live without my lover—I'll fly to seek him.

Meter: Rhyming distich of 8 + 8-syllable lines.

Ya rabb, komo bibreyo—*"Oh God, how can I live"*

From a panegyric for Abu Ishaq Nahman ibn Azhar. The muwashshaha is less erotic than the preceding one, and alludes to (Jewish) biblical traditions. The poet claims to be drawn to Ibn Azhar like a girl whose lover is leaving her, and the kharja is introduced as her words.

¿Ya rabb, komo bibreyo kon eshte al-kallaq? ¡Ya man qabl an yusallam yuhaddid bi-al-firaq!	Oh God, how can I live with this impetuous man? Oh, even before he's been greeted he threatens to leave!

Meter: Rhyming distich of 7 + 6-syllable lines (with vowel elision in final hemistich).

Anonymous and Yehuda Halevi

Komo si filiolo alieno—*"As if you were someone else's little son"*

Attached to an anonymous muwashshaha in Arabic as well as to one in Hebrew by Yehuda Halevi, the former a love poem for a girl, the latter a panegyric for Abu al-Hasan Meir ibn Qamniel. In the Arabic muwashshaha, the girl sings this in grief at her lover's absence; in Halevi's, Ibn Qamniel sings it to his friends.

Komo si filiolo alieno, non maish adormesh en mio sheno.	As if you were someone else's little son, you no longer sleep on my breast.

Provenance: Probably first half of the twelfth century.
Meter: Two hemistichs of 10 syllables each.

Abu Bakr Yahya ibn al-Sayrafi

Bokella al-'iqdi—*"Mouth of pearls"*

In a muwashshaha that combines amatory and panegyric material. The kharja is presented as sung by girls ecstatic at the sight of the "pearls of his mouth."

Bokella al-'iqdi,   dolje komo al-shuhdi,
  ben, beija-me.
Habibi ji 'indi   ad union amando   komo
  yawmi.

Mouth of pearls, sweet as honey,
  come, kiss me!
Lover, come to me, to be joined
  in love as before.

Provenance: Ibn al-Sayrafi died in 1174.
Meter: Rhyming distich of 6 + 6 + 4-syllable lines.

Anonymous

Mamma, ayy habibi—*"Mother, what a lover!"*

The muwashshaha that precedes this kharja is a love poem addressed by a male speaker to a young man called Ahmad; his beauty is such that a girl spoke thus to her mother about his charms.

¡Mamma, ayy habibi!   ¡Shua al-jumella
  saqrella
e el qollo albo   e bokella hamrella!

Mother, what a lover! His locks are fair,

His neck white, and his mouth is red!

Provenance: Anonymous Arabic kharja of uncertain date.
Meter: Rhyming distich of 6 + 7-syllable lines.

Anonymous

Amanu, ya habibi—*"Mercy, my lover!"*

From a love poem to a wondrous "gazelle." When the beloved appeared, the poet burst into tears, and she addressed him with these words.

¡Amanu, ya habibi!   Al-wahsh me no ferash.
Bon beija mia bokella   awshak tu no irash.

Mercy, my lover! Don't leave me alone.
Kiss my mouth well—you won't want to
  go so quickly.

Provenance: Anonymous Arabic muwashshaha of uncertain date.
Meter: Rhyming distich of 7 + 6-syllable lines.

CHAPTER 7
FRANCE

Occitan (Provençal)

Provence is often thought of as the cradle of Western European vernacular lyric. Although this is by no means entirely true, there is a remarkable flowering of lyric here from the eleventh century on, and here arises the literary convention of *fin'amor* or courtly love. *Fin'amor* finds its classic expression in the canso, the song in which the lover declares his devotion to his lady. The tenso, a poetic debate, draws on the same love code. And the alba crystallizes here as, typically, an exchange between warning watchman and castle lady in the arms of her illicit lover. Less courtly in style, the pastourelle (in Occitan, *pastorela*), with its dialogue between knight and shepherdess, links gender difference to distinctions in social class.

By far the greater part of this poetry is in the male voice, but some of it is woman's song, notably the work of the women troubadours or trobairitz, who give their own stamp to the genres used by their male counterparts, especially the canso and to a lesser extent the tenso. Outside the trobairitz corpus, songs exclusively in the female voice are rare in Occitan. They tend to be in the non-courtly style, with simple, repetitive language, and a strong musical element. It has been widely assumed, without any firm evidence, that anonymous "popularizing" *chansons de femme* are male-authored. Whether this is so or not, certainly the femininity constructed by the trobairitz is more complex than that in most of the male-authored and anonymous poems—courtly and uncourtly.

For a general introduction to the troubadours, see the essays in the collections edited by F.R.P. Akehurst and Judith Davis (*A Handbook of the Troubadours*, 1995) and by Simon Gaunt and Sarah Kay (*The Troubadours*, 1999), especially those on the trobairitz by Matilda Bruckner in the former and Tilde Sankovitch in the latter. See also the introduction to the edition edited by Bruckner with Laurie Shepard and Sarah White, *Songs of the Women Troubadours* (1995, 2000). For Marcabru, see the general Introduction as well as the sections on individual poems, in the edition by Gaunt with Ruth Harvey and Linda Paterson (2000). On the Comtessa de Dia and Castelloza, see Bruckner, "Fictions of the Female Voice," in *Medieval Woman's Song*, ed. Klinck and Rasmussen (1992, 2002). On musical composition and performance by women, see Susan Boynton, "Women's Performance of the Lyric Before 1500," in Klinck and Rasmussen (2002). On women's voices in Marcabru and the Comtessa de Dia, see Fredric Cheyette and Margaret Switten, "Women in Troubadour Song" (1998). For a fictional recreation of the Comtessa de Dia, see Irmtraud Morgner, *The Life and Adventures of Trobadora Beatrice*, translated by Jeanette Clausen (1976, 2000).

Marcabru

A la fontana del vergier—*"At the spring in the orchard"*

Marcabru is notable for his distinctive take on conventional forms, but he may have helped to initiate rather than to modify them. He is a composer of religious and political polemics as well as love poems. *A la fontana* blends the *chanson de croisade* ("crusade song") with elements of the *pastorela*, although the girl encountered here is "daughter of a castle's lord," not a peasant. The setting, the narrative frame, and the woman's impassioned words resemble those in *En un vergier sotz fuella d'albespi*.

I	A la fontana del vergier,	At the spring in the orchard,
	on l'erb'es vertz josta.l gravier,	where the grass is green down to the bank,
	a l'ombra d'un fust domesgier,	in the shade of a fruit tree,
	en aiziment de blancas flors	taking solace in the white flowers
5	e de novelh chant costumier,	and in the habit of a new song,
	trobey sola, ses companhier,	I found alone, without companion,
	selha que no vol mon solatz.	the girl who rejects my society.
II	So fon donzelh' ab son cors belh,	She was a maiden, of lovely form,
	filha d'un senhor de castelh;	daughter of a castle's lord.
10	e quant ieu cugey que l'auzelh	While I supposed that the birds,
	li fesson joy e la verdors,	the greenery, and the sweetness
	e pel dous termini novelh,	of the young season would give her joy,
	qu'ela entendes mon favelh,	and that she'd listen to my words,
	tost li fon sos afars camjatz.	suddenly her manner changed.
III 15	Dels huelhs ploret josta la fon	Tears flowed from her eyes beside the spring
	e del cor sospiret preon.	and she sighed from the bottom of her heart.
	"Jhesus," dis elha, "reys del mon,	"Jesus," she said, "king of the world,
	per vos mi creys ma grans dolors,	because of you my great grief grows,
	quar vostra anta mi cofon,	for the injury done you confounds me:
20	quar li mellor de tot est mon	the best men in all this world
	vos van servir, mas a vos platz.	are going to serve you—such is your pleasure.
IV	Ab vos s'en vai lo mieus amicx,	Because of you my lover is going away.
	lo belhs e.l gens e.l pros e.l ricx.	He's handsome, well-bred, brave, and noble.
	Sai m'en reman lo grans destricx,	All that's left to me here is great distress,
25	lo deziriers soven e.l plors.	constant desire and weeping.
	Ay! mala fos reys Lozoicx	Alas! Evil befall King Louis,
	que fay los mans e los prezicx	who issues the orders and the edicts
	per que.l dols m'es el cor intratz!"	that have brought grief into my heart!"
V	Quant ieu l'auzi desconortar,	When I heard her lamenting,
30	ves lieys vengui josta.l riu clar:	I came up to her by the clear stream.
	"Belha," fi.m ieu, "per trop plorar	"Fair lady," I said, "With too much weeping
	afolha cara e colors;	you mar your face and your complexion,
	e no vos cal dezesperar,	and there's no cause for you to despair,
	que selh qui fai lo bosc fulhar	for He who makes the trees bud
35	vos pot donar de joy assatz."	can give you joy in plenty."

VI   "Senher," dis elha, "ben o crey
     que Dieus aya de mi mercey
     en l'autre segle per jassey,
     quon assatz d'autres peccadors;
40   mas say mi tolh aquelha rey
     don joy mi crec; mas pauc mi tey,

     que trop s'es de mi alonhatz."

"Lord," she said, "I truly believe
that God will have mercy on me
in the other world, forever,
with many other sinners.
But here He takes away the very thing
that feeds my joy, for my lover thinks
    little of me,
since he's gone so far away."

Provenance: Provence. Marcabru lived ca. 1127–50; this poem can be dated by its reference to the Second Crusade, organized by Louis VII in 1147.
Meter: Six *coblas singulars* (individually rhymed stanzas) of 7 octosyllabic lines.

L'autrier jost'una sebissa—*"The other day, by a hedgerow"*

This poem is more clearly a *pastorela*, and the earliest unmistakable example of the genre in a European vernacular. Marcabru plays deftly with class and manners, as the shepherdess neatly undermines the knight's confident superiority. He flatters her by telling her she is a "courtly peasant," a contradiction, but she sees through his wiles. While her language is down-to-earth, his switches between courtliness and crudity, reflecting the discordance between his suave exterior and his real intentions. Though Marcabru appears to identify with the knight, the "I" of the poem, it is the shepherdess who wins the contest of wits.

I   L'autrier jost'una sebissa
     trobei tozeta mestissa,
     de joi e de sen masissa,
     si con fillia de vilaina
5   chap' e gonel' e pellissa
     viest, e camiza traslissa,
     sotlars e caussas de laina.

The other day, by a hedgerow,
I met a common little girl,
full of high spirits and good sense.
Like the daughter of a peasant woman,
she wore a cape, a tunic lined with fur,
a rough chemise,
shoes, and woolen stockings.

II   A leis vinc per la chalmissa.
     "Bela," fiz m'ieu, "res faitissa,
10   dol ai car lo fregz vos fissa."
     "Segner," so.m ditz la vilaina,
     "merce Dieu e ma noirissa,
     pauc o prez si.l venz m'erissa
     c'alegreta.n soi e sana."

I approached her across the heath.
"Pretty girl," I said, "you beautiful thing,
it pains me that you're pierced by the cold."
"Milord," said the peasant girl,
"I thank God and my nurse,
I don't care if the wind ruffles me,
for I'm happy and healthy."

III 15 "Bella," fiz m'ieu, "douc' e pia,
     destortz me soi de la via
     per far ab vos compagnia,
     c'anc aitals toza vilaina
     non dec ses pareil-paria
20   gardar aitanta bestia
     en aital terra, soldaina."

"Pretty girl," I said, "sweet and dear,
I've come out of my way
to keep you company,
for a country girl like you
shouldn't, without a good companion,
tend all these animals
alone, in a place like this."

IV   "Don," fetz ella, "qi qe.m sia,
     ben conosc sen o folia.

     La vostra pareillaria,
25   segner," so.m diz la vilaina,
     lai on s'estai, si s'estia,

"Sir," she said, "whatever I am,
I know the difference between sense and
    stupidity.
As for your company,
milord," said the country girl,
"let it stay where it's supposed to be.

car tals la cuid' en bailia
tener, no.n a mas l'ufaina."

For anyone who thinks she has it to keep,
has no more than a fantasy."

V   "Bella, per lo mieu veiaire,
30   cavalers fo vostre paire
        qe.us engenrec en la maire
        car fon corteza vilaina.
        On plus vos gart m'es bellaire,
        et ieu per lo joi m'esclaire—
35   si.m fossetz un pauc umana."

"Pretty girl, as I see it,
he must have been a knight,
the father who conceived you in your mother,
and she was a courtly peasant.
The more I look at you, the happier I am,
and I brighten with joy—
if only you'd be a bit more humane to me."

VI   "Don, tot mo ling e mon aire
        vei revertir e retraire
        al vezoig et a l'araire,
        segner," so.m diz la vilaina,
40   "qe tals si fai cavalgaire
        qe deuri' atretal faire
        los seis jorns en la setmana."

"Sir, my lineage and my ancestry
I see going all the way back
to the sickle and the plough,
milord," said the peasant girl.
"But people who claim to be knights
ought to act like them
six days a week."

VII   "Bella," fiz m'ieu, "gentils fada
        vos faizonec cant fos nada:
45   fina beutat esmerad' a
        e vos, corteza vilaina,
        e seria.us ben doblada
        ab sol un' atropellada,
        mi sobra e vos sotraina."

"Pretty girl," I said, "a noble fairy
shaped you when you were born.
Delicate, perfect beauty
is found in you, courtly peasant girl,
and it would be increased twofold
by just one coupling,
me over and you under."

VIII 50 "Segner, tan m'avetz lauzada
        qe tota.n soi enoiada.
        Pos em pretz m'avetz levada,
        segner," so.m ditz la vilaina,
        "per so m'auretz per soudada
55   al partir: bada fols bada,
        en la muz' a meliaina!"

"Lord, you've praised me so much
that I'm quite annoyed.
Since you've talked me up so high,
milord," said the peasant girl,
"you'll get me as your payment
when we part: gape, you fool,
open-mouthed, at noon!"

IX   "Toz' estraing cor e salvatge
        adomesz' om per usatge.
        Ben conosc al trespassatge
60   d'aital tozeta vilaina
        pot hom far ric companjatge,
        ab amistat de paratge,
        se l'us l'autre non engana."

"Girl, your hard, savage heart
a man can subdue with practice.
I know well that when someone runs across
a little peasant girl like you,
he can have splendid company
and excellent friendship,
as long as one doesn't cheat the other."

X   "Don, om cuitatz de folatge
65   jur' e pliu e promet gatge.
        Tant fariatz omenatge,
        segner," so.m diz la vilaina,
        "mais ieu per un pauc d'intratge

        non voil jes mon pieuzelatge
70   chamjar per nom de putana."

"Sir, a man carried away by folly
swears, and pleads, and gives pledges.
This is the kind of homage you would pay,
milord," said the peasant girl,
"but I don't want—for the sake of a paltry
  entrance fee—
to exchange my virginity
for the name of a whore."

XI   "Bella, tota criatura
        revertei' a ssa natura.
        Pareillar pareillatura
        devem, eu et vos, vilaina,
75   a l'ombra lonc la pastura
        car plus n'estaretz segura
        per far pareilla dousaina."

"Pretty girl, every creature
reverts to its own nature.
We should join in companionship,
you and I, peasant girl,
in the shade by the pasture;
it'll be safer for you there
to join in that sweet way."

XII	"Don, hoc, mas segon drechura
	encalz fols sa folatura,
80	cortes cortez' aventura,
	e.l vilas ab sa vilaina,
	qu'en tal luec fa senz frachura,
	don om non garda mezura:
	so ditz la genz cristiana."

"Yes, sir, but it's appropriate
for a fool to pursue his folly,
a courtly man his courtly adventure,
and a peasant a peasant girl,
for there's no wisdom
unless one observes moderation—
that's what the Christians say."

XIII 85 "Toz," anc de vostra figura
non vi una plus tafura
en tota gent christiana."

"Girl—about your behaviour—
I've never seen anything sneakier
in the whole of Christendom."

XIV "Don, lo chavetz nos aüra
qe tals bad' a la penchura
90 c'autre n'espera la maina."

"Sir, the owl gives us this augury:
one man gapes at a picture,
when another expects the real thing."

Meter: Seven-line stanzas rhyming in pairs, that is, *coblas doblas*. Two 3-line *tornadas* (envoys). The word *vilaina* appears as a rhyming refrain in the middle line of every stanza.

Comtessa de Dia

Ab ioi et ab ioven m'apais—*"I feed on joy and youth"*

Three of the Comtessa de Dia's four extant cansos are included here. Whereas most woman's songs are love complaints, *Ab ioi* proclaims the delight of satisfied love. In the closing *tornada*, the Comtessa addresses her lover by the senhal "Floris," a name from medieval romance (some manuscripts read simply *Amics*, "friend"). In troubadour songs, a senhal, or code name, is often used to preserve anonymity, secrecy being one of the requirements of *fin'amor*.

I Ab ioi et ab ioven m'apais
e iois e iovens m'apaia,
que mos amics es lo plus gais
per qu'eu sui coindeta e gaia;
5 e pois eu li sui veraia
be.is taing q'el me sia verais,
c'anc de lui amar no m'estrais
ni ai cor que m'en estraia.

I feed on joy and youth,
and joy and youth nourish me,
for my lover is the happiest man—
that's why I'm joyful and happy too.
And since I'm true to him,
it's appropriate he should be true to me.
For I've never strayed from loving him,
nor have I the heart to stray.

II Mout mi plai car sai que val mais
10 cel q'ieu plus desir que m'aia,
e cel que primiers lo m'atrais,
Dieu prec que gran ioi l'atraia
e qui que mal l'en retraia,
non creza, fors qu'ie.l retrais;
15 c'om cuoill maintas vetz los balais
ab q'el mezeis se balaia.

He pleases me much, for I know his worth,
the man whom I want most to possess me,
and to him who first brought my lover to me,
I pray God send great joy.
If anyone says ill of my lover,
let him not believe it—only what I say.
For people often make birch-rods
and get the chastisement themselves.

III Dompna que en bon pretz s'enten
deu ben pausar s'entendenssa
en un pro cavallier valen,
20 pos ill conois sa valenssa,
que l'aus amar a presenssa;
e dompna, pois am'a presen,
ia pois li pro ni.ll'avinen
no.n diran mas avinenssa.

A lady whose heart's set on high esteem
must steadily set her heart
on a fine, valiant cavalier.
Since she knows his valor
let her dare to love him openly.
And when a lady loves openly
good and gracious souls
will say nothing ungracious of her.

IV 25 Q'ieu n'ai chausit un pro e gen	I've chosen a fine and noble man
per cui pretz meillura e genssa,	in whom honor's increased and refined,
larc et adreig e conoissen,	generous, accomplished and wise,
on es sens e conoissenssa;	a man of good sense and understanding.
prec li que m'aia crezenssa,	I urge him to have faith in me
30 ni hom no.il puosca far crezen	and let no one make him believe
q'ieu fassa vas lui faillimen,	that I'd do him wrong,
sol non trob en lui faillensa.	as long as I find no wrong in him to me.
V Floris, la vostra valenssa	Floris, your valor
sabon li pro e li valen,	is well known to the good and brave,
35 per q'ieu vos qier de mantenen,	so I ask—if you please—
si.us plai, vostra mantenenssa.	keep me in your good keeping.

Provenance: Provence. The exact identity of the Comtessa is unknown. Possibly she is to be located in the circle of poets including Raimbaut d'Aurenga in the second half of the twelfth century.
Meter: Four *coblas doblas* of 8 octosyllabic lines; 4-line *tornada*. The poem uses derived rhyme: alternate masculine and feminine rhymes using different forms of the same word.

A chantar m'er de so q'ieu no volria—*"It's my task to sing of what I would not wish"*

An outspoken poem, in which the Comtessa de Dia professes to be in an extremity of love but never loses the sense of her own dignity and worth. The Comtessa alludes to two figures who seem to come from a lost medieval romance, identifying herself with the male, Seguis, and her lover with the female, Valenssa. *A chantar* combines the pride of the silent lofty lady adored by male admirers with the frank sexuality of the earthy persona who speaks in lower-style songs like *Quant lo gilos*. The poem ends with a sting in the tail.

I A chantar m'er de so q'ieu no volria,	It's my task to sing of what I would not wish—
tant me rancur de lui cui sui amia,	I've so much pain from him whose friend I am,
car eu l'am mais que nuilla ren que sia;	for I love him more than anything in the world.
vas lui no.m val merces ni cortesia	With him, kindness and courtesy do me no good,
5 ni ma beltatz ni mos pretz ni mos sens,	neither my beauty, nor reputation, nor understanding.
c'atressi.m sui enganada e trahia	I'm cheated and betrayed—
com degr'esser, s'ieu fos desavinens.	as I'd deserve if I were graceless.
II D'aisso.m conort car anc non fis faillenssa,	I comfort myself with this: I've done no wrong,
amics, vas vos per nuilla captenenssa,	friend, ever, to you, in any way,
10 anz vos am mais non fetz Seguis Valenssa,	but I love you more than Seguis did Valenssa.
e platz mi mout que eu d'amar vos venssa,	It pleases me much that I outdo you in love,
lo mieus amics, car etz lo plus valens;	my friend, for you're the worthiest;
mi faitz orgoil en digz et en parvenssa	to me you're proud in word and deed,
e si etz francs vas totas autras gens.	and yet so generous to everyone else.
III 15 Meraveill me cum vostre cors s'orgoilla,	I marvel your heart's so full of pride,
amics, vas me per q'ai razon qe.m doilla;	friend, towards me—which gives me cause to lament.
non es ies dreitz c'autr'amors vos mi toilla	it's not right another love draws you from me—
per nuilla ren qe.us diga ni.us acoilla,	not for any words or welcome she gives you.
e membre vos cals fo.l comenssamens	You remember how it was,

20	de nostr'amor, ia Dompnedieus non vuoilla	the beginning of our love. Now God forbid
	q'en ma colpa sia.l departimens.	I'd be to blame for it all ending.

IV	Proessa grans q'el vostre cors s'aizina	The magnanimity that dwells in you
	e lo rics pretz q'avetz m'en ataina,	and your rich merit give me pause
	c'una non sai loindana ni vezina	for I know no woman, far or near,
25	si vol amar vas vos no si aclina;	who won't incline towards you if she feels like loving.

	mas vos, amics, etz ben tant conoissens	But you, friend, are so perceptive
	que ben devetz conoisser la plus fina,	you should perceive who is most devoted
	e membre vos de nostres covinens.	and remember our contract.

| V | Valer mi deu mos pretz e mos paratges | My standing and rank should benefit me, |
| 30 | e ma beutatz e plus mos fins coratges, | as should my beauty—and my loyal heart even more. |

	per q'ieu vos man lai on es vostre estatges	And so, I'm sending you, where you reside,
	esta chansson que me sia messatges,	this song, to be my messenger.
	e voill saber, lo mieus bels amics gens,	And I want to know, my handsome, noble friend,

| | per que m'etz vos tant fers ni tant salvatges, | why you're so harsh and rude to me— |
| 35 | no sai si s'es orgoills ni mals talens. | I know not whether it's pride or ill will. |

| VI | Mas aitan plus vuoill li digas, messatges, | But all the more I want you to tell him, messenger, |
| | q'en trop orgoill ant gran dan maintas gens. | excessive pride brings many to a fall. |

Meter: Five *coblas singulars* of 7 decasyllabic lines; 2-line *tornada*.

Estat ai en greu cossirier—*"I have been in sore distress"*

Another bold declaration of love. Again, the Comtessa de Dia appropriates the more active, male, role by comparing herself with the male partner Floris and her lover with the female partner Blanchefleur. A well-known pair from medieval romance, the two were children brought up together and devoted to each other. Once more, the Comtessa manages to combine outspoken passion with self-possession and wit. Note the provocative conclusion.

I	Estat ai en greu cossirier	I have been in sore distress
	per un cavallier q'ai agut,	for a knight who was once mine.
	e vuoil sia totz temps saubut	And I want this to be known for all time:
	cum eu l'ai amat a sobrier.	how I loved him beyond measure.
5	Ara vei q'ieu sui trahida	Now I see that I'm betrayed,
	car eu non li donei m'amor,	because I denied him my love
	don ai estat en gran error	and I've been in great confusion
	en lieig e qand sui vestida.	both in bed and when I'm clothed.

II	Ben volria mon cavallier	How I wish I could hold my knight
10	tener un ser en mos bratz nut,	one night naked in my arms.
	q'el s'en tengra per ereubut	He'd be overjoyed—
	sol q'a lui fezes cosseillier;	if he could just make me his pillow.
	car plus m'en sui abellida	For I take more delight in him
	no fetz Floris de Blanchaflor;	than Floris did in Blanchefleur.
15	eu l'autrei mon cor e m'amor	My heart and my love are his,
	mon sen, mos huoills e ma vida.	my mind, my eyes, and my life.

III	Bels amics, avinens e bos,	Handsome friend, gracious and good,
	cora.us tenrai en mon poder,	when will I have you in my power?
	e que iagues ab vos un ser,	Oh that I could lie with you one night
20	e qe.us des un bais amoros?	and give you a passionate kiss.
	Sapchatz, gran talan n'auria	You know, I'd dearly like
	qe.us tengues en luoc del marit	to hold you in a husband's place,
	ab so que m'aguessetz plevit	as long as you promised me
	de far tot so qu'eu volria.	to do everything I'd wish.

Meter: Three stanzas of 8 octosyllabic lines, the first two being *coblas doblas*.

Raimbaut d'Aurenga and a Lady

Amics, en gran cosirier—*"Friend, I'm in great distress"*

A lively battle of wits between the well-known troubadour and a woman speaker. In this tenso (debate) the two speakers try to outdo each other in protesting their love. Because of the resemblance to the opening line of the Comtessa de Dia's *Estat ai en greu cosirier*, and the statement in a *vida* (life) that she loved Raimbaut, the woman has sometimes been identified with the Comtessa. The female-voice stanzas may be composed by a trobairitz, or, possibly, seeing that the lady is anonymous and there is no manuscript attribution to her, by Raimbaut himself.

I	"Amics, en gran cosirier	"Friend, I'm in great distress
	sui per vos e en grieu pena	for you, and in great suffering.
	e del mal q'ieu en sufier	The pain I suffer for you
	non cug qe vos sentas gaire.	I think you scarcely feel at all.
5	Doncs, per qe.us metes amaire	Then why become a lover
	pos a mi laissas tot lo mal,	when you leave all the pain to me?
	qar amdui no.l partem egal."	Why don't we share it equally?"
II	"Don', amors ha tal mestier,	"Lady, it's the function of love,
	pos dos amics encadena,	When it binds two friends together,
10	q'el mal q'an e l'alegrier	to make each one in their own way
	sen chascus so.ill es veiaire;	feel joy or pain.
	q'ieu pens, e no sui gabaire,	I think—and I'm not mocking you—
	qe la dura dolor coral	that the painful suffering of heart
	ai ieu tota a mon cabal."	falls entirely to my share."
III 15	"Amics, s'acses un cartier	"Friend, if you had a quarter
	de la dolor qe.m malmena	of the suffering I'm burdened with
	ben viras mon enconbrier,	you'd see well what I have to endure,
	mas no.us cal del mieu dan gaire	but you're scarcely troubled at all at my distress.
	qe, qan no m'en puesc estraire,	For—though I can't extricate myself—
20	com qe m'an vos es comunal,	what I feel is the same to you,
	an me ben o mal atretal."	whether it's good or ill."
IV	"Donna, qar ist lauzengier	"Lady, since these slanderers
	qe m'an tout sen e alena,	who've taken my mind and my breath away
	son nostr'angoissos gerrier	are our most bitter foes,
25	lais m'en, no per talen vaire,	I'm quitting—not because my inclination's changed;
	qar no.us son pres, q'ab lur braire	I can't be with you now, for with their talk

	nos an basti tal joc mortal	they've played us such a deadly game
	qe no iauzem iauzen iornal."	we can't enjoy one day of joy."

V		
	"Amics, nul gratz vos refier	"Friend, I give you no thanks
30	quar le mieus dans vos refrena	that my ill fortune keeps you
	de vezer me, qe.us enqier,	from seeing me, as I ask you.
	e si vos fas plus gardaire	And since you're more protective
	del mieu qez ieu non vueilh faire,	of my injury than I wish to be,
	be.us tenc per sobreplus leial	I think you're more loyal
35	que no son cil de l'ospital."	than the Knights Hospitaller."

VI		
	"Donna, ieu tem a sobrier	"Lady, I'm very much afraid
	q'aur perdi e vos arena,	that I lose gold, and you just sand,
	qe per ditz de lauzengier	that by the words of slanderers
	nostr'amor tornes en caire,	our love is coming to grief.
40	per so deg tener en gaire	So I've much more cause to be on guard
	trop plus que vos, per San Marsal,	than you, by St. Martial,
	qar es la res qi plus mi val."	for you're the thing I value most."

VII		
	"Amics, tan vos sai aleugier	"Friend, I know you're so light
	en fach d'amoroza mena	in the ways of love
45	quez ieu cuid de cavallier	that I think you've been transformed
	siaz devengutz camiaire;	from a knight into a money-changer.
	e deg vos o ben retraire,	And I must rebuke you,
	qar ben pareis qe pensas d'al	for you seem to be thinking of another,
	pueis del miei pensamen no.us cal."	since my trouble doesn't worry you."

VIII 50		
	"Domna, ia mais esparvier	"Lady, let me nevermore carry a sparrowhawk
	non port ni catz ab serena	or go hunting with a falcon,
	s'anc pueis qe.m des ioi entier	if ever—since you've been giving me full joy—
	fui de null'autr'anqistaire,	I've looked for another;
	ni no sui aital bauzaire;	I'm no such cheat!
55	mas per enveia.l deslial	It's out of envy that false people
	m'o alevon e.m fan venal."	accuse me and make me base."

IX		
	"Amics, creirai vos per aital	"Friend, I'll believe you on one condition:
	q'aisi.us aia toztemps leial."	that you always stay as faithful as this."

X		
	"Domna, aissi m'aures lial	"Lady, I'll be so faithful to you
60	qe ia mais non pensarai d'al."	that I'll never think of anyone else."

Provenance: Region around Orange; Raimbaut lived ca. 1144–73.
Meter: Seven-line *coblas unissonans* (stanzas with the same rhymes); first 5 lines of 7 syllables, last 2 of 8; two 2-line *tornadas*.

Castelloza

Mout avetz faich lonc estatge—*"Long is the time you've been away"*

Castelloza assumes the role of a devoted lover wooing an unresponsive beloved, that is, the typical posture of the male suitor in the canso. However, in doing so she also takes the initiative and rejects the passive stance conventionally assigned to ladies. Thus, there is a piquant admixture of defiance in her long-suffering fidelity and her claim to be on the verge of death. The poem ends optimistically, with an invitation that her man surely won't be able to resist.

I   Mout avetz faich lonc estatge,

Long is the time you've been away,

amics, pois de mi.us partitz,

friend, since you left me,

et es mi greu e salvatge

and it's painful and harsh to me,

car me iuretz e.m plevitz

because you've sworn and promised me

5   que als iorns de vostra vida

that all the days of your life

non acsetz dompna mas me,

you'd accept no lady but me.

e si d'autra vos perte

If you've devoted yourself to another

mi avetz morta e trahida,

you have killed and betrayed me,

c'avia en vos m'esperanssa

for I placed my hope in you

10   que m'amassetz ses doptanssa.

that you'd love me unwaveringly.

II   Bels amics, de fin coratge

Fair friend, with true devotion

vos amei puois m'abellitz,

I've loved you since you gave me pleasure,

e sai que fatz hi follatge,

and I know that doing so is folly

que plus m'en etz escaritz

for you treat me all the more distantly

15   c'anc non fis vas vos ganchida;

because I was never disloyal to you.

e si.m fasetz mal per be,

If you render me evil for good

be.us am e no m'en recre,

I still love you well, nor will cease to do.

mas tant m'a amors sazida

But love has mastered me so completely

qu'eu non cre que benananssa

I don't think I can possess

20   pousca aver ses vostr'amanssa.

happiness without your love.

III Mout aurai mes mal usatge

I'll be a sad example

a las autras amairitz,

to the other ladies in love,

c'om sol trametre messatge

for usually the man sends a message

e motz triatz e chausitz,

in measured and well-chosen words.

25   et eu tenc me per garida,

But I think I'm cured,

amics, a la mia fe,

friend, by my faith,

qan vos prec, c'aissi.m cove,

when I woo you—it pleases me so.

qe.ill plus pros n'es enriquida

The most noble lady increases in worth

s'a de vos calc'aondanssa

if you favor her

30   de baisar o d'acoindanssa.

with your kisses or your company.

IV Mal ai'eu, s'anc cor volatge

Woe betide me if I've ever been changeable

vos aic, ni.us fui camiairitz,

or inconstant toward you,

ni drutz de negun paratge

or ever desired another lover

per mi non fo encobitz;

however high in rank he was.

35   anz sui pensiva e marrida

Instead, I'm pensive and sad

car de m'amor no.us sove

because you're not mindful of my love.

e si de vos iois no.m ve,

And if no joy comes to me from you

tost mi trobaretz fenida,

soon you'll find I'm dead,

car per pauc de malananssa

for it takes only a little sickness

40   mor dompna s'om tot no.il lanssa.

to kill a lady, if a man doesn't banish it
completely.

V   Tot lo maltraich e.l dampnatge

All the ill-treatment and the harm

que per vos m'es escaritz

I suffer at your hands

vos grazir fan mos lignatge

make you dear to my relatives,

e sobre totz mos maritz.

and my husband above all.

45   E s'anc fetz vas mi faillida

If ever you did me an injury

perdon la.us per bona fe,

I pardon you in good faith

e prec [que veingnaz a me

and beg [you to come to me

depueis que] auretz auzida

as soon as] you've heard

ma chansson qe.us fai fianssa,

my song—for I give you my pledge:

50   sai trobetz bella semblanssa.

you'll find a sweet welcome.

Provenance: Auvergne, early thirteenth century. Castelloza was married to Turc de Mairona (Meyronne).
Meter: *Coblas unissonans* of ten 7-syllable lines.

Anonymous

En un vergier sotz fuella d'albespi—*"In an orchard, under the leaves of a hawthorn tree"*

This alba, with its narrative framing the woman's voice and its garden setting, does not quite conform to the classic Occitan form, but does feature the typical refrain and watchman's warning. There is an intense eroticism in the woman's eagerness to "do everything," "play a new game," and drink in her lover's breath like a "sweet breeze," but the extravagance of her protestations is tempered by restraint and economy in the stylized depiction of the scene, so that the little drama remains idealized, its details suggestive rather than graphic. With this compare the German alba or *Tagelied* by Wolfram von Eschenbach, later.

I En un vergier sotz fuella d'albespi

In an orchard, under the leaves of a hawthorn tree

tenc la dompna son amic costa si
tro la gayta crida que l'alba vi,
Oy Dieus! Oy Dieus! de l'alba tan tost ve.

the lady holds her lover by her side,
until the watchman cries he sees the dawn:
Oh God! Oh God! The dawn! How soon it comes!

II 5 "Plagues a Dieu ia la nueitz non falhis
ni.l mieus amicx lonc de mi no.s partis
ni la gayta iorn ni alba no vis,
Oy Dieus! Oy Dieus! de l'alba tan tost ve.

"Would God the night were not already ending,
nor my lover parting far from me,
nor the watchman seeing day or dawn!
Oh God! Oh God! The dawn! How soon it comes!

III Bels dous amicx, baizem nos yeu e vos
10 aval e.ls pratz on chanto.ls auzellos
tot o fassam en despieg del gilos,
Oy Dieus! Oy Dieus! de l'alba tan tost ve.

Fair, sweet friend, let you and me kiss
in the meadow where the little birds sing:
let's do everything in spite of that jealous man.
Oh God! Oh God! The dawn! How soon it comes!

IV Bels dous amicx, fassam un ioc novel
yns el iardi on chanton li auzel

Fair, sweet friend, let's play a new game
down in the meadow, where the birds are singing,

15 tro la gaita toque son caramelh,
Oy Dieus! Oy Dieus! de l'alba tan tost ve.

until the watchman rings his bell.
Oh God! Oh God! The dawn! How soon it comes!

V Per la doss'aura qu'es venguda de lay
del mieu amic belh e cortes e gay—
del sieu alen ai begut un dous ray,
20 Oy Dieus! Oy Dieus! de l'alba tan tost ve."

In the sweet breeze that's come from there,
from my fair, courteous, merry friend—
I've drunk a sweet vapor of his breath.
Oh God! Oh God! The dawn! How soon it comes!"

VI La dompna es agradans e plazens
per sa beutat la gardon mantas gens

The lady is gracious and pleasing.
Many look at her for her beauty,

et a son cor en amar leyalmens,	and she holds her heart in loyal love.
Oy Dieus! Oy Dieus! de l'alba tan tost ve.	Oh God! Oh God! The dawn! How soon it comes!

Provenance: Provence; date uncertain.
Meter: Six *coblas singulars* of 3 decasyllabic lines and a 1-line refrain.

Anonymous

Quant lo gilos er fora—*"When that jealous man's away"*

A light-hearted *balada*, a song probably composed to accompany dancing. It belongs to the *chanson de malmariée* genre, better attested in North France; see the examples later. The problems of cuckoldry and wife beating are treated playfully here, as in many a song of this type. Contrast this poem with the high-style *canso*.

	Quant lo gilos er fora,	When that jealous man's away,
	bels ami,	fair friend come
	vene.vos a mi!	and visit me!
I	Balada coint' e gaia—	I'm singing a dance-song, pretty and gay—
5	Quant lo gilos er fora—	when that jealous man's away—
	faz, cui pes ni cui plaia—	please or displease whom it may—
	Qant lo gilos—	when that jealous man—
	pel dolz cant qe m'apaia,	It cheers me, this sweet roundelay
	que.us audi	I've heard you sing
10	seir e de mati.	morn and eve to me.
	Quant lo gilos er fora,	When that jealous man's away,
	bels ami,	fair friend come
	vene.vos a mi!	and visit me!
II	Amic, s'eu vos tenia—	Friend, if I could have you stay—
15	Quant lo gilos—	when that jealous man's away—
	dinz ma chambra garnia—	in my chamber garnished and gay—
	Qant lo gilos—	when that jealous man—
	de joi vos baisaria,	with joyful kisses I'd repay.
	qar n'audi	For I've heard
20	ben dir l'autre di.	your praises recently.
	Quant lo gilos er fora,	When that jealous man's away,
	bels ami,	fair friend come
	vene.vos a mi!	and visit me!
III	Se.l gilos mi menaza—	If my jealous husband should threaten and say—
25	Quant lo gilos—	when that jealous man's away—
	de baston ni de maça—	with stick or with club he'll do what he may—
	Quant lo gilos—	when that jealous man—
	del batre si se.l faza,	let him beat me if that's his way.
	que.us afi:	I promise you
30	mon cor no.s cambi!	a heart that's true, unchangingly!
	Quant lo gilos er fora,	When that jealous man's away,
	bels ami,	fair friend come
	vene.vos a mi!	and visit me!

Provenance: Provence; date uncertain, probably thirteenth century.
Meter: *Balada*; three 7-line *coblas unissonans* with a 3-line refrain, which also opens the poem. Longer and shorter lines of stanzas and refrain are linked by rhymes; the first line of the refrain recurs within the stanza.

Anonymous

Quan vei los praz verdesir—*"When I see the fields grow green"*

This poem has the courtly vocabulary and aristocratic speaker characteristic of the *canso*, but its refrain and anonymous attribution are more characteristic of lower-style songs. The poem moves from pain to joy, from longing for love to satisfied recollection, as memory evokes the presence of the beloved, and the speaker ends with a proclamation of her power over her lover. Compare the role of memory in Sappho 16, earlier, where, similarly, the poet recreates in her mind the physical presence of her lover.

I	Quan vei los praz verdesir	When I see the fields grow green,
	e pareis la flors granada,	and the bright flowers appear,
	adoncas pens e consir	then I think and meditate
	d'amors qu'aissi m'a lograda,	on love, which has so overpowered me
5	per un pauc non m'a tuada;	that it's almost killed me;
	tan soven sospir	I often sigh,
	c'anc non vi tan fort colada	for I was never so assailed—
	senes colp ferir.	without even a blow being struck.
	Aei.	Aei!
II 10	Tota noit sospir e pes	Each night I sigh and lie awake,
	e tressalh tot'endormida	and cry aloud in my sleep,
	per oc, car veiaire m'es	because it seems to me
	que.l meus amics me reissida.	that my lover is waking me.
	A Deus, com serai garida	Oh God, my sickness would be cured
15	s'aissi devengues	if it happened so,
	una noit per escarida	and one night by chance
	qu'a me s'en vengues.	he came to me.
	Aei.	Aei!
III	Domna qui Amors aten	A lady who waits for love
20	ben deu aver fin coratge;	should have a noble soul;
	tal n'i a qu'ades la pren	there are some men who would take her up,
	pois la laissa per folatge;	then leave her thoughtlessly.
	mas eu l'en tenh fin coratge	But I love with a noble soul
	aissi leialmen	so faithfully
25	qu'anc domna del mieu paratge	that no lady of my rank
	non o fetz tan gen.	ever kept love so well.
	Aei.	Aei!
IV	Domna qui amic non a	A lady who has no lover,
	ben si gart que mais non aia	let her take care never to have one:
30	qu'amors ponh oi e dema	love's piercing pains
	ni tan ni quan non s'apaia;	give her no rest at all;
	senes colp fai mort, e plaia	love strikes her dead without a blow; its wounds
	ia non garira	will never be healed,
	per nul metge que i en aia,	by any doctor in the world,

| 35 | s'Amors non lo.i da. | except for Love itself. |
| | Aei. | Aei! |

V	Messagier, levatz mati	Messenger, rise in the morning
	e vai m'en la gran iornada,	and make me a long day's journey:
	la chançon a mon ami	take this song to my friend
40	li portatz en sa contrada;	in the region where he is;
	digas li que mout m'agrada	tell him it delights me
	quan membre del son	when I think of the song
	qu'el mi ditz quan m'ac baizada	that he sang me when he kissed me
	soz mon paveillon.	beneath my canopy.
45	Aei.	Aei!

VI	Dins ma chambr'encortinada	In my curtained chamber
	fon el a lairon,	he was secretly;
	dins ma chambra ben daurada	in my gilded chamber
	fo il en preison.	he was in captivity.

Provenance: Provence; date uncertain.
Meter: Five *coblas singulars* of 8 lines; final 4-line *tornada*.

Occitan or Northern French

Anonymous

A l'entrade del tens clar—"*At the beginning of the fair season*"

A humorous and lively *balada*, in which the girls attending the "April Queen" chase away the tiresome jealous men who will spoil their fun. The girls express a preference for lovers over husbands. The song seems to be associated with a mime performed in spring celebrations where a young woman is chosen as queen—more commonly as May Queen on the first day of that month.

I	A l'entrade del tens clar—eya!	At the beginning of the fair season—eya!
	pir ioie recomençar—eya!	to begin our amusement—eya!
	e pir ialous irritar—eya!	and to annoy a jealous husband—eya!
	vol la regine mostrar	the queen wants to show
5	k'ele est si amourouse.	that she's in love.
	A la vi', a la vie, ialous!	Away, away with you, jealous ones!
	Lassaz nos, lassaz nos	Leave us free, leave us free,
	ballar entre nos, entre nos.	to dance together, dance together.

II	Ele a fait pir tot mandar—eya!	She's had it proclaimed far and wide—eya!
10	non sie iusq'a la mar—eya!	as far as the coast of the sea—eya!
	pucele ni bachelar—eya!	that every maiden and bachelor—eya!
	que tuit non venguent dançar	must come to dance
	en la dance ioiouse.	in the merry dance.
	A la vi', a la vie, ialous!	Away, away with you, jealous ones!
15	Lassaz nos, lassaz nos	Leave us free, leave us free,
	ballar entre nos, entre nos.	to dance together, dance together.

III	Lo reis i vent d'autre part—eya!	The king is coming from far away—eya!
	pir la dance destorbar—eya!	to interrupt the dance—eya!
	que il est en cremetar—eya!	for he's in a panic—eya!
20	que on no li vuelle emblar	that someone might run away
	la regine avrillouse.	with the April Queen.

A la vi', a la vie, ialous!	Away, away with you, jealous ones!
Lassaz nos, lassaz nos	Leave us free, leave us free,
ballar entre nos, entre nos.	to dance together, dance together.

IV 25 Mas pir neient lo vol far—eya!   But she wants him not at all—eya!
       k'ele n'a soing de viellart—eya!   for she's no need of an old man—eya!
       mais d'un legeir bachelar—eya!   but a lively bachelor—eya!
       ki ben sache solaçar   who knows well how to charm
       la donne savorouse.   a sexy lady.
30   A la vi', a la vie, ialous!   Away, away with you, jealous ones!
          Lassaz nos, lassaz nos   Leave us free, leave us free,
          ballar entre nos, entre nos.   to dance together, dance together.

V   Qui donc la veist dançar—eya!   Whoever could see her dance—eya!
       e son gent cors deportar—eya!   moving her graceful body—eya!
35   ben puist dire de vertat—eya!   could well say in truth—eya!
       k'el mont non aei sa par   that the world has not the equal
       la regine ioiouse.   of our merry queen.
          A la vi', a la vie, ialous!   Away, away with you, jealous ones!
          Lassaz nos, lassaz nos   Leave us free, leave us free,
40   ballar entre nos, entre nos.   to dance together, dance together.

Provenance: Northern France?; thirteenth century.
Meter: *Balada*; 5 *coblas unissonans* of 5 lines with a refrain word after the first 3; 3-line refrain.

Northern French

The lyric forms cultivated by the troubadours begin to appear in Northern France from the twelfth century on: for example, the *grand chant courtois* (corresponding to the canso), the *jeu parti* (a northern version of the debate poem—not included here), the *aube*, and the pastourelle. But particularly prolific in the north are two kinds of *chanson de femme*: the *chanson de toile*, which is only attested there, and the *chanson de malmariée*, which is much more abundant than in the south. *Malmariées* often take the metrical form of dance songs: *ballette*, resembling the Occitan *balada*, and *rondeau*. The *ballette* later evolves into the *ballade*. Much of the woman's voice poetry from the north is lively and outspoken—and not particularly courtly. However, the *grand chant* style can be seen in some of the songs, especially the more serious ones, and persists to the end of the Middle Ages. In the later, Middle French, period (the fourteenth and fifteenth centuries), the *ballade, rondeau*, and *virelai*, "formes fixes" originally based on dance-songs, become the dominant lyric genres, and can be used for graver subjects. By this time, texts and music have come to be conceived as separate things, and poems are more likely to be composed in writing.

For a broad selection of trouvère songs and melodies, see *Songs of the Troubadours and Trouvères*, ed. Samuel Rosenberg et al. (1998); on performance Christopher Page, *Voices and Instruments of the Middle Ages* (1987), and Maria Coldwell, "*Jouglaresses* and *Trobairitz*," in *Women Making Music*, ed. Jane Bowers and Judith Tick (1986). The significant contribution of women poets is asserted by Joan Grimbert in the Introduction to *Songs of the Women Trouvères*, ed. Eglal Doss-Quinby et al. (2001). On women and gender relations, see Simon Gaunt, *Gender and Genre in Medieval France* (1995), and Jane Burns et al., "Feminism and the Discipline of Old French Studies," in *Medievalism and the*

Modernist Temper, ed. Howard Bloch and Stephen Nichols (1996); on the *chanson de toile* Burns, "Sewing Like a Girl," in *Medieval Woman's Song*, ed. Klinck and Rasmussen (2002). Further, Kevin Brownlee, *Poetic Idenity in Guillaume de Machaut* (1984); *Eustache Deschamps: Selected Poems*, ed. Ian Laurie, Deborah Sinnreich-Levi, David Curzon, and Jeffrey Fiskin (2003). The Norton Critical Edition *Selected Writings of Christine de Pizan*, ed. Renate Blumenfeld-Kosinski (1997) provides a useful introduction; for two of Christine's poems of widowhood, see Jane Taylor, "Mimesis Meets Artifice," in *Christine de Pizan 2000*, ed. John Campbell and Nadia Margolis (2000).

Richard de Semilly

L'autrier tout seus chevauchoie mon chemin—"*I was riding all alone the other day*"

A pastourelle, with elements of the *malmariée*. Probably because of the influence of the latter, the two participants are treated as co-conspirators rather than antagonists, and they seem to be more or less equal in rank. Both the young man riding out and the young woman he encounters are equally eager to play the game of illicit love.

I   L'autrier tout seus chevauchoie mon chemin.
A l'oissue de Paris par un matin
oï dame bele et gente en un jardin
ceste chançon noter:
5   "Dame qui a mal mari,
s'el fet ami,
n'en fet pas a blasmer."

I was riding all alone the other day.
At the gate of Paris in the morning
I heard a fair, noble lady in a garden
singing this song:
"If a lady has a bad husband
and she takes a lover,
she's not to blame."

II   Vers li me trés, si li dis: "Suer dites moi,
pour quoi parlez vous d'ami? Est ce desroi?"
10   "Sire, je le vous dirai mult bien pour quoi,
ja nel vous qier celer:
Dame qui a mal mari,
s'el fet ami,
n'en fet pas a blasmer.

I went to her and said, "Sister, tell me,
why do you speak of a lover? Is it from folly?"
"Sir, I'll tell you exactly the reason;
I don't want to hide it from you:
If a lady has a bad husband
and she takes a lover,
she's not to blame.

III 15   A un vilain m'ont donee mi parent,
qui ne fet fors aüner or et argent,
et me fet d'ennui morir assez souvent,
q'il ne me let joer.
Dame qui a mal mari,
20   s'el fet ami,
n'en fet pas a blasmer."

My parents gave me to a boorish man
who does nothing but heap up gold and silver
and keeps me dying of frustration constantly
because he won't let me have fun.
If a lady has a bad husband
and she takes a lover,
she's not to blame."

IV   Je li dis: "Ma douce suer, se Dex me saut,
vez ci vostre douz ami qui ne vos faut;

venez vous en avec moi, et ne vos chaut,
25   si le lessiez ester.
Dame qui a mal mari,
s'el fet ami,
n'en fet pas a blasmer."

I said to her, "Sweet sister, so save me God,
you don't lack a pleasant lover; you see one here.
Come off with me—don't give it a thought—
and let your husband be.
If a lady has a bad husband
and she takes a lover,
she's not to blame."

V	"Sire, je n'iroie pas hors de Paris.	"Sir I wouldn't go outside Paris—
30	J'auroie perdu heneur més a touz dis,	I'd have lost my honour forever after.
	més ici l'acoupirai, se trouver puis,	But I'll cheat on him here, if I can find
	nul qui me vueille amer.	someone who wants to love me.
	Dame qui a mal mari,	If a lady has a bad husband
	s'el fet ami,	and she takes a lover,
35	n'en fet pas a blasmer."	she's not to blame."

VI	Qant je vi qu'avecques moi ne vout venir,	When I saw she wouldn't come with me,
	je li fis le gieu d'amors au departir.	I played the game of love with her and went away.
	Puis me pria et requist qu'au revenir	Then she begged and requested me, when I returned
	alasse a li parler.	to talk to her again.
40	"Dame qui a mal mari,	"If a lady has a bad husband
	s'el fet ami,	and she takes a lover,
	n'en fet pas a blasmer."	she's not to blame."

Provenance: Richard de Semilly was composing in the region of Paris around 1200.
Meter: *Rotrouenge*, that is, a folk-song with simple structure and refrain. Six stanzas of 3 long and 1 short line; 3-line refrain. Final lines of stanza and refrain rhyme together.

Maroie de Diergnau

Mout m'abelist quant je voi revenir—*"It does me good to see"*

The beginning of a what promises to be a lively poem, more or less in the *grand chant* style. In a nice contrast to the usual springtime setting, the speaker, confident in her youth and beauty, refuses to be downcast by the winter weather.

Mout m'abelist quant je voi revenir	It does me good to see
yver, gresill et gelee aparoir,	winter return, when hail and frost appear,
car en toz tans se doit bien resjoïr	for at all seasons a pretty girl
bele pucele, et joli cuer avoir.	should be happy, and have a light heart.
5 Si chanterai d'amors por mieuz valoir,	So I'll sing of love, to raise my spirits,
car mes fins cuers plains d'amorous desir	for my noble heart, full of desire for love
ne mi fait pas ma grant joie faillir.	won't let my great joy fail.

Provenance: First half of the thirteenth century. Diergnau was a faubourg of Lille, and Maroie a contemporary of Andrieu Contredit d'Arras, who died ca. 1248.
Meter: Stanza of seven 10-syllable lines; the remaining stanzas are missing.

Anonymous

Bele Yolanz en chambre koie—*"Fair Yolande, quiet in her chamber"*

Both this and the following poem, found together in Manuscript U, are *chansons de toile* (sewing songs), supposedly sung by women at their needlework, and often, as here, featuring women doing embroidery. Typically, the poem begins with the word "bele" and a woman's name. In its simple exposition and dramatic dialogue, the *chanson de toile* resembles the Old French epic or *chanson de geste*—as well as the later English ballad. Often serious, sometimes tragic, the genre takes a humorous turn in this example.

I	Bele Yolanz en chambre koie	Fair Yolande, quiet in her chamber,
	sor ses genouz pailes desploie.	spreads out silk upon her knees,
	Cost un fil d'or, l'autre de soie.	sews a gold thread, then a silk.
	Sa male mere la chastoie:	Her cruel mother scolds her:
5	"Chastoi vos en, bele Yolanz.	"I'm scolding you, fair Yolande.
II	Bele Yolanz, je vos chastoi:	Fair Yolande, I'm scolding you:
	ma fille estes, faire lo doi."	you're my daughter; I must do so."
	"Ma dame mere, et vos de coi?"	"My lady mother, why must you?"
	"Je le vos dirai, par ma foi:	"I'll tell you, by my faith:
10	Chastoi vos en, bele Yolanz."	I'm scolding you, fair Yolande."
III	"Mere, de coi me chastoiez?	"Mother, why are you scolding me?
	Est ceu de coudre ou de taillier,	Is it for the way I sew and snip,
	ou de filer, ou de broissier,	or spin or card?
	ou se c'est de trop somillier?"	Or have I been sleeping too long?"
15	"Chastoi vos en, bele Yolanz.	"I'm scolding you, fair Yolande.
IV	Ne de coudre ne de taillier,	Not for sewing or snipping,
	ne de filer, ne de broissier,	not for spinning or carding,
	ne ceu n'est de trop somillier;	not for sleeping too long;
	mais trop parlez au chevalier.	but for talking too much with a knight.
20	Chastoi vos en, bele Yolanz.	I'm scolding you, fair Yolande.
V	Trop parlez au conte Mahi,	You talk too much with Count Mahi,
	si en poise vostre mari.	and that bothers your husband.
	Dolanz en est, jel vos affi.	It makes him unhappy, I promise you.
	Nel faistes mais, je vos en pri.	Do it no more, I beg you.
25	Chastoi vos en, bele Yolanz."	I'm scolding you, fair Yolande."
VI	"Se mes mariz l'avoit juré,	"If my husband had sworn it,
	et il et toz ses parentez,	he and all his relatives,
	mais que bien li doie peser,	however much it bothers him
	ne lairai je oan l'amer."	I'll never leave off loving."
30	"Covegne t'en, bele Yolanz."	"Suit yourself, fair Yolande."

Provenance: Northern France; first half of the thirteenth century?
Meter: Six stanzas of 5 octosyllabic lines, including a 1-line refrain.

Anonymous

Quant vient en mai, que l'on dit as lons jors (Bele Erembors)— *"When it befalls in May, called the time of long days"*

Another *chanson de toile*, sometimes called *Bele Erembors*. Only a small part of this is in the woman's voice, but the return of the lover is presented from her point of view—literally, as she sees him from her window, calls out to him, protests her fidelity, and persuades him to climb the stairs and come to her.

I	Quant vient en mai, que l'on dit as lons jors,	When it befalls in May, called the time of long days,
	que Franc de France repairent de roi cort,	that the Franks are returning from the royal court

Reynauz repaire devant el premier front;	Raynaut comes first, in the front rank.
si s'en passa lez lo meis Arembor,	As he passed by the house of Erembors,
5 ainz n'en dengna le chief drecier amont.	he didn't even deign to raise his head.
E Raynaut, amis!	Oh, Raynaut, my love!

II Bele Erembors a la fenestre au jor	Fair Erembors sits at the window in the light,
sor ses genolz tient paile de color,	holding colored cloth on her lap.
voit Frans de France qui repairent de cort	She sees the Franks returning from the royal court
10 et voit Raynaut devant el premier front.	and she sees Raynaut coming first, in the front rank.
	She said her thought out loud:
En haut parole, si a dit sa raison:	
E Raynauz, amis!	Oh, Raynaut, my love!

III "Amis Raynauz, j'ai ja veü cel jor	"Raynaut, my love, I've seen the day before
se passissoiz selon mon pere tor,	when if you were passing by my father's tower,
15 dolanz fussiez se ne parlasse a vos."	you'd be grief-stricken if I didn't speak to you."
"Ja.l mesfaïstes, fille d'empereor;	"Yes, but you've done wrong, daughter of an emperor,
autrui amastes, si obliastes nos."	you've loved elsewhere, and forgotten us."
E Raynauz, amis!	Oh, Raynaut, my love!

IV "Sire Raynauz, je m'en escondirai;	"Sir Raynaut, I'll tell you truly.
20 a cent puceles sor sainz vos jurerai,	Before a hundred virgins, on relics I'll swear to you,
a trente dames que avuec moi menrai,	before thirty ladies I'll bring with me,
c'onques nul home fors vostre cors n'amai.	that I've never loved any man but you.
Prennez l'emmende et je vos baiserai."	Accept my oath, and I'll give you a kiss."
E Raynauz, amis!	Oh, Raynaut, my love!

V 25 Li cuens Raynauz en monta lo degré,	Count Raynaut climbed up the staircase,
gros par espaules, greles par lo baudré;	broad-shouldered, slim-waisted
blonde ot lo poil, menu recercelé.	with fair hair in close curls.
en nule terre n'ot si biau bacheler.	In no land was there such a handsome young man.
Voit l'Erembors, si comence a plorer.	When Erembors sees him she begins to weep.
30 E Raynauz, amis!	Oh, Raynaut, my love!

VI Li cuens Raynauz est montez en la tor,	Count Raynaut has climbed up the tower,
si s'est assis en un lit point a flors;	he's sat down on a bed embroidered with flowers.
dejoste lui se siet bele Erembors.	Beside him sits Fair Erembors.
. . .	. . .
35 Lors recomencent lor premieres amors.	They take up again the love they'd had before.
E Raynauz, amis!	Oh, Raynaut, my love!

Provenance: Lorraine, thirteenth century.
Meter: Stanzas of 5 decasyllabic, monorhymed, or assonanced lines; 5-syllable refrain.

Anonymous

Jherusalem, grant damage me fais—"*Jerusalem, you do me great injury*"

A *chanson de croisade* in which the speaker cries out passionately against the religious claims that are taking her lover away from her. As in many woman's songs, a personal and private attachment is asserted against a social commitment—here, to organized religion. The abstraction of the Crusades becomes concretized in the personified city of Jerusalem, here treated as the woman's rival.

I	Jherusalem, grant damage me fais, qui m'as tolu ce que je pluz amoie.	Jerusalem, you do me great injury for you've taken away the one I love most of all.
	Sachiez de voir ne vos amerai maiz, quar c'est la rienz dont j'ai pluz male joie;	Know this for sure: I'll love you no more, for it's the thing from which I have the saddest joy.
5	et bien sovent en souspir et pantais si qu'a bien pou que vers Deu ne m'irais, qui m'a osté de grant joie ou j'estoie.	Very often I sigh and lament over it so much I nearly turn from God who's deprived me of the great joy I had.
II	Biauz dous amis, com porroiz endurer la grant painne por moi en mer salee,	Fair, sweet friend, how could you bear great pain for me on the salt sea,
10	quant rienz qui soit ne porroit deviser la grant dolor qui m'est el cuer entree? Quant me remembre del douz viaire cler que je soloie baisier et acoler, grant merveille est que je ne sui dervee.	for nothing on earth could express the great grief that's entered my heart? When I think of the sweet, bright face that I used to kiss and draw close, it's a great wonder I don't go mad.
III 15	Si m'aït Deus, ne puis pas eschaper: morir m'estuet, teus est ma destinee, si sai de voir que qui muert por amer trusques a Deu n'a pas c'une jornee. Lasse! mieuz vueil en tel jornee entrer	God save me, I cannot escape; I must die—such is my destiny. I know for sure that whoever dies for love to reach God needs no more than a day. Unhappy me! I'd rather take that journey of a day,
20	que je puisse mon douz ami trover que je ne vueill ci remaindre esguaree.	so I could find my sweet friend, than remain here in my despair.

Provenance: Northern France; thirteenth century? Attributed in the manuscript rubric to Gautier d'Épinal and in the manuscript table of contents to Jean de Neuville. Both attributions are doubtful.

Meter: Three stanzas of 7 decasyllabic lines. The second and third stanzas are *coblas doblas* linked by the same rhymes. This linking suggests that some stanzas may be missing.

Adam de la Halle

Fi, maris, de vostre amour—*"Fie, husband, on your love"*

A lively and defiant *chanson de malmariée* for singing and dancing. The poem is a round or *rondeau*. Compare this with the more literary rondeau by Guillaume de Machaut, later.

	Fi, maris, de vostre amour, car j'ai ami! Biaus est et de noble atour: fi, maris, de vostre amour!	Fie, husband, on your love, for I've a lover! He's handsome, cuts a fine figure. Fie, husband, on your love!
5	Il me sert et nuit et jour, pour che l'aim si. Fi, maris, de vostre amour, car j'ai ami!	He serves me night and day. That's why I love him so. Fie husband, on your love, for I've a lover!

Provenance: Picardy. Adam de la Halle was born in Arras, and was active there in the second half of the thirteenth century.
Meter: *Rondeau*: a short poem with the opening refrain repeated between the other lines and linked to them by rhyme. Here, an 8-line poem with lines of 7 and 4 syllables, line 1 repeated in line 4, lines 1–2 in lines 7–8.

Anonymous

Au cuer les ai, les jolis malz—*"I have the sweet sickness at heart"*

Chanson de malmariée in the form of a *ballette*. Typically, the speaker's husband is boorish (a *vilains*), avaricious, and physically repellent; no doubt her lover is handsome, generous, and courtly. This and the following two poems, all anonymous and all in the Lorraine dialect, are found close together in Manuscript I.

	Au cuer les ai, les jolis malz.	I have the sweet sickness at heart.
	Coment an guariroie?	What cure can I find?
I	Kant li vilains vait a marchiet,	When the boor goes to market, here's why:
	il n'i vait pais por berguignier,	he doesn't go to bargain and buy,
5	mais por sa feme a esgaitier	but to watch his wife in case someone comes by
	que nuns ne li forvoie.	with seduction in mind.
	Au cuer les ai, les jolis malz.	I have the sweet sickness at heart.
	Coment an guariroie?	What cure can I find?
II	Vilains, car vos traites an lai,	Boor, take yourself away from me!
10	car vostre alainne m'ocidrait.	Your breath could be the death of me.
	Bien sai c'ancor departirait	I know we should sever immediately
	Vostre amor et la moie.	your love and mine.
	Dieus, j'ai a cuer les jolis malz.	God, I have the sweet sickness at heart.
	Coment an guariroie?	What cure can I find?
III 15	Vilains, cuidiez vos tout avoir,	Boor, is this what you expect to do,
	et belle dame et grant avoir?	have a pretty wife and money too?
	Vos avereiz lai hairt on col,	A noose is what is waiting for you,
	Et mes amins lai joie.	and for my lover a good time.
	Dieus, j'ai a cuer les jolis malz.	God, I have the sweet sickness at heart.
20	Coment an guariroie?	What cure can I find?

Provenance: Lorraine; thirteenth century?
Meter: *Ballette*: Three 4-line stanzas with a 2-line refrain, which also opens the poem; the last line of stanzas and the refrain are linked by rhyme.

Anonymous

Por coi me bait mes maris—*"Why does my husband beat poor wretched me"*

Another *chanson de malmariée* and *ballette*. The crude husband gets his just deserts, and the wife pays him back for his brutality. Rhyming diminutives applied to the speaker do much to establish the saucy tone. Contrast with this their use for genuine pathos in Christine de Pizan's *Seulete sui*, later.

	Por coi me bait mes maris,	Why does my husband beat
	laisette?	poor wretched me!
I	Je ne li de rienz meffis,	I've done him no wrong,
	ne riens ne li ai mesdit	I've said him no ill—
5	fors c'acolleir mon amin	just received my lover
	soulete.	privately.
	Por coi me bait mes maris,	Why does my husband beat
	laisette?	poor wretched me!

II	Et s'il ne mi lait dureir	If he won't let me alone
10	ne bone vie meneir,	to lead the sweet life,
	je lou ferai cous clameir,	I'll get him called cuckold,
	a certes.	I guarantee.
	Por coi me bait mes maris,	Why does my husband beat
	laisette?	poor wretched me!

III 15	Or sai bien que je ferai	I know what I'll do
	et coment m'an vangerai:	to take my revenge.
	avec mon amin geirai	I'll lie with my lover
	nüete.	nakedly.
	Por coi me bait mes maris,	Why does my husband beat
20	laisette?	poor wretched me!

Provenance: Lorraine; thirteenth century.
Meter: *Ballette*.

Anonymous

Entre moi et mon amin—*"My lover and I"*

An *aube*. The setting, "in a wood near Bethune," is more pastoral and less aristocratic than in the (usual) Occitan alba, and it is the lark, not the watchman, that warns the lovers they must part. The lark as unwelcome herald of morning to clandestine lovers is a motif that finds its most famous expression in *Romeo and Juliet*, Act 3, Scene 5.

I	Entre moi et mon amin,	My lover and I
	en un boix k'est leis Betune,	in a wood near Bethune
	alainmes juwant mairdi	sported last Tuesday
	toute lai nuit a la lune,	all night beneath the moon,
5	tant k'il ajornait	until day began to dawn
	et ke l'alowe chantait	and the lark to sing,
	ke dit: "Amins, alons an."	saying, "Friend, we must go."
	Et il respont doucement:	And he replies gently,
	"Il n'est mie jours,	"Day hasn't yet come.
10	saverouze au cors gent;	Lovely girl with your body sweet,
	si m'aït amors,	so help me Love,
	l'alowette nos mant."	the lark's song is deceit."

II	Adont se trait pres de mi,	Then he draws close to me—
	et je ne fu pas anfruine;	I didn't take it amiss;
15	bien trois fois me baixait il,	a good three times he kissed me,
	ausi fix je lui plus d'une,	and more than once I returned his kiss—
	k'ainz ne m'anoiait.	I took no offence!
	Adonc vocexiens nous lai	Then we could have wished

ke celle neut durest sant,
20 mais ke plus n'alest dixant:
    "Il n'est mie jours,
    saverouze au cors gent;
    si m'aït amors,
    l'alowette nos mant."

this night to last a hundred more,
with no need to say,
    "Day hasn't yet come.
    Lovely girl with your body sweet,
    so help me Love,
    the lark's song is deceit."

Provenance: Lorraine; thirteenth century?
Meter: Two assonanced *coblas doblas* of 8 lines; 4-line refrain.

Guillaume de Machaut

Celle qui nuit et jour desire (Le Livre du Voir-Dit 727–39)—*"She who night and day desires"*

This *rondeau* accompanies a letter supposedly sent to Guillaume de Machaut by a young lady who has fallen in love with his poetic reputation. On the basis of an anagram at at the end of the *Voir-Dit* ("True Story") she has been identified with Péronne (or Péronnelle) d'Armentières. The letter is sent toward the beginning of a courtly-love relationship initiated by the girl and conducted largely by correspondence. At this point, Guillaume is sick and depressed; receipt of the letter effects a marvellous cure. Scholars disagree as to whether the lady and her part of the correspondence are fictional. Thus, the poem included here contains a structural "defect," regarded by some as evidence that Machaut is not the author (see Meter). In this little poem, the speaker addresses the elderly poet in the high style, with a mixture of romantic affection, protectiveness, and devoted admiration.

Celle qui nuit et jour desire
de vous véoir
sui, pour oster vostre cuer d'ire:
n'a nulle autre riens tant ne tire
730 ne n'a voloir,
    celle qui nuit et jour desire
    de vous véoir,
com de véoir vostre martyre:
qu'à son pooir,
735 elle sera dou garir mire.
    Celle qui nuit et jour desire
    de vous véoir
    sui, pour oster vostre cuer d'ire.

She who night and day desires
to see you
am I, to rid your heart of ire.
She is drawn to no other creature so,
nor does she wish to be,
    she who night and day desires
    to see you,
and likewise to see your suffering,
which as best she can
she would minister to and cure.
    She who night and day desires
    to see you
    am I, to rid your heart of ire.

Provenance: Rheims. Guillaume de Machaut lived ca. 1300–77. The *Voir-Dit* records near-contemporary events that would have taken place between ca. 1362 and 1365.
Meter: *Rondeau*. The third line of the refrain should be repeated on its second appearance, but its inclusion would fit awkwardly with the sense.

Eustache Deschamps

Il me semble, a mon avis—*"In my opinion, it seems to me"*

Disciple of Guillaume de Machaut, and friend of Chaucer and Christine de Pizan, Eustache Deschamps was an extremely prolific writer of poems in various genres.

This *virelai* adopts the persona of a young, coquettish but virginal, girl. The poem maintains a delicate balance between titillation and irony as the speaker itemizes all her desirable points. Of course, the "earthly paradise" of the penultimate stanza is an illusion, and her beauty is no one's to keep forever.

I	Il me semble, a mon avis,	In my opinion, it seems to me,
	que j'ay beau front et doulz viz	I have a fair forehead and a pleasant face,
	et la bouche vermeillette;	a little red mouth.
	dittes moy se je suis belle.	Tell me if I'm pretty!
II 5	J'ay vers yeulx, petis sourcis,	I have green eyes and narrow brows,
	le chief blont, le nez traitis,	fair hair, a straight nose,
	ront menton, blanche gorgette;	a round chin, a white neck.
	sui je, sui je, sui je belle? etc.	Oh, am I, am I, am I pretty!
III	J'ay dur sain et hault assis,	I have firm breasts, and a fair height,
10	lons bras, gresles doys aussis	long arms and slender fingers too,
	et par le faulz sui greslette;	and in the waist I'm very slim.
	dittes moy se je suis belle.	Tell me if I'm pretty!
IV	J'ay bonnes rains, ce m'est vis,	I have good haunches, it seems to me,
	bon dos, bon cul de Paris,	a good back, a nice bum in the Paris style,
15	cuisses et gambes bien faictes;	shapely thighs and shapely legs.
	sui je, sui je, sui je belle? etc.	Oh, am I, am I, am I pretty!
V	J'ay piez rondès et petiz,	My feet are plump and small,
	bien chaussans, et biaux habis,	my shoes neat, and my clothes fine,
	je sui gaye et joliette;	I'm, lively and attractive.
20	dittes moy se je sui belle.	Tell me if I'm pretty!
VI	J'ay mantiaux fourrez de gris,	I've coats trimmed with gray fur,
	j'ay chapiaux, j'ay biaux proffis	I've hats—I've plenty of money,
	et d'argent mainte espinglette;	I've lots of pretty silver pins.
	sui je, sui je, sui je belle? etc.	Oh, am I, am I, am I pretty!
VII 25	J'ay draps de soye et tabis,	I've clothes of satin and watered silk,
	J'ay draps d'or et blans et bis,	I've clothes of gold, and white, and grey.
	J'ay mainte bonne chosette;	I have many nice little things.
	dittes moy se je sui belle.	Tell me if I'm pretty!
VIII	Que .XV. ans n'ay, je vous dis;	I'm only fifteen years old, I admit.
30	moult est mes tresors jolys,	my special treasure is a lovely thing,
	s'en garderay la clavette;	and I'll keep the key to it.
	sui je, sui je, sui je belle? etc.	Oh, am I, am I, am I pretty!
IX	Bien devra estre hardis	The man who'd be my lover
	cilz qui sera mes amis,	must be a bold fellow
35	qui ara tel damoiselle;	to have a girl like me.
	dittes moy se je sui belle.	Tell me if I'm pretty!
X	Et par Dieu je li plevis	And by God I swear to him
	que tres loyal, se je vis,	I'll be very loyal if I live,
	li seray, si ne chancelle;	and I won't waver.
40	sui je, sui je, sui je belle? etc.	Oh, am I, am I, am I pretty!

XI	Se courtois est et gentilz,
	vaillant apres, bien apris,
	il gaignera sa querelle;
	dittes moy se je sui belle.

If he's courteous and noble,
valiant, and educated too,
he'll win his contest.
Tell me if I'm pretty!

XII 45 C'est un mondains paradiz
que d'avoir dame toudiz
ainsi fresche, ainsi nouvelle;
sui je, sui je, sui je belle? etc.

It's an earthly paradise
to have a lady forever
who's so fresh and young.
Oh, am I, am I, am I pretty!

XIII Entre vous acouardiz,
50 pensez a ce que je diz:
cy fine ma chansonnette;
sui je, sui je, sui je belle?

You cowards, think about this.
Listen to my words.
Here's the end of my little song.
Oh, am I, am I, am I pretty!

Provenance: Eustache Deschamps lived ca. 1340–ca. 1404.
Meter: *Virelai:* the opening lines form a refrain that is subsequently repeated after alternate stanzas. This example, which is unusually long, has 4-line stanzas using the same rhymes throughout.

Christine de Pizan

Seulete sui et seulete vueil estre—*"Alone I am and alone wish to be"*

Christine de Pizan was married at fifteen, to a man ten years older, and after she became a widow at twenty-five composed many poems about her bereavement. This is probably the most famous. The insistent, ritualistic repetition makes it a kind of ceremonial lament that both celebrates and exorcizes her grief. Like the poem that follows it here, *Seulete sui* adopts the *ballade* convention of addressing itself to a "prince" or head of a *puy* (literary society)—by this time probably a purely imaginary figure.

I Seulete sui et seulete vueil estre,
seulete m'a mon doulx ami laissée,
seulette sui, sanz compaignon ne maistre,
seulette sui, dolente et courroussiée,
5 seulette sui, en languour mesaisiée,
seulette sui, plus que nulle esgarée,

seulete sui sans ami demourée.

Alone I am and alone wish to be;
alone has my dear one left me.
Alone I am, without partner or master;
alone I am, lamenting and embittered;
alone I am, languishing, distressed.
Alone I am, more than any woman who has
    lost her way.
Alone I'm left with no beloved friend.

II Seulette suis à huis ou à fenestre,
seulette sui en un englet muciée,
10 seulette sui pour moy de plours repaistre,
seulette sui, dolente ou appaysiée,
seulette sui. Rien n'est qui tant me siée.
Seulette sui, en ma chambre enserrée,
seulette sui sans ami demourée.

Alone I am, at door and window;
alone in a corner, hidden away.
Alone I am; I've had my fill of tears;
alone I am, lamenting or consoled.
Alone I am; there's nothing so suits me.
Alone I am in my chamber, closeted.
Alone I'm left with no beloved friend.

III 15 Seulette sui par tout et en tout estre.
Seulette sui, où je voise où je siée,
seulette sui plus qu'aultre riens terrestre,
seulette sui, de chacun delaissiée,

Alone I am in each place, everywhere;
alone I am, whether I walk or sit.
Alone I am, more than any creature on earth;
alone I am, by everyone abandoned.

	seulette sui, durement abaissiée,	Alone I am, cruelly brought low.
20	seulette sui, souvent toute esplourée,	Alone I am, often worn out with weeping;
	seulette sui sanz ami demourée.	alone I'm left with no beloved friend.

IV	Princes, or est ma douleur commenciée.	Prince, now has my grief begun:
	Seulette sui, de tout dueil menaciée,	alone I am, facing every sorrow;
	seulette sui, plus tainte que morée,	alone I am, more darkened than a Moorish girl.
25	seulette sui sanz ami demourée.	Alone I'm left with no beloved friend.

Provenance: Christine de Pizan, who lived ca. 1364–ca. 1430, was born in Italy, but spent most of her life in France. This poem was written ca. 1395.

Meter: *Ballade*: 3 stanzas with a refrain and often an envoy; here, stanzas of seven 10-syllable lines; 4-line envoy.

Doulce chose est que mariage—*"Marriage is a sweet thing"*

Written a considerable number of years after her husband's death, this lyric seems to speak of Christine's own happy marriage. As a medieval poem in praise of marriage it is unusual, though not unparalleled.

I	Doulce chose est que mariage,	Marriage is a sweet thing,
	je le puis bien par moy prouver,	as I have proved for myself.
	voire, à qui mari bon et sage	It's true when one's husband is kind and good
	a, comme Dieux m'a fait trouver.	like the one God granted me to find.
5	Louez en soit il qui sauver	Praised be He, because it was His will
	le me vueille, car son grant bien	to keep him for me. The great kindness
	de fait je puis bien esprouver,	of his nature I can feel indeed.
	et certes le doulx m'aime bien.	I know my gentle husband loves me well.

II	La premier nuit du mesnage	The first night of our marriage
10	tres lors, peus je bien esprouver	from the beginning I could feel
	son grant bien, car oncques oultrage	his great kindness, for he never did amiss,
	ne me fist dont me deust grever.	nor anything of which I might complain.
	Mais, ains qu'il fust temps de lever,	But before it was time to get up,
	cent fois baysa, si com je tien,	he kissed me a hundred times, just as I like,
15	sans villenie autre rouver,	without asking any indignity.
	et certes, le doulx m'aime bien.	I know my gentle husband loves me well.

III	Et disoit par si doulx lengage:	And he said to me in gentle words,
	"Dieux m'a fait à vous arriver,	"God granted me to come to you,
	doulce amie, et pour vostre usage	sweetheart, and for your service
20	je croy qu'il me fist eslever."	I believe he brought me up."
	Ainsi ne fina de resver	And so he went on dreaming
	toute nuit en si fait maintien,	all night in that way
	sans autrement soy desriver,	without any change.
	et certes, le doulx m'aime bien.	I know my gentle husband loves me well.

IV 25	Princes, mais il me fait desver	But, Prince, I'm carried away
	quant il me dit qu'il est tout mien;	when he tells me that he is all mine;
	de doulçour me fera crever,	for joy he'll make my heart burst.
	et certes, le doulx m'aime bien.	I know my gentle husband loves me well.

Meter: *Ballade*; stanzas of 8 octosyllabic lines; 4-line envoy.

CHAPTER 8

MEDIEVAL EUROPE: LATIN AND MACARONIC

In the Middle Ages, nonreligious Latin and macaronic verse (partly in Latin, partly in the vernacular) was composed as a pastime by clerics. This verse is often witty or ironic, qualities emphasized by the insistent rhymes of the Latin, with their repeated inflectional endings. Woman's song forms a small, but significant, portion of the corpus. These poems can be graceful and charming; they can also be bawdy or rough, dealing frankly with sexual matters and with the seamy side of life. In the harsher poems, an ironic detachment contrasts with the suffering described, and suggests both the bitter disillusionment of the speaker and the distance of a male author. It is possible, though, that some of these poems, especially the more lyrical ones, were composed by women, perhaps in a convent.

Most of the examples that follow come from two collections compiled in Germany (the manuscript of the Cambridge Songs was preserved in England). The three short pieces from the Cambridge collection all contain echoes of the Hebrew love poetry found in the Song of Songs (or Song of Solomon) and interpreted allegorically by later Judaic and Christian tradition. Especially noteworthy is the idea of love-longing: *languens* (CC 14A.1), *languet* (CC 40.24), *languore* (CC 49.5), recalling the often-quoted *quia amore langueo* ("because I am languishing with love"), Song 2.5 and 5.8. Interestingly, this collection also includes a classical Latin poem about love that may be in a woman's voice, Horace, *Odes* 3 (the Neobule poem, copied as CC 46).

See Anne Schotter, "Woman's Song in Medieval Latin," in Plummer's *Vox Feminae* (1981). For the Cambridge Songs miscellany, see the Introduction to Jan Ziolkowski's edition (1994). For the *Carmina Burana*, see the introductory essay on goliardic poetry (i.e., the recreational poetry of medieval clerics) in Edward Blodgett and Arthur Swanson's translation, *The Love Songs of the Carmina Burana* (1987). See also Ann Astell, *The Song of Songs in the Middle Ages* (1990).

Medieval Latin

Anonymous

Plangit nonna, fletibus—*"A nun is crying"*

The lament of the young nun, confined in a convent against her will, is a well-developed medieval genre, with examples in the vernaculars as well as in Latin. Compare the later, Castilian, *Agora que soy niña*. The following Latin

representative of the genre combines defiance with pathos, and the repugnance
with which the young woman's living conditions are described is striking.

I	Plangit nonna, fletibus	A nun is crying,
	inenarrabilibus	weeping inexpressibly,
	condolens gemitibus-	accompanying her lamentations
	que consocialibus:	with groans.
5	Heu misella!	Oh, poor me!
	nichil est deterius	Nothing is worse
	tali vita!	than such a life,
	Cum enim sim petulans	for someone sexy and lusty
	et lasciva,	like me.
II 10	Sono tintinnabulum,	I ring the bell,
	repeto psalterium,	repeat the psalms,
	gratum linquo somnium	have to leave pleasant dreams
	cum dormire cuperem—	when I'd like to sleep.
	heu misella!—	Oh, poor me!
15	pernoctando vigilo	I have to do a vigil all night
	cum non vellem;	when I don't want to.
	iuvenem amplecterer	How glad I'd be
	quam libenter!	to put my arms around a young man!
III	Fibula non perfruor,	I can't take pleasure in jewellery,
20	flammeum non capio,	I'll never wear a wedding veil;
	strophium assumerem,	I'd like to put on a headdress,
	diadema cuperem,	a fine diadem.
	heu misella!—	Oh, poor, me!
	Monile arriperem	I'd steal a necklace
25	si valerem,	if I could.
	pelles et herminie	It would be nice to wear
	libet ferre.	furs and ermine.
IV	Ago trabe circulum,	I walk round and round the floor,
	pedes volvo per girum,	trace my steps in a circle,
30	flecto capud supplicum,	bow my head in prayer,
	non ad auras tribuo,	never get outside.
	heu misella!	Oh, poor me!
	Manus dans, in cordibus	I stretch out my hands in appeal,
	rumpo pectus,	break my heart in my breast,
35	linguam tero dentibus	bite my tongue with my teeth.
	verba promens.	as I utter these words.
V	Lectus est in pissinis,	My bed is in a black hole;
	filtris non tappetibus,	it's made of felt, not rich fabrics,
	cervical durissimum,	with a hard pillow
40	subter filtrum palea—	and underneath a filling of straw.
	heu misella!	Oh, poor me!
	Vescor lance misera	The food I eat is wretched
	et amara,	and bitter;
	e succis farinule	it tastes only of flour
45	et caseo.	and cheese.
VI	Tunica teterrima,	My tunic is filthy,
	interula fetida	my underwear stinks;
	stamine conposita;	it's coarse and rough.
	cenosis† obicibus—	I'm in a foul prison.
50	heu misella!—	Oh, poor me!

fex cupedes adolens	There's smelly dirt
inter pilos,	in my pretty hair,
atque lens perferitur,	and I have to endure lice
scalpens carnes.	scratching my skin.

VII 55	Iuvenis, ne moreris!	Young man don't wait!
	faciam quod precipis;	I'll do what you ask.
	dormi mecum! si non vis,	Sleep with me! If you don't want to,
	tedet plura dicere—	there's no point in saying more.
	heu misella!—	Oh, poor me!
60	atque magis facere,	No use doing more,
	perdens vitam—	Wasting my life.
	cum possim eruere	But at least
	memetipsam.	I can kill myself.

Provenance: Eleventh century.
Meter: Nine-line stanzas with irregular assonance and rhyme. The fifth line forms a refrain.

Anonymous

Nam languens amore tuo *(Carmina Cantabrigiensia 14A)—"For longing with love of you"*

Possibly this evocative piece is a fragment of something longer; only the feminine inflection of *nuda* points unmistakably to a female speaker. The woman looking out over the sea is reminiscent of Ariadne, except that here she seems to be expecting a returning lover. Ovid (though not Catullus) was well known in the Middle Ages and may have been an influence. As in the following two poems, there are also echoes of the Song of Songs.

	Nam languens	For longing
	amore tuo	with love of you
	consurrexi	I arose
	diluculo	at dawn,
5	perrexi-	and went
	que pedes nuda	barefoot
	per nives et	through the snow
	per frigora,	and cold,
	atque maria	and scanned
10	rimabar mesta,	the waste sea,
	si forte ventivola	if perhaps your windblown sails
	vela cernerem,	I might discern,
	aut frontem navis	or glimpse
	conspicerem.	the prow of your ship.

Provenance: Germany, early eleventh century.
Meter: Lines 1–8 and 14 of 4 syllables; 9–10 and 12–13 of 5; line 11 of 7. The alternate lines rhyme. Could also be treated as (for the most part longer) lines rhyming in pairs.

Anonymous

Levis exsurgit zephirus *(Carmina Cantabrigiensia 40)—"The light breeze rises"*

A woman contrasts the beauty and burgeoning of spring with her own listless unhappiness. Probably, but not certainly, a love lament, or part of one. Again, the

femininity of the speaker rests on a single inflection, the feminine ending of *sola*.
Compare Rinaldo d'Aquino's *Ormai quando flore*, later, which also begins with
a conventional spring opening, and delays the information that the speaker
is a woman.

Levis exsurgit zephirus	The light breeze rises,
et sol procedit tepidus,	the warm sun comes forth,
iam terrra sinus aperit,	and now the earth opens her bosom
dulcore suo difluit.	and exudes her sweetness.
5 Ver purpuratum exiit,	Bright spring comes out,
ornatus suos induit,	and puts on her lovely clothing,
aspergit terram floribus,	strewing the earth with flowers
ligna silvarum frondibus.	and the branches of the trees with leaves.
Struunt lustra quadrupedes	The beasts are building their lairs,
10 et dulces nidos volucres,	and the sweet birds their nests
inter ligna florentia	as, in the flowery branches,
sua decantant gaudia.	they sing out their happiness.
Quod oculis dum video	While I see this with my eyes,
et auribus dum audio,	and hear it with my ears,
15 heu pro tantis gaudiis	alas, instead of all these joys
tantis inflor suspiriis.	I breathe in nothing but sighs.
Cum mihi sola sedeo	While I sit alone and grow pale
et hec revolvens palleo,	thinking of these things,
si forte capud sublevo,	if by chance I raise my head,
20 nec audio nec video.	I neither hear nor see.
Tu, saltim veris gratia,	You, for the sake of spring,
exaudi et considera	should listen, and consider
frondes, flores, et gramina;	the leaves, the flowers, and the grass;
nam mea languet anima.	for my heart is sore.

Provenance: Germany, early eleventh century.
Meter: Six stanzas of 4 octosyllabic lines rhyming in pairs.

Anonymous

Veni, dilectissime *(Carmina Cantabrigiensia 49)—"Come, sweetheart"*

A young woman boldly invites her lover to come and satisfy her desire. The
voluptuous language, with its talk of longing for love and the lover approach-
ing his beloved's door is reminiscent of the Song of Songs 5.4–8. This piece,
along with some of the other love poetry in the manuscript, has been subse-
quently erased by a medieval censor; hence the gaps in the text.

Veni, dilectissime,	Come, sweetheart,
et a et o!	ah!
gratam me invisere,	to visit me, your pleasure,
et a et o!	ah!

5	In languore pereo,	in longing I perish,
	et a et o!	ah!
	venerem desidero,	I yearn for love,
	et a et o et a et o!	ah!

10	...	...
	...	...
	...	...
	...	...

	Si cum clave veneris,	If you come with your key,
	et a et o!	ah!
15	mox intrare poteris,	you shall promptly enter,
	et a et o et a et o!	ah!

Provenance: Germany; early eleventh century.
Meter: Seven-syllable lines; strophic arrangement uncertain—perhaps 4 stanzas of two rhyming lines with a refrain after each.

Anonymous

Huc usque, me miseram *(Carmina Burana 126)—"Until now, poor wretched me"*

Lament of a pregnant girl; there is a casual tone to the description of her humiliation that may imply the attitude of a male poet and audience. But her wretchedness and suffering are inescapable.

I	Huc usque, me miseram!	Until now, poor wretched me,
	rem bene celaveram	I'd concealed things well,
	et amavi callide.	and loved cunningly.
II	Res mea tandem patuit,	Finally, my secret's out,
5	nam venter intumuit,	for my belly's swollen up,
	partus instat gravide.	showing I'm pregnant and soon due.
III	Hinc mater me verberat,	On one side my mother beats me,
	hinc pater improperat,	on the other my father yells at me,
	ambo tractant aspere.	both of them are hard on me.
IV 10	Sola domi sedeo,	All alone I sit at home;
	egredi non audeo	I daren't go out
	nec inpalam ludere.	and amuse myself in public.
V	Cum foris egredior,	If I go outdoors,
	a cunctis inspicior,	everybody looks at me
15	quasi monstrum fuerim.	as if I were a monster.
VI	Cum vident hunc uterum,	When they see my belly,
	alter pulsat alterum,	one pokes the other,
	silent, dum transierim.	and they're silent till I've gone past.
VII	Semper pulsant cubito,	People always nudge each other,
20	me designant digito,	point at me with a finger
	ac si mirum fecerim.	as if I'd performed a marvel;

VIII	Nutibus me indicant,	Criticize me with nodding heads,
	dignam rogo iudicant,	think I should be burnt on the pyre,
	quod semel peccaverim.	just because I've sinned once.

IX 25	Quid percurram singula?	Why should I tell each little thing?
	ego sum in fabulo	I'm the subject of a story;
	et in ore omnium.	I'm in everybody's mouth.

X	Ex eo vim patior,	Because of him I suffer this abuse.
	iam dolore morior,	I'm so miserable I'm dying.
30	semper sum in lacrimis.	I'm always in tears.

XI	Hoc dolorem cumulat,	And this adds to my troubles,
	quod amicus exulat	that my lover's gone off
	propter illud paululum.	because of that trifle.

XII	Ob patris sevitiam	On account of his father's rage,
35	recessit in Franciam	he's taken off to France
	a finibus ultimis.	right out of the country.

XIII	Sum in tristitia	I'm lonesome
	de eius absentia	because of his absence.
	in doloris cumulum.	What a pile of trouble I've had!

Provenance: South Germany or Austria, early thirteenth century.
Meter: Three-line stanzas. The first two lines rhyme together; the final line has a separate rhyme scheme and links the stanzas.

Macaronic (Bilingual)

Anonymous

Floret silva nobilis *(Carmina Burana 149)—"The fine wood is blooming"*

Another spring song. As in *CC 40*, the burgeoning of spring prompts feelings of love-longing. It is not clear whether the Latin stanza gave rise to the German or vice-versa. Compare this poem with *CB 174A, Chume, chume, geselle min*, later.

I	Floret silva nobilis	The fine wood is blooming
	floribus et foliis.	with flowers and leaves.
	ubi est antiquus	Where is he
	meus amicus?	who used to be my lover?
5	hinc equitavit!	He has ridden away!
	eia! quis me amabit?	Alas, who will love me?
	Floret silva undique;	The wood is in bloom everywhere;
	nah mime gesellen ist mir we!	for my lover my heart is sore.

II	Grünet der walt allenthalben.	The wood grows green on every side.
10	wa ist min geselle also lange?	Where then is my lover of old?
	der ist geriten hinnen.	He has ridden away!
	owi! wer sol mich minnen?	Alas, who will love me?
	Floret silva undique;	The wood is in bloom everywhere;
	nah mime gesellen ist mir we!	for my lover my heart is sore.

Provenance: South Germany or Austria, early thirteenth century.
Meter: Two stanzas of couplets, rhyming or assonanced: 6-line Latin stanza, 4-line German stanza, plus macaronic refrain.

Anonymous

Ich was ein chint so wolgetan (Carmina Burana 185)—"I was such a lovely girl"

The bitter lament of a deflowered girl, this poem draws on the pastourelle tradition. There is a sharp contrast between the vulnerability of the speaker and the knowing complacency of her seducer, the distance between the two underlined by that between the German and the Latin—although both languages are used by both characters.

I	Ich was ein chint so wolgetan,	I was such a lovely girl
	virgo dum florebam,	while I flourished as a virgin.
	do brist mich diu werlt al,	The whole world praised me,
	omnibus placebam.	everybody liked me.
5	Hoy et oe!	Hoy and oe!
	maledicantur tilie	Cursed be the linden trees
	iuxta viam posite!	planted by the way.
II	Ia wolde ih an die wisen gan,	When I set out for the meadows
	flores adunare,	to pick flowers,
10	do wolde mich ein ungetan	a crude fellow decided
	ibi deflorare.	to deflower me there.
	Hoy et oe!	Hoy and oe!
	maledicantur tilie	Cursed be the linden trees
	iuxta viam posite!	planted by the way.
III 15	Er nam mich bi der wizen hant,	He took me by the white hand,
	sed non indecenter,	but not indiscreetly;
	er wist mich diu wise lanch	he led me along the meadow
	valde fraudulenter.	very deceitfully.
	Hoy et oe!	Hoy and oe!
20	maledicantur tilie	Cursed be the linden trees
	iuxta viam posite!	planted by the way.
IV	Er graif mir an daz wize gewant	He took me by the white dress
	valde indecenter,	most indiscreetly,
	er fürte mih bi der hant	he led me along by the hand,
25	multum violenter.	very fiercely.
	Hoy et oe!	Hoy and oe!
	maledicantur tilie	Cursed be the linden trees
	iuxta viam posite!	planted by the way.
V	Er sprach: "vrowe, gewir baz!	He said, "Lady, let's go over there:
30	nemus est remotum.	That grove is lonely."
	dirre wech, der habe haz!"	Woe betide that road we took!
	planxi et hoc totum.	I had cause to lament it.
	Hoy et oe!	Hoy and oe!
	maledicantur tilie	Cursed be the linden trees
35	iuxta viam posite!	planted by the way.

VI   "Iz stat ein linde wolgetan
            non procul a via,
            da hab ich mine herphe lan,
            tympanum cum lyra."
40   Hoy et oe!
                maledicantur tilie
                iuxta viam posite!

VII   Do er zu der linden chom,
            dixit: "sedeamus,"
45   —diu minne twanch sêre den man—
            "ludum faciamus!"
                Hoy et oe!
                maledicantur tilie
                iuxta viam posite!

VIII 50   Er graif mir an den wizen lip,
            non absque timore,
            er sprah: "ich mache dich ein wip,
            dulcis es cum ore!"
                Hoy et oe!
55   maledicantur tilie
                iuxta viam posite!

IX   Er warf mir üf daz hemdelin,
            corpore detecta,
            er rante mir in daz purgelin
60   cuspide erecta.
                Hoy et oe!
                maledicantur tilie
                iuxta viam posite!

X   Er nam den chocher unde den bogen,
65   bene venabatur!
            der selbe hete mich betrogen.
            "ludus compleatur!"
                Hoy et oe!
                maledicantur tilie
70   iuxta viam posite!

"There stands a fine linden tree
not far from the path.
I've left my harp there,
my drum, and lyre."
    Hoy and oe!
    Cursed be the linden trees
    planted by the way.

When he came to the linden tree,
he said, "Let's sit down."—
Love really constrained him—
"Let's play a game!"
    Hoy and oe!
    Cursed be the linden trees
    planted by the way.

He took me by the white body,
not without my trembling.
He said, "I'll make you a woman—
your face is so pretty!"
    Hoy and oe!
    Cursed be the linden trees
    planted by the way.

He pulled up my little shift,
leaving my body bare.
He broke into my little fortress
with his erect spear.
    Hoy and oe!
    Cursed be the linden trees
    planted by the way.

He took the quiver and the bow.
Well he did his hunting!
That's how he betrayed me.
"End of the game!"
    Hoy and oe!
    Cursed be the linden trees
    planted by the way.

Provenance: South Germany or Austria, early thirteenth century.
Meter: Four-line stanzas of alternating longer and shorter lines, alternate lines rhyming or assonanced; refrain of 3 lines rhyming together.

CHAPTER 9

GERMANY

German lyrics of the early and high Middle Ages, from the mid-twelfth century on, include a small but wide-ranging body of woman's voice poetry, some of it in the form of complete poems (*Frauenlieder*) and some in stanzas (*Frauenstrophen*), which may alternate with male-voice poetry. Much of this woman's song is clearly influenced by the courtly love conventions stemming from Provence. But some of it, particularly the early pieces from south Germany and Austria, may derive from indigenous sources of inspiration. Many of the German *Frauenlieder*, unlike the French *chansons de femme*, are completely integrated into the world of courtly verse, rather than being contrastive to it. Of the language groups included in this anthology, it is the German corpus that shows the widest spectrum of poetic effects. Some of the short, early lyrics are striking for the vividness with which they evoke a single emotion. Other, longer poems can be complex and ambiguous, creating shifting perspectives and playing with expectations. Particularly striking and rich in texture are Wolfram von Eschenbach's *Sîne klâwen* and Walther von der Vogelweide's *Under der linden*.

For an overview see Olive Sayce, *The Medieval German Lyric 1150–1300* (1982); also Marion Gibbs and Sidney Johnson, *Medieval German Literature*, Part Five (1997). On woman's voice poetry, see William Jackson, "The Woman's Song in Medieval German Poetry," in Plummer's *Vox Feminae* (1981). On Reinmar see Jackson, *Reinmar's Women* (1981); also Ingrid Kasten, "The Conception of Female Roles," in *Medieval Woman's Song*, ed. Klinck and Rasmussen (1987, 2002). For Walther von der Vogelweide, see Rasmussen, "Representing Woman's Desire," in Albrecht Classen, *Women as Protagonists and Poets* (1991) and "Reason and the Female Voice," in Klinck and Rasmussen (2002). On Neidhart, see Rasmussen, *Mothers and Daughters*, chapter six.

Anonymous

Dû bist mîn, ich bin dîn—*"I am all yours, you all mine"*

This little poem, one of the oldest German lyrics, is appended to a Latin love-letter written by a nun. The lost key and the speaker's heart as the lover's prison may be compared with imagery of secret access and sexual enclosure in other poems, like the more carnal *Veni, dilectissime*, earlier.

Dû bist mîn, ich bin dîn.	I am all yours, you all mine:
des solt dû gewis sîn.	of that you should be sure.
dû bist beslozzen	You're locked up
in mînem herzen,	in my heart,
5 verlorn ist daz sluzzelîn:	and the key is lost.
dû muost ouch immêr darinne sîn.	Always I'll keep you there.

Provenance: South Germany, twelfth century.
Meter: Three rhyming couplets; lines of varying length.

Anonymous

Waere diu werlt alle mîn (Carmina Burana 145a)—
"Were all the world mine"

A brief and sweeping declaration of feeling. This one is hard to contextualize. It has been transferred from a woman's to a man's voice by a corrector's change of "king" to "queen" in the manuscript.

Waere diu werlt alle mîn	Were all the world mine,
von deme mere unze an den Rîn,	from the sea to the Rhine,
des wolt ich mich darben,	I'd relinquish it all
daz chunich von Engellant	to have the King of England
5 laege an mînen armen.	lying in my arms!

Provenance: Bavaria, twelfth century?
Meter: Five lines of unequal length rhyming aabcb; lines 4–5 may form a longer line with caesura.

Anonymous

Chume, chume, geselle min (Carmina Burana 174A)—"Come, my love, come to me"

An example of the medieval German Wechsel, "exchange," in which two voices speak in alternate stanzas. Here, each desiring lover calls to the other to come. As a love duet this type of poem seems to have had ancient antecedents, judging by Aristophanes's parody (see earlier). These stanzas echo the immediately preceding ones in Latin, beginning Veni, veni, venias. Chume, chume, geselle mîn may have inspired the Latin verses or been prompted by them. Compare the macaronic Floret silva nobilis, earlier.

Chume, chume, geselle min,	Come, my love, come to me,
ih enbite harte din!	I summon you, urgently!
ih enbite harte din,	I summon you, urgently,
chum, chum, geselle min!	come my love, come to me!
5 Süzer roservarwer munt,	Rose-colored mouth so sweet,
chum unde mache mich gesunt!	come and make me complete!
chum unde mache mich gesunt,	Come and make me complete,
süzer roservarwer munt!	rose-colored mouth so sweet!

Provenance: Twelfth century?
Meter: Monorhymed stanzas of four 4-stress lines.

Anonymous

Mich dunket niht sô guotes—*"Nothing seems to me so fine"*

Like the preceding lyrics, this poem crystallizes the speaker's longing. The rose and the birdsong embody the sweetness of love but are also transcended by it.

Mich dunket niht sô guotes noch sô lobesam	Nothing seems to me so fine and fit to praise
sô diu liehte rôse und diu minne mîns man.	as the bright rose and my man's love.
diu kleinen vogellîn	The little birds
diu singent in dem walde, dêst menegem	that sing in the wood make many a heart
herzen liep.	light.
5 mir enkome mîn holder geselle, ine hân der	But if my true love stays away, summer's
sumerwunne niet.	joy is nought.

Provenance: Twelfth century?
Meter: Long line; modified Nibelungen stanza.

Anonymous

"Mir hât ein ritter," sprach ein wîp—*" 'A knight has served me,'*
a woman said"

The poem alludes to the courtly convention of *Frauendienst* (love-service) whereby a knight "serves" his lady as if she were his feudal lord. But this speaker, designated a *wîp* (woman), rather than a *frouwe* (lady) also expresses her own urgent desires. The ability of love to transcend the bleakness of winter is a variation of the usual spring setting. Compare Maroie de Diergnau, earlier.

"Mir hât ein ritter," sprach ein wîp,	"A knight has served me," a woman said,
"gedienet nâch dem willen mîn.	"all according to my will.
ê sich verwándèlt diu zît,	Before the turning of the year,
sô muoz ime doch gelônet sîn.	he must be repaid.
5 Mich dunket winter unde snê	Winter and snow seem to me
schoene bluomen unde klê,	fair flowers and sweet clover,
swenne ich in umbevangen hân.	if I have him in my arms.
und waerz al der welte leit,	Though the whole world take it ill,
sô muoz sîn wille an mir ergân."	he shall have his will of me!"

Provenance: Twelfth century?
Meter: Four-stress lines rhyming or assonanced ababccdxd.

Der von Kürenberg

Ich zôch mir einem valken—*"I trained me a falcon"*

Both this and the following poem center on the image of a falcon, whose freedom to fly away contrasts with the speaker's fixity. Here, the falcon seems to represent the speaker's lost lover. The significance of the other lands to which it has flown is rather mysterious. Are the "other lands" the territory of another woman? Or have they a more transcendental meaning? The poem expresses yearning, but not jealousy, and ends with a prayer for union, perhaps in another world. Contrast this with *Tapina in me*, later.

Ich zôch mir einem valken   mêre danne ein jâr.
dô ich in gezamete,   als ich in wolte hân,
und ich im sîn gevidere   mit golde wol bewant,
er huop sich ûf vil hôhe   und vlouc in
    ándèriu lant.

Sît sach ich den valken   schône vliegen,

er vuorte an sînem vuoze   sîdîne riemen,
und was im sîn gevidere   alrôt guldîn.
got sende sî zesamene,   die gelieb wéllen
    gerne sîn!

I trained me a falcon more than a year.
When I'd tamed him to my bidding
and twined his feathers with fair gold thread,
he sprang up high and flew to other lands.

Since then I've seen that falcon in splendid
    flight,
trailing silk ribbons from his feet,
his feathers all bright red-gold.
God reunite lovers who long to be at one!

Provenance: South Germany or Austria; mid-twelfth century. The author, "the man from Kürenberg," is actually anonymous. Kürenberg may be Kürnberg Castle, near Linz.
Meter: Long lines with caesura, rhyming in pairs; modified Nibelungen stanza.

Dietmar von Aist

Ez stuont ein vrouwe alleine—*"There stood a lady alone"*

Another falcon poem. Here the speaker envies the bird its unchecked freedom to choose where it wishes to settle. She too has made her choice—and been criticized for it. Subtly, too, the poem implies a contrast between the waiting woman and a roving lover, as well as between her solitary independence and the general run of women.

Ez stuont ein vrouwe alleine
und warte über heide
unde warte ir liebes,
sô gesách si valken vliegen.
5   "sô wol dir, valke, daz du bist!
du vliugest, swar dir liep ist,
du erkíusest dir in dem walde
einen bóum, der dir gevalle.
alsô hân ouch ich getân:
10   ich erkôs mir selbe einen man,
den erwélten mîniu ougen.
daz nîdent schoene vrouwen.
owê, wan lânt si mir mîn liep?
joch engérte ich ir dekeines trûtes niet!"

There stood a lady alone
looking over the heath,
looking for her lover,
when she saw a falcon flying.
"How fortunate, falcon, you are!
You fly where you want,
you choose for yourself in the wood
any tree that pleases you.
I too have done that:
I have chosen myself a man
whom my eyes picked out.
Fair ladies are jealous of me.
Alas, why won't they allow me my love?
For I grudge them none of their sweethearts."

Provenance: South Germany or Austria, between 1150 and 1180. The Aist is a tributary of the Danube.
Meter: Four-stress lines rhyming or assonance in pairs. Could also be treated as long lines with internal rhyme.

Hartmann von Aue

Diz waeren wunneclîche tage—*"These would be delightful days"*

It is not completely clear whether the speaker's loss is caused by parting or by death. But the finality of the separation and the commendation of the beloved to

God suggest that this poem may be a lament for a lover or husband who has died. The speaker contrasts her own suffering with an imagined woman who has never known the joy of love and so has been spared its sorrow.

I Diz waeren wunneclîche tage,
der sî mit vröiden möhte leben.
nu hât mir got ein swaere klage
ze dirre schoenen zît gegeben,
5 der mit leider niemer wirdet buoz:
ich hân verlórn éinen man,
daz ich vür wâr wol sprechen muoz,
daz wîp nie liebern vriunt gewan.
dô ich sîn pflac, dô vröit er mich:
10 nu pflege sîn got, der pfliget sîn baz
    danne ich.
	These would be delightful days,
	if one could live in joy.
	Now God has given me heavy suffering
	during this pleasant time,
	pain for which, sadly, there'll never be a cure:
	I've lost a man
	of whom I can truly say
	that a woman never won a dearer friend.
	While I took care of him he gave me joy.
	Now God care for him, who keeps him
	    better than I.

II Mîn schade waer niemanne reht erkant, ern diuhte in grôzer klage wert. an dem ich triuwe und êre ie vant und swes ein wîp an manne gert, 5 Der ist alze gaehes mir benomen. des mac mir unz an mînen tôt niemer niht ze staten komen, ine müeze lîden sende nôt. der nû iht liebers sî beschehen, 10 diu lâze ouch daz an ir gebaerden sehen.	No one has rightly understood my loss who would not call him worthy of lament, in whom I ever found truth and honor, and whatever a woman desires in a man. He's been all too roughly snatched from me. Until the day I die nothing can compensate me for him. I must suffer endless distress. A woman more fortunate than I will show it in her bearing.
III Got hât vil wol zuo zir getân, sîn liep sô leidez ende gît, diu sich ir beider hât erlân: der gêt mit vröiden hin diu zît. 5 Ich hân klage sô manigen liehten tac, und ir gemüete stêt alsô, daz sî mir niht gelouben mac. ich bin von liebe worden vrô: sol ich der jâre werden alt, 10 daz giltet sich mit leide tûsentvalt.	God has treated that woman well— since love ends in such pain— who has kept free of both: time passes joyfully for her. On many a bright day I have pain, while her spirits are so high that she cannot believe me. I've been made happy through love. Should I live to be old in years, I'll pay for it with sorrow a thousandfold.

Provenance: Southwest Germany; late twelfth century.
Meter: Ten-line stanzas of 4-stress lines (lines 5 and 10 of five stresses) rhyming ababcdcdee.

Reinmar der Alte

War kan iuwer schoener lîp?—*"Where has your beauty gone?"*

Reinmar is well known for the *Frauenlieder* and *Frauenstrophen* in which he presents an anxiously loving woman with sympathy and sensitivity—but contrast this poem with the one that follows.

I "War kan iuwer schoener lîp?
wer hat iu, saelic vrouwe, den benomen?
ir wâret ein wunneclîchez wîp,
nu sint ir gar von iuwer varwe komen.
5 Dâst mir leit und müet mich sêre.
swer des schuldic sî, den velle got und nem
    im al sîn êre."
	"Where has your beauty gone?
	Who has stolen it, blessed lady?
	You were a beautiful woman,
	now you have left your brightness behind.
	It makes me sad and hurts me sorely.
	Whoever's guilty, let God punish him and
	    take his honor away"

II   "Wâ von solt ich schoene sîn
     und hôhes muotes als ein ander wîp?
     ich h'ân des willen mîn
     niht mêre wan sô vil, ob ich den lîp
5   Mac behüeten vor ir nîde,
     die mich zîhent unde machent, daz ich
       einen ritter mîde.

III Solhe nôt und ander leit
     hât mir der varwe ein michel teil benomen.
     doch vröuwet mich sîn sicherheit,
     daz er lobte, er wolte schiere komen.
5   Weste ich, ob ez alsô waere,
     sô engehôrte ich nie vor maniger wîle
       mir ein lieber maere.

IV   Ich gelache in iemer an,
     kumt mir der tac, daz in mîn ouge ersiht.
     wand ichs niht verlâzen kan
     vor liebe, daz mir alsô wol geschiht.
5   Ê ich danne von im scheide,
     sô mac ich sprechen 'gên wir brechen
       bluomen ûf der heide.'

V   Sol mir disiu sumerzît
     mit manigem liehten tage alsô zergân,
     daz er mir niht nâhen lît,
     dur den ich alle ritter hân gelân,
5   ôwê danne schoenes wîbes!
     sôn kam ich nie vor léidè in groezer angest
       mînes lîbes.

VI   Mîne vriunde mir dicke sagent—
     und liegent—, daz mîn niemer werde rât.
     wol in, daz si mich sô klagent!
     wie nâhen in mîn leit ze herzen gât!
5   Swenne er mich getroestet eine,
     sô gesiht man wol, daz ich vil selten
       iemer iht geweine."

"Why should I be so beautiful,
and high-spirited like another woman?
I have won no more of my desire
than to preserve myself
from those spiteful ones
who mock me and keep me from
  a knight.

This grief and other suffering too
has bereft me of my beauty—much of it.
Yet his assurance heartens me,
when he promised he would come back soon.
If I knew it were so,
it would be the dearest news I'd heard in a
  long while.

I'll smile at him constantly
if the day comes that my eyes look upon him.
I'll not be able to stop,
for love, so fortunate I'll be.
Before I leave him then, I may well say,
'Let's go and pluck flowers on the
  heath!'

If this summer season
with many a bright day must pass by,
without his lying beside me,
the man for whom I've left all other knights,
then alas for my beauty!
Grief's never made me fear so for my
  looks.

Often my friends say to me—
and they lie!—that it does me no good.
Well for them, that they lament me so.
My grief comes close to their hearts.
When he solaces me alone,
full seldom they'll see me
  weep."

Provenance: Austria, late twelfth or early thirteenth century. Originally from Hagenau in Alsace, Reinmar was later connected with the Viennese court. He died ca. 1210.
Meter: Six-line stanzas. Lines of varying length rhyming ababcc.

Zuo niuwen vröuden stât mîn muot—*"With prospect of new joys, my heart"*

A celebration of satisfied love. The manuscript attribution of this poem to Reinmar was contested by earlier scholars because of its outspoken female persona.

I   "Zuo niuwen vröuden stât mîn muot
     vil schône," sprach ein schoenez wîp.
     "ein ritter mînen willen tuot:
     der hât geliebet mir den lîp.
5   Ich wil im iemer holder sîn
     denne keinem mâge mîn.
     ich getúon ime wîbes triuwe schîn.

"With prospect of new joys, my heart
is high," a lovely woman said.
"A knight does my will,
who's fallen in love with me.
I'll always be truer to him
than to any of my kin.
I'll show him what a woman's devotion is.

II	Diu wîle schône mir zergât,		How pleasantly time goes for me
	swenne er an mîme arme lît		when he lies in my arms
	und ér mich zuo íme gevángen hât.		and clasps me to him.
	daz ist ein wunnenclîche zît.		It's a delightful moment.
5	Sô ist mîn trûren gar zergán		Then my sorrow's all gone,
	und bin ál die wochen wol getân.		I'm happy all the week,
	ei, waz ich dene vröuden hân!"		oh! what joy I have then!"

Meter: Seven-line stanzas. Lines of varying length rhyming ababccc.

Wolfram von Eschenbach

Sîne klâwen durch die wolken sint geslagen—*"Its claws tear through the clouds"*

Better known as a composer of romances, notably *Parzival*, Wolfram has left us seven lyrics, five of them albas or *Tagelieder*. In this dramatic *Tagelied* the dawn is depicted as a bird of prey tearing red streaks through the clouds with its talons. As in the classic Occitan alba, the poem takes the form of a dialogue between the lady in the arms of her lover and the friendly castle watchman. Wolfram manages to evoke both the sensibility of the woman and her physical presence from the silent lover's point of view. Consummation and imminent parting fuse in the poem's climactic ending.

I	"Sîne klâwen		"Its claws
	durch die wolken sint geslagen,		tear through the clouds,
	er stîget ûf mit grôzer kraft;		It rises with great strength!
	ich sich in grâwen		I see light in the grey,
5	tegelîch, als er wil tagen:		as if day begins,
	den tac, der im geselleschaft		the day that must break in upon
	Erwenden wil, dem werden man,		his tryst, this honorable man,
	den ich mit sorgen în verliez.		whom I warily let in.
	ich bringe in hinnen, ob ich kan.		I'll spirit him away if I can,
10	sîn vil mánigiu tugent mich daz leisten		the man whose many virtues bade me serve
	hiez."		him."

II	"Wahtaer, du singest,		"Watchman, your song
	daz mir manige vreude nimt		snatches away much joy from me
	unde mêret mîn klage.		and swells my sorrow.
	maer du bringest,		You bring news
5	der mich leider niht gezimt,		that is no pleasure to me, I fear,
	immer morgens gegen dem tage.		each morning at the break of day.
	Diu solt du mir verswîgen gar.		You should be silent.
	daz gebiut ich den triuwen dîn		I ask your fidelity,
	des lôn ich dir, als ich getar,		for which I'll reward you—as best I dare—
10	sô belîbet híe dér geselle mîn."		then my lover will stay here with me."

III	"Er muoz et hinnen		"He must depart,
	balde und ân sûmen sich.		be gone without delay;
	nu gip im urloup, süezez wîp.		Now give him leave to go, sweet woman.
	lâze in minnen		Let him love you
5	her nâch sô verholn dich,		later, in secrecy,
	daz er behalte êre unde den lîp.		so he may keep his honor and his life.

Er gap sich mîner triuwen alsô,
                              He gave himself to my safe-keeping asking
                                   this—

daz ich in braehte ouch wider dan.   that I should bring him out again.
ez ist nu tac. Naht was ez, dô   It is now day. It was night when
10   mit drücken an brúst dîn kus mir in an   close-pressing to your breast, you won him
    gewan."   from me with your kiss."

IV   "Swaz dir gevalle,   "Whatever you please,
    wahtaer, sinc und lâ den hie,   watchman, sing, and leave him here,
    der minne brâht und minne enpfienc.   who brought love and took it in return.
    von dînem schalle   At your cry
5   ist er und ich erschrocken ie,   he's always filled with dread—and so am I,
    sô nínder der mórgenstern ûf gienc   even before the morning star rises
    Ûf in, der her nâch minne ist komen,   on him, who came here for love,
    noch ninder lûhte tages lieht.   even before bright day starts.
    du hâst in dicke mir benomen   You keep snatching him from me—
10   von blanken armen, und ûz herzen niht."   taking him from white arms—but never from
                                   the heart."

V   Von den blicken,   At the beams
    die der tac tet durch diu glas,   the day sent through the glass,
    und dô wahtaere warnen sanc,   and as the watchman sang in warning,
    si muose erschricken   she had to tremble
5   durch den, der dâ bî ir was.   for the man at her side.
    ir brüstlîn an brust si dwanc.   Against his breast she pressed her little
                                   breasts.

Der rîter ellens niht vergaz;   The knight remembered to be bold—
des wold in wenden wahtaers dôn: although the watchman would have hindered
                                   him.

urloup nâh und nâher baz   Leave-taking close—and closer yet—
10   mit kusse und anders gap in minne lôn.   with kissing and other things love gave them
                                   their reward.

Provenance: South Germany. Wolfram lived ca. 1170–1217.
Meter: Ten-line stanzas of varying line length, rhyming aabaabcdcd.

Walther von der Vogelweide

Under der linden—"Under the linden"

The best known *Frauenlied* of the German Middle Ages by one of the most celebrated poets. *Under der linden* is deceptive, for though its language and syntax present an appearance of innocence and simplicity, its tone is quite elusive. Is the speaker being modest or daring? Is she a rustic maiden or a high-born lady? The poem is influenced by the pastourelle genre. In its account of seduction under a lime tree it also resembles *Ich was ein chint so wolgetan*, earlier.

I   Under der linden   Under the linden
    an der heide,   on the heath,
    dâ unser zweier bette was,   where the bed of us two lovers was,
    dâ mugent ir vinden   there you can see
5   schône beide   prettily together
    gebrochen bluomen unde gras.   broken flowers and grass.
    Vor dem walde in einem tal,   By the wood in a vale—
       tandaradei,   tandaraday—
    schône sanc diu nahtegal.   sweetly sang the nightingale.

II Ich kam gegangen	I came on my way
zuo der ouwe,	to the meadow,
dô was mîn friedel komen ê.	where my lover had come before.
dâ wart ich enpfangen,	There I was taken—
5 hêre frowe,	Holy Mary!—
daz ich bin sælic iemer mê.	and I'm happy for it evermore.
Kuster mich? wol tûsentstunt,	He kissed me a thousand times—
tandaradei,	tandaraday—
seht, wie rôt mir ist der munt.	see how red is my mouth!
III Dô hât er gemachet	There he'd made
alsô rîche	so finely
von bluomen eine bettestat.	a bed all out of flowers.
des wirt noch gelachet	It will make them smile
5 inneclîche,	secretly
kumt iemen an daz selbe pfat,	if someone comes that way; surely
Bî den rôsen er wol mac,	from the roses they will tell—
tandaradei,	tandaraday—
merken, wâ mirz houbet lac.	see just where my head lay.
IV Daz er bî mir læge,	That he lay with me
wessez iemen,	no one should know—
nun welle got, sô schamt ich mich.	God forbid! I'd be so ashamed.
wes er mit mir pflæge,	What he did with me
5 niemer niemen	let no one ever
bevinde daz, wan er und ich,	know that, but him and me,
Und ein kleinez vogellîn,	and a little bird—
tandaradei,	tandaraday—
daz mac wol getriuwe sîn.	who I'm sure will keep our faith.

Provenance: Born in Austria, Walther lived ca. 1170–1230, and composed at various German-speaking courts.
Meter: Stanzas of 8 lines plus refrain word, rhyming abcabcdxd.

Otto von Botenlauben

Waere Kristes lôn niht alsô süeze—"Were Christ's reward not so sweet"

A *chanson de croisade* or *Kreuzlied* in the form of a *Wechsel*. The speakers seem to be Otto and his wife. As in other crusade poems, the claim of human love is juxtaposed with that of religious duty, but in this poem love is its own religion, for the man almost as strong as Christian faith and for the woman stronger.

I "Waere Kristes lôn niht alsô süeze,	"Were Christ's reward not so sweet
so enlieze ich niht der lieben frouwen mîn,	I'd never leave my beloved lady,
diech in mînem herzen dicke grüeze:	whom I greet in my heart again and again.
sie mac vil wol mîn himelrîche sîn,	Well may she be my heaven,
5 swâ diu guote wone al umbe den Rîn.	and the dear homeland around the Rhine.
herre got, nu tuo mir helfe schîn,	Lord God, now grant me your aid
daz ich mir und ir erwerbe noch die	to win your grace for her and me!"
hulde dîn!"	
II "Sît er giht ich sî sîn himelrîche,	"Since he says I'm his heaven,
sô habe ich in zuo gote mir erkorn,	I've chosen him as my god,
daz er niemer fuoz von mir entwîche.	never to depart a footstep from me.

herre got, lâ dirz niht wesen zorn.	Lord God, take it not in anger!
5 erst mir in den ougen niht ein dorn,	He's no thorn in the side to me,
der mir hie ze fröiden ist geborn.	he who was born to be my joy here.
kumt er mir niht wider, mîn spilnde fröide	Should he not return, my radiant joy's all
ist gar verlorn."	gone."

Provenance: End of twelfth or first half of thirteenth century. Botenlauben is near Kissingen. Otto was in Palestine between 1197 and 1217, married Beatrice, daughter of the Seneschal of Jerusalem, and died in 1244 or 1245. It is not certain which crusade prompted this poem. **Meter**: Seven-line stanzas, lines 1–6 with 6 stresses, final line 8 stresses; rhyming ababccc.

Neidhart

Der meie der ist rîche *(Sommerlied 2)*—*"May is mighty"*

Neidhart's poems are traditionally divided into *Sommerlieder* (Summer Songs) and *Winterlieder* (Winter Songs), depending on their settings. Both depict peasant life, sometimes coarsely, sometimes lyrically as in the example that follows, and always with an element of irony. Neidhart himself appears in the persona of a charming man from Reuental. This mother–daughter dialogue resembles many Galician-Portuguese poems, but Neidhart's girl is quite openly lusting after her young man.

I	Der meie der ist rîche:	"May is mighty:
	er füeret sicherlîche	truly it leads
	den walt an sîner hende.	the wood in its train.
	der ist nu niuwes loubes vol: der winter	It's in new bloom now: the winter's
	hât ein ende.	over.
II	"Ich fröu mich gegen der heide	I delight in the heath
	ir liehten ougenweide	and the bright look
	diu uns beginnet nâhen,"	it's preparing for us."
	sô sprach ein wolgetâniu maget; "die wil	Thus said a pretty maid. "I'll seize the
	ich schône enpfâhen.	moment.
III	Muoter, lât ez ân melde!	Mother, don't complain about it!
	jâ wil ich komen ze velde	I will surely come to the meadow
	und wil den reien springen;	and dance in a ring,
	jâ ist es lanc, daz ich diu kint niht niuwes	for it's long since I've heard the maidens sing
	hôrte singen."	a new song."
IV	"Neinâ, tohter, neine!	"No, daughter, no!
	ich hân dich alterseine	I've reared you alone
	gezogen an mînen brüsten:	at my breast.
	nu tuo ez durch den willen mîn, lâz dich der	Now do my will, and don't go wishing
	man niht lüsten."	for men."
V	"Den ich iu wil nennen,	"I'll tell you his name,
	den muget ir wol erkennen.	for you must know him.
	ze dem sô wil ich gâhen.	The man I want to go to,
	er ist genant von Riuwental: den wil ich	he's called von Reuental; him I'll
	umbevâhen.	embrace.
VI	Ez gruonet an den esten,	The branches grow so green with leaves
	daz alles möhten bresten	that the trees must break

die boume zuo der erden.
nu wizzet, liebiu muoter mîn,   ich belige
  den knaben werden.

VII Liebiu muoter hêre,
  nâch mir sô klaget er sêre.
  sol ich im des niht danken?
  er spricht, daz ich diu schœnest sî   von
    Beiern unz in Vranken."

and fall to the earth.
You know, dear mother, I will lie with
  the young man.

Dear, honored mother
he laments over me so sadly—
shouldn't I thank him for it?
He says I'm the prettiest girl from
  Bavaria to France."

Provenance: Bavaria or Austria, first half of thirteenth century. Neidhart was probably born between 1180 and 1190, was active in the area of Vienna, and died ca. 1240.
Meter: Four-line stanzas; three 7-syllable lines, fourth 15 syllables, long line with caesura.

CHAPTER 10

ITALY

The influence of the troubadours is first seen in Italian verse in the work of the aristocratic poets at the cosmopolitan court of Frederick II of Sicily, between 1220 and 1250. All the poetry of the Sicilian School, as it is called, is on the theme of love, and its sentiments tend to be conventional. The two characteristic forms are the *canzone*, the rather elaborate song of courtly love corresponding to the canso, and the newly invented sonnet. Later in the thirteenth century, Northern Italian poets compose in the same modes. The poems that follow range from the graceful *Dolce meo drudo*, by King Frederick, to the energetic *Mamma lo temp'è venuto*, which draws on a more earthy tradition.

For further reading, see the two anthologies by Frede Jensen: *The Poetry of the Sicilian School* (1986), and *Tuscan Poetry of the Duecento* (1994). Also, in German, Ulrich Mölk's essay in the festschrift for Margot Kruse, "'Frauenlieder' des Duecento im Gewande der Ballade," in *Gestaltung-Umgestaltung*, ed. Bernhard König and Jutta Lietz (1990).

Sicilian

King Frederick II of Sicily

Dolze meo drudo, eh! vatène?—*"My sweet love, are you leaving?"*

The lady is distressed that her lover must leave her; he responds with assurances of his loyalty. This exchange expresses some typical sentiments of courtly love, notably the man's subjection to the woman's authority. Although he must go, his heart remains with her.

I	"Dolze meo drudo, eh! vatène?	"My sweet love, are you leaving?
	Meo sire, a Deo t'acomanno,	My lord, I commend you to God,
	chè ti diparti da mene,	for you are going away from me,
	ed io tapina rimanno.	and I remain, wretched.
5	Lassa! La vita m'è noia,	Poor me! Life is a burden to me,
	dolze la morte a vedire,	and death sweet to look upon,
	ch'io non pensai mai guerire	for I have not expected ever to recover,
	membrando me fuor di gioia.	when I think that I am without joy.
II	Membrandome che ten vai,	When I think that you are going away,
10	lo cor mi mena gran guerra;	my heart puts me through great trouble,
	di ciò che più disiai	for the man whom I have most desired
	mi tolle lontana terra.	a distant land takes from me.

Or se ne va lo mio amore,	Now my love is leaving,
ch'io sovra gli altri l'amava;	whom I have loved more than all others;
15 biasmomi de la Toscana,	I blame Tuscany,
che mi diparte lo core."	which is taking my heart's love away."
III "Dolce mia donna, lo gire	"My sweet lady, the journey
non è per mia volontate,	is not of my wishing,
chè mi convene ubidire	for I must obey
20 quelli che m'à 'n potestate:	him who has me at his command.
or ti conforta s'io vaio	Now comfort yourself if I go,
e già non ti dismagare,	and don't be dismayed,
ca per null'altra d'amare,	for, love, I won't betray you
amor, te non falseraio.	by loving anyone else.
IV 25 Lo vostro amore mi tene	Your love holds me
ed àmi in sua segnoria,	and has me in its power,
ca lealmente m'avene	for it befits me
d'amar voi sanza falsia.	to love you loyally without deceit.
Di me vi sia rimembranza,	May you remember me,
30 no mi agiate 'n obrìa,	don't let me be forgotten,
c'avete in vostra balìa	for you have in your power
tutta la mia disianza.	all my desire.
V Dolze mia donna, commiato	My sweet lady, I ask permission
domando sanza tenore;	to go without delay.
35 che vi sia racomandato,	Let my heart be commended to you,
chè con voi riman mio core;	for it remains behind with you.
cotal' è la memoranza	Such is the memory
degli amorosi piaciri	of love's pleasures,
che non mi posso partiri	that I can't depart,
40 da voi, donna, in leanza."	lady, from my loyalty to you."

Provenance: Son of the German emperor Henry VI, Frederick was born in 1194, became king of Sicily in 1198, was crowned emperor in 1220, and died in 1250.
Meter: Eight-line stanzas of 8-syllable lines rhyming ababcddc.

Rinaldo d'Aquino

Ormai quando flore—*"Now, when things are in bloom"*

Troubadour conventions are reflected here in the refining effect of love, gratification as a reward, the importance of one's worth or reputation, and the need for secrecy. In delaying the information that the speaker is a woman (only apparent in line 28, with the feminine participle *amata*), and in depicting her conflicting feelings, the poem, whose opening sounds like a typical spring song, is more unusual—and more complex.

I Ormai quando flore	Now, when things are in bloom
e mostrano verdura	and meadow and countryside
le prate e la rivera,	show their greenery,
li auselli fan sbaldore	the birds make merry
5 dentro da la frondura	among the leaves,
cantando in lor manera:	singing in their way:
infra la primavera, che ven presente	in spring which now comes
frescamente così frondita,	so fresh and leafy,
ciascuno invita d'aver gioia intera.	each bird invites to perfect joy.

II 10 Confortami d'amore	The perfume of the flowers
l'aulimento dei fiori	and the song of the birds
e 'l canto de li auselli;	rouse me to love.
quando lo giorno appare,	When day breaks,
sento li dolci amori	I hear the sweet loves
15 e li versi novelli,	and the new verses
chè fan sì dolci e belli e divisati	when they make their songs so sweet
lor trovati a provasione;	and well modulated, with keen rivalry
a gran tenzone stan per li arbuscelli.	in a great contest, as they sit in the bushes.

III Quando l'aloda intendo	When I hear the lark and nightingale
20 e rusignuol vernare	sing their spring songs,
d'amor lo cor m'afina,	my heart is refined with love,
e magiormente intendo	and I feel all the more
ch'è legno d'altr'affare	that it's made of a strange wood
chè d'arder no rifina.	which never ceases to burn.
25 Vedendo quell'ombrina del fresco bosco,	Seeing that shady place in the fresh wood
ben cognosco ca cortamente	I know well that soon
serà gaudente l'amor che mi china.	the love that sways me will find its satisfaction.

IV Mi china, ch'eo so amata,	It sways me, for I am loved
e già mai non amai:	and have never loved before.
30 ma 'l tempo mi 'namura	But the season makes me fall in love
e fami star pensata	and causes me to think
d'aver mercè ormai	of having my reward henceforth
d'un fante che m'adura;	from a boy who adores me.
e saccio che tortura per me sostene	I know he suffers torment for me
35 e gran pene. L'un cor mi dice	and great pain. Half of my heart tells me
che si disdice, e l'altromi sicura.	it's not permitted; the other reassures me.

V Però prego l'Amore,	Therefore, I pray Love,
che mi 'ntende e mi svoglia	who drives me and sweeps me away
come la foglia vento,	like a leaf in the wind,
40 che no mi faccia fore	not to take away from me
quel che presio mi toglia	what would deprive me of my reputation,
e stia di me contento.	but to be satisfied.
Quelli c'à intendimento d'avere intera	He who longs to possess perfect joy
gioia e ciera de lo mio amore	and manifestation of my love in secret
45 senza romore, no nde à compimento.	will not find the fulfilment he seeks.

Provenance: Southern Italy. Rinaldo was composing within the period ca. 1235–75. He may have been the brother of Thomas Aquinas.

Meter: Stanzas of 6 shorter and 3 longer lines rhyming abcabbcdec. The last 3 lines of each stanza rhyme internally with the end of the preceding line.

Anonymous

Compiangomi, laimento e di cor doglio—*"I lament, bewail, and grieve from my heart"*

The speaker has lost her lover because of her cruelty. She blames herself.

I Compiangomi, laimento e di cor doglio	I lament, bewail, and grieve from my heart,
e dico "oi lasso meve, com faragio,	and I say, "Poor me, what should I do,
pensando c'ò perduta la speranza	to think that I've lost the hope
del dolze aulente in cui comando soglio	of my beloved, whom, with his consent,

5 averlo in mia balìa, ed or non l'agio?"	I used to have in my power, and now no longer have."
Donato à lo suo core in altr'amanza.	He's given his heart to another love.
Ben è ragione ch'io degia penari,	It's right that I should suffer,
da poi li fui crudera,	because I was cruel to him,
salvagia e dura e fera	rude, severe, and harsh
10 ver gli amorosi dolzi risguardari.	in return for his sweet, amorous glances.

II Da meve è straniato lo più gente,	From me he's become estranged, the noblest man
quelli ch'aver solea in comandamento:	that I ever used to have at my command.
tornato m'è lo bene in grande affanno,	My good has turned to great anguish,
perdut'ò la speranza lungiamente,	my hope I've long since lost,
15 l'amoroso, compiuto e buon talento;	my lover, my good and perfect wish.
lo suo sollazo m'è tornato a danno.	The comfort I had from him is turned to harm.
Ched io l'amava di sì buona menti	That I loved him with true heart
mostrar no gliell volia	I did not wish to show him,
per temenza ch'avia	for fear I had
20 de li parlieri falsi maldicenti.	of false, slanderous tattle-tales.

III A gran ragione si partio doglioso,	With good reason he's departed in sadness
da ch'io non volsi avere pietanza	because I wouldn't have pity on him
di quelli che m'amava sanza inganno;	who loved me without deceit.
e però lo mio core sta pensoso	And therefore my heart is pensive,
25 ed à gran doglia de la rimembranza	and suffers greatly at the memory
che gli à donato Amore in tale affanno.	which Love has given him of such pain.
Dunque, s'io son colpata per ragione,	Then if by rights I'm guilty,
degiami giudicare;	he ought to pass judgement on me,
ca ben voglio durare	for I'm willing to endure
30 la quale pena piace a lo mio amore.	whatever pain is pleasing to my love.

Provenance: Sicily? Mid-thirteenth century.
Meter: Ten-line stanzas of longer and shorter lines rhyming abcabcdeed.

Anonymous

Tapina in me, c'amava uno sparvero!—"*Alas for me! I loved a hawk*"

An early example of the sonnet. The hawk-lover here invites comparison with *Ich zôch mir einem valken*, earlier, but in the present poem the lover has clearly defected to another lady, though here too yearning rather than jealousy is the dominant emotion. The closing words suggest also the speaker's envy of her lover's freedom, energy, and mobility. The poem is the first half of a *tenzone* or debate, in which a male speaker replies, protesting his loyalty, in the second half.

I Tapina in me, c'amava uno sparvero!	Alas for me! I loved a hawk!
Amaval tanto ch'io me ne moria!	I loved him almost to death!
A lo richiamo ben m'era manero,	He was trained to my call,
ed unque troppo pascer no'l dovia.	and I'd no need to overfeed him.

II 5 Or è montato e salito sì altero,	Now he has risen, and climbed so high,
assai più alto che far non solia,	far higher than he used to do,
ed è assiso dentro a uno verzero;	and he's sitting in an orchard;
un'altra donna lo tene in balìa.	another lady has him in her keeping.

III	Sparvero mio, ch'io t'avea nodrito,
10	sonaglio d'oro ti facea portare
	per che dell'uccellar fosse più ardito.

My hawk, whom I had nurtured,
I made you wear a bell of gold
so you'd be the keener in hunting.

IV   Or se' salito sì come lo mare
    ed ài rotti li geti e se' fugito,
    quando eri fermo nel tuo uccellare!

Now you've risen like the sea.
You tore your jesses and flew away,
once you were confident in your hunting.

Provenance: Sicily? Mid-thirteenth century.
Meter: Sonnet, rhyming abab,abab,cdc,dcd.

Northern Italian

La Compiuta Donzella

A la stagion che 'l mondo foglia e fiora—*"In the season when
the world puts out leaves and flowers"*

One of three sonnets attributed to the "Accomplished Young Lady of Florence."
Here the speaker laments because she has been betrothed against her will. In the
poem that follows in the manuscript, the speaker expresses her desire to enter a
convent. Possibly these poems are autobiographical, but nothing is known of this
young lady, whose situation is the reverse of that in *Mamma lo temp'è venuto,*
later. "Flower and leaf," "leaf and flower" frame the poem, plaintively contrast-
ing spring joy with the speaker's unhappiness.

I   A la stagion che 'l mondo foglia e fiora

In the season when the world puts out leaves
   and flowers

    acresce gioia a tutti fin' amanti:
    vanno insieme a li giardini alora
    che gli auscelletti fanno dolzi canti;

joy grows in all noble lovers;
they go together to the gardens
when the birds sing sweet songs.

II 5   la franca gente tutta s'inamora,
    e di servir ciascun tragges' inanti,
    ed ogni damigella in gioia dimora;
    e me, n'abondan marrimenti e pianti.

All gentlefolk are in love,
and everyone is drawn first to love-service,
and every maiden lives in joy,
but as for me, I'm full of sadness and
   weeping.

III	Ca lo mio padre m'ha messa 'n errore,
10	e tenemi sovente in forte doglia:
	donar mi vole a mia forza segnore,

For my father has put me in distress
and keeps me constantly in great misery.
He wants to give me to a husband against
   my will.

IV   ed io di ciò non ho disio né voglia,
    e 'n gran tormento vivo a tutte l'ore;
    però non mi ralegra fior né foglia.

But I neither desire nor wish this,
and I live in great torment all the time.
That's why I find no joy in flower and leaf.

Provenance: Florence, second half of the thirteenth century. Nothing is known about the
woman the manuscript designates "La Compiuta Donzella di Firenze." *Compiuta*, "accom-
plished" may or may not be her actual name.
Meter: Sonnet, rhyming abab,abab,cdc,dcd.

Anonymous

Mamma, lo temp'è venuto—*"Mother, the time has come"*

Both this and the following lyric are found in the Memoriali Bolognese, a huge collection of legal records, in which, to prevent later tampering, the notaries filled up the blank spaces with jottings. The present poem is a vehement exchange between daughter and mother. The former rather aggressively demands that her mother let her get married, and the latter warns of dire consequences if she has relations with a man. The emphasis is on the girl's sexual rather than social expectations, and she speaks of her feelings in quite uninhibited terms. Stanza III mentions figures from French epic: Roland and Morando are associated with Charlemagne; the Knight without Fear with the hero Guiron le Courtois ("the Courtly").

	"Mamma, lo temp'è venuto	"Mother, the time has come
	ch'eo me voria maritare	when I'd like to be married
	d'un fante che m'è sí plazuto	to a boy who's so pleasing to me
	no'l te podria contare.	that I couldn't describe it to you.
I 5	Tanto me plaze 'l so fatto,	His manner pleases me so much,
	li soi portament'e i scemblanti	his bearing and his appearance
	che, ben te lo dico entrasatto,	that, I tell you, in a word,
	sempre 'l voria aver davanti;	I'd always want to have him before me.
	e 'l drudo meo ad onne patto	And I want my lover
10	del meo amor vòi' che se vanti.	to boast of my love on any terms.
	Matre, lo cor se te sclanti	Mother, may your heart burst
	s'tu me lo vòi contrariare.	if you want to forbid me this.
	Mamma, lo temp'è venuto	Mother, the time has come
	ch'eo me voria maritare	when I'd like to be married
15	d'un fante che m'è sí plazuto	to a boy who's so pleasing to me
	no'l te podria contare."	that I couldn't describe it to you."
II	"Eo te 'l contrario en presente,	"I forbid you most urgently,
	figliola mia maledetta:	my accursed daughter,
	de prender marito en presenti	to take a husband so precipitately.
20	troppo me par ch'aibi fretta.	It seems to me you're in too much haste.
	Amico non hai né parente	You have no friend nor relative
	che 'l voglia, tant'èi picoletta.	who would wish it—you're so young
	tanto me par' garzonetta,	you seem to me such a little girl.
	non èi da cotai fatti fare."	You're not ready to do such things."
25	"Mamma, lo temp'è venuto	"Mother, the time has come
	ch'eo me voria maritare	when I'd like to be married
	d'un fante che m'è sí plazuto	to a boy who's so pleasing to me
	no'l te podria contare.	that I couldn't describe it to you.
III	Matre, de flevel natura	Mother, it's because of your weak nature
30	te ven che me vai sconfortando	that you go making me uneasy
	de quello ch'eo sun plu segura	about him of whom I'm surer
	non fo per arme Rolando	than Roland was of his sword,
	né 'l cavalier sens paura	or the Knight without Fear
	né lo bon duso Morando.	or the good Duke Morando.
35	Matre, 'l to dir sia en bando,	Away with your words, mother,
	ch'eo pur me vòi' maritare.	for I still want to marry.
	Mamma, lo temp'è venuto	Mother, the time has come
	ch'eo me voria maritare	when I'd like to be married
	d'un fante che m'è sí plazuto	to a boy who's so pleasing to me
40	no'l te podria contare."	that I couldn't describe it to you."

IV   "Figlia, lo cor te traporta
né la persona non hai:
tosto podriss'esser morta
s'usassi con om, ben lo sai.

45   Or, figlia, per Deo, sii acorta
né no te gli ametter zamai,
ch' a la ventura, che sai
morte 'n pudrisse portare."
    "Mamma, lo temp'è venuto
50   ch'eo me voria maritare
d'un fante che m'è sí plazuto
no'l te podria contare.

V   Matre, tant'ho 'l cor azunto,
la voglia amorosa e conquisa,
55   ch'aver voria lo meo drudo
visin plu che non è la camisa.
Cun lui me staria tutt'a nudo
né mai non voria far devisa:
eo l'abrazaria en tal guisa
60   che 'l cor me faria allegrare.
    Mamma, lo temp'è venuto
ch'eo me voria maritare
d'un fante che m'è sí plazuto
no'l te podria contare."

"Daughter, your heart is carrying you away,
and you're not grown up yet.
It might be instant death
if you have dealings with a man, you
    know well.
Now, daughter, in God's name, be wise,
and don't ever give yourself to him,
for in that event, as you know,
you could meet your death."
    "Mother, the time has come
when I'd like to be married
to a boy who's so pleasing to me
that I couldn't describe it to you.

Mother, my heart's so captured,
my love-longing has so overpowered me,
that I'd want to have my lover
closer to me than my shift.
I'd be with him quite naked,
and I'd never want to separate from him.
I'd embrace him so
it would delight my heart.
    Mother, the time has come
when I'd like to be married
to a boy who's so pleasing to me
that I couldn't describe it to you."

Provenance: North Italy or Tuscany; copied in 1282.
Meter: *Ballata grande* of 8-line rhyming stanzas, with an opening 4 lines recurring as refrain.
Cf. the French *ballette*.

Anonymous

Pàrtite, amore, adeo—*"Leave me, my love, adieu"*

An alba. Fearing that her husband will come, the speaker warns her lover to leave.
The morning bell suggests a somewhat urban setting, rather than a castle or a
garden, but the situation is not expanded, and it is likely the poem is incomplete.

I   Pàrtite, amore, adeo,
chè tropo ce se' stato:
lo maitino è sonato,
zorno me par che sia.

II 5 Pàrtite, amor, adeo;
che non fossi trovata
in sí fina cellata
como nui semo stati:
or me bassa, oclo meo;
10   tosto sïa l'andata,
tenendo la tornata
como di 'namorati;
siché per speso usato
nostra zoglia renovi,
15   nostro stato non trovi
la mala celosia.

Leave me, my love, adieu.
You've stayed here too long;
the morning bell has sounded,
It seems the day is here.

Leave me, my love, adieu,
lest I be discovered
in this sweet intimacy
that we have had.
Now kiss me, light of my eyes.
let it be farewell immediately,
counting on a return,
as lovers do,
so that, by frequent practice
our happiness is renewed,
and our relationship is not discovered
by mean jealousy.

III	Pàrtite, amore, adeo,	Leave me, my love, adieu,
	e vane tostamente,	and go immediately,
	ch'one toa cossa t'azo	for I've made ready all your things
20	pareclata in presente.	to leave at once.

Provenance: Bologna; copied in 1286.
Meter: Probably fragment of a *ballata grande*.

CHAPTER 11
SPAIN AND PORTUGAL

Galician-Portuguese

The over 500 Galician-Portuguese *cantigas de amigo* ("songs about a lover") constitute a genre that is both contrastive and complementary to the male-voice *cantigas de amor* ("songs about love"). Older scholarship regarded the *cantigas de amigo* as reflective of an indigenous popular poetry, as distinct from the *cantigas de amor*, modelled on the courtly Occitan canso. However, more recent analyses have emphasized the similarity of the two genres, both practiced by the same poets. Nearly all of the authors are identified by—male—name. Sometimes the poems are designated as *cantigas de refran* ("songs with refrain"), as opposed to the more linguistically complex *cantigas de meestria* ("songs of master-craft"). The most typical structure is a parallelistic poem with a refrain and *leixa-pren*, "leaving and taking up," that is, the incorporation of an earlier line into a later stanza according to a fairly strict pattern. The best of these poems are characterized by a haunting simplicity of language and subtly varied incremental repetition.

For Galician-Portuguese poetry more generally, see the introduction to Frede Jensen's anthology of *Medieval Galician-Portuguese Poetry* (1992); also Mercedes Brea's collected edition, *Lírica profana galego-portuguesa* (1996). On the *cantigas de amigo* as a genre, see Kathleen Ashley, "Voice and Audience," in Plummer (1981), and Esther Corral, "Feminine Voices" in Klinck and Rasmussen (2002); for a suggestive translation of selected poems, Barbara Fowler's *Songs of a Friend* (1996).

Martin Codax

Ondas do mar de Vigo—*"Waves of the Bay of Vigo"*

A *marinha* or "sea song." The speaker stands by the shore and addresses her longing to the sea, whose swelling waves seem to embody her own intense feelings. Martin Codax is one of only two composers of cantigas for which the music has been preserved. Though a woman speaks, the evocation of loving, longing femininity suggests a male author's perspective.

I	Ondas do mar de Vigo,	Waves of the Bay of Vigo,
	se vistes meu amigo?	have you seen my love?
	e ai Deus, se verrá cedo!	Oh God, will he come soon!
II	Ondas do mar levado,	Waves of the stormy sea,
5	se vistes meu amado!	have you seen my beloved?
	e ai Deus, se verrá cedo!	Oh God, will he come soon!

III	Se vistes meu amigo, o por que eu sospiro! e ai Deus, se verrá cedo!	Have you seen my love, the one for whom I sigh? Oh God, will he come soon!
IV 10	Se vistes meu amado por que ei gran coidado! e ai Deus, se verrá cedo!	Have you seen my beloved, the one for whom I've great distress? Oh God, will he come soon!

Provenance: Galicia. Martin Codax was probably from Vigo and composed around the mid-thirteenth century.

Meter: Distichs with a refrain line; *coblas alternas* (alternate stanzas linked by rhyme or assonance); parallelistic structure and *leixa-pren*.

Ai Deus, se sab' ora meu amigo—*"God! does my lover know"*

Again, the speaker longs for her lover; the poem dwells on her loneliness. No one watches over her except her own weeping eyes.

I	Ai Deus, se sab' ora meu amigo com'eu senlheira estou en Vigo e vou namorada.	God! does my lover know how I am alone in Vigo— and I'm in love.
II 5	Ai Deus, se sab' ora meu amado com'eu en Vigo senlheira manho e vou namorada.	God! does my beloved know how I stay alone in Vigo— and I'm in love.
III	Com'eu senlheira estou em Vigo e nulhas guardas non ei comigo e vou namorada.	How I am alone in Vigo, and I have no guardians with me— and I'm in love.
IV 10	Com'eu en Vigo senlheira manho e nulhas guardas migo non trago e vou namorada.	How I stay alone in Vigo, bringing no guardians with me— and I'm in love.
V 15	E nulhas guardas non ei comigo, ergas meus olhos que choran migo e vou namorada.	And I have no guardians with me except my eyes, which are weeping for me— and I'm in love.
VI	E nulhas guardas migo non trago, ergas meus olhos que choran ambos e vou namorada.	Bringing no guardians with me, except my eyes—both weeping— and I'm in love.

Meter: Distichs with a shorter refrain line; *coblas alternas*; parallelistic structure and *leixa-pren*.

Nuno Fernandes Torneol

Levad', amigo, que dormides as manhanas frias—*"Rise, my friend, sleeping in the chill morning"*

A dawn song of a highly unusual kind. While the Occitan *alba* describes a lovers' parting and the typical Galician-Portuguese *alborada* a lovers' meeting at dawn, here the speaker bids her lover to leave and accuses him of destroying their love. The vernal branches and birds that we might expect as the setting for a love encounter are here broken and silenced by the cruel lover. By the end of the poem the joyful refrain has become ironic.

I	Levad', amigo, que dormides as manhanas frias;
	todalas aves do mundo d'amor dizian:
	
	   leda m' and' eu.
		Rise, my friend, sleeping in the chill morning.
		All the birds in the world have been carolling of love.
		   Joyful go I!

II
 	
5
	Levad', amigo, que dormide-las frias manhanas;
	todalas aves do mundo d'amor cantavan:
	
	   leda m' and'eu.
		Rise, my friend, sleeping in the morning chill.
		All the birds in the world have been singing of love—
		   joyful go I!

III	Todalas aves do mundo d'amor dizian;
	
	do meu amor e do voss'en ment'avian:
	
	   leda m' and' eu.
		All the birds in the world have been carolling of love—
		my love and yours they had in mind.
		   Joyful go I!

IV 10	Todalas aves do mundo d'amor cantavan;
	
	do meu amor e do voss'i enmentavan:
	
	   leda m' and' eu.
		All the birds in the world have been singing of love—
		it was my love and yours of which they trilled.
		   Joyful go I!

V
 	
15
	Do meu amor e do voss'en ment'avian;
	
	vós lhi tolhestes os ramos en que siian:
	
	   leda m' and' eu.
		My love and yours they had in mind.
		You have broken off the branches on which they were perched.
		   Joyful go I!

VI	Do meu amor e do voss'i enmentavan;
	
	vos lhi tolhestes os ramos en que pousavan:
	
	   leda m' and' eu.
		It was my love and yours of which they trilled.
		You have broken off the branches on which they reposed.
		   Joyful go I!

VII
 	
20
	Vós lhi tolhestes os ramos en que siian,
	
	e lhis secastes as fontes en que bevian:
	
	   leda m' and' eu.
		You have broken off the branches on which they were perched,
		you have dried up the fountains from which they drank.
		   Joyful go I!

VIII	Vós lhi tolhestes os ramos en que pousavan,
	
	e lhis secastes as fontes u se banhavan:
	
	   leda m' and' eu.
		You have broken off the branches on which they reposed,
		you have dried up the fountains in which they bathed.
		   Joyful go I!

Provenance: Nuno Fernandes Torneol composed at the court of Alfonso X of Castile and Leon around the mid-thirteenth century.
Meter: Distichs with a shorter refrain line; *coblas alternas*; parallelistic structure and *leixa-pren*.

Vi eu, mia madr', andar—"*I saw the ships going, mother*"

Another *marinha*. The speaker goes to the harbor in the hope that her lover will have come back from the sea. She looks for him in vain. Compare *Nam languens*, earlier.

I	Vi eu, mia madr', andar
	as barcas eno mar:
	  e moiro-me d' amor.
		I saw the ships going, mother,
		the ships on the sea.
		  I'm dying of love!

II
5
	Foi eu, madre, veer
	as barcas eno ler:
	  e moiro-me d' amor.
		I went to see, mother,
		the ships on the ocean.
		  I'm dying of love!

III	As barcas eno mar
	e foi-las aguardar:
	  e moiro-me d' amor.
		The ships on the sea—
		I went to look for them.
		  I'm dying of love!

IV 10	As barcas eno ler
	e foi-las atender:
	  e moiro-me d' amor.
		The ships on the ocean—
		I went to wait for them.
		  I'm dying of love!

V
 	
15
	E foi-las aguardar
	e non o pud' achar:
	  e moiro-me d' amor
		I went to look for them,
		but could not find him.
		  I'm dying of love!

VI	E foi-las atender
	e non o pud' i veer:
	  e moiro-me d' amor.
		I went to wait for them,
		but could not see him there.
		  I'm dying of love!

VII
20
	E non o achei i,
	o que por meu mal vi:
	  e moiro-me d' amor.
		I didn't find him there—
		the man whom to my sorrow I saw.
		  I'm dying of love!

Meter: Distichs with a refrain line; *coblas alternas*; parallelistic structure and *leixa-pren*.

Martin de Ginzo

Treides, ai mia madr', en romaria—*"Come, my mother, on pilgrimage"*

The *romaria* or "pilgrimage song" is specific to the Galician-Portuguese *cantigas de amigo*. In the poems of this genre, a girl plans to meet her lover at a shrine to which she is making a pilgrimage.

I
 	
5
	Treides, ai mia madr', en romaria
	orar u chaman Santa Cecilia:
	  e, louçana irei,
	  ca ja i est' o que namorei,
	  e, louçana, irei.
		Come, my mother, on pilgrimage
		to pray where they worship Saint Cecilia.
		  I'll go, in loveliness,
		  for already the one I love is there.
		  I'll go, in loveliness.

II
 	
10
	E treides migo, madre, de grado,
	ca meu amigu' é por mi coitado:
	  e, louçana, irei,
	  ca ja i est' o que namorei,
	  e, louçana, irei.
		Come with me, mother, please,
		because my lover is in distress for me.
		  I'll go, in loveliness.
		  for already the one I love is there.
		  I'll go, in loveliness.

III
 	
15
	Orar u chaman Santa Cecilia,
	pois m'aduss' o que eu ben queria:
	
	  e, louçana, irei,
	  ca ja i est' o que namorei,
	  e, louçana, irei.
		To pray where they worship Saint Cecilia.
		Since she has brought back to me the one
		    I love so.
		  I'll go, in loveliness.
		  for already the one I love is there.
		  I'll go, in loveliness.

IV Ca meu amigu' é por mi coitado,	Because my lover is in distress for me
e, pois, eu non farei seu mandado?	and then, why shouldn't I obey him?
e, louçana, irei,	I'll go, in loveliness.
ca ja i est' o que namorei,	for already the one I love is there.
20 e, louçana, irei.	I'll go, in loveliness.

Provenance: Probably Galicia; second half of the thirteenth century.
Meter: Distichs with a refrain of 3 shorter lines; *coblas alternas*; parallelistic structure and *leixa-pren*.

Pero Meogo

Digades, filha, mia filha velida—*"Tell me, daughter, my lovely daughter"*

Pero Meogo composed several *cantigas de amigo* in which a girl mentions mountain stags, implying a disturbing male, feral element in her sheltered world. Here their muddying of the water is both her masking of and her symbolism for an encounter with her lover.

I	"Digades, filha, mia filha velida:	"Tell me, daughter, my lovely daughter,
	porque tardastes na fontana fria?"	why you lingered by the chilly stream."
	"Os amores ei"	"I'm in love."
II	"Digades, filha, mia filha louçana:	"Tell me daughter, my graceful daughter,
5	porque tardastes na fria fontana?"	why you lingered by the stream so chilly."
	"Os amores ei."	"I'm in love."
III	"Tardei, mia madre, na fontana fria,	"I lingered, my mother, by the chilly stream—
	cervos do monte a áugua volvian.	the water was stirred up by the mountain stags.
	Os amores ei.	I'm in love.
IV 10	Tardei, mia madre, na fria fontana,	I lingered, my mother, by the stream so chilly.
	cervos do monte volvian a áugua:	The mountain stags were stirring up the water.
	Os amores ei."	I'm in love."
V	"Mentir, mia filha, mentir por amigo;	"You're lying, my daughter, lying for your lover.
	nunca vi cervo que volvess' o rio."	I never saw a stag stirring up the river."
15	"Os amores ei."	"I'm in love."
VI	"Mentir, mia filha, mentir por amado;	"You're lying, my daughter, lying for your beloved.
	nunca vi cervo que volvess' o alto."	I never saw a stag stirring up the deep water."
	"Os amores ei."	"I'm in love."

Provenance: Probably Galicia; second half of the thirteenth century.
Meter: Distichs with a shorter refrain line; *coblas alternas*; parallelistic structure and *leixa-pren*.

Mendinho

Sedia-m'eu na ermida de San Simion—*"I was at the sanctuary of Saint Simon"*

This poem is both a *marinha* and a *romaria*. Here parallelistic incremental repetition is powerfully suggestive of the encroaching waves of the sea that threaten to engulf the speaker. This movement toward a climax in which the woman will "die" also has erotic implications.

I	Sedia-m'eu na ermida de San Simion	I was at the sanctuary of Saint Simon,
	e cercaron-mi as ondas, que grandes son:	and the waves, the huge waves, rolled around me,
	en atendend'o meu amigo,	waiting for my lover,
	en atendend'o meu amigo!	waiting for my lover!
II 5	Estando na ermida ant'o altar,	I was at the sanctuary before the altar,
	e cercaron-mi as ondas grandes do mar:	and the huge waves of the sea rolled around me,
	en atendend'o meu amigo!	waiting for my lover,
	en atendend'o meu amigo!	waiting for my lover!
III	E cercaron-mi as ondas, que grandes son,	And the waves, the huge waves, rolled around me—
10	non ei i barqueiro, nen remador:	I have no boatman, nor oarsman—
	en atendend'o meu amigo!	waiting for my lover,
	en atendend'o meu amigo!	waiting for my lover!
IV	E cercaron-mi as ondas do alto mar,	And the waves of the deep sea rolled around me—
	non ei i barqueiro, nen sei remar:	I have no boatman, nor can I row—
15	en atendend'o meu amigo!	waiting for my lover,
	en atendend'o meu amigo!	waiting for my lover!
V	Non ei i barqueiro, nen remador,	I have no boatman, nor oarsman,
	morrerei fremosa no mar maior:	lovely as I am, I'll die in the swelling sea,
	en atendend'o meu amigo!	waiting for my lover,
20	en atendend'o meu amigo!	waiting for my lover!
VI	Non ei i barqueiro, nen sei remar,	I have no boatman, nor can I row,
	morrerei fremosa no alto mar:	lovely as I am, I'll die in the deep sea,
	en atendend'o meu amigo!	waiting for my lover,
	en atendend'o meu amigo!	waiting for my lover.

Provenance: Galicia; late thirteenth century? Mendinho may have come from Vigo, since the sanctuary of Saint Simon is on an island there.
Meter: Distichs with a refrain of 2 identical lines; *coblas alternas*; parallelistic structure and *leixa-pren*.

Airas Nunez

Oí oj'eu ûa pastor cantar—*"Today I heard a shepherdess singing"*

A kind of pastourelle, but instead of the narrator meeting a shepherdess, in this poem he finds her singing alone, and secretly listens. The narrator's delicacy here contrasts with his open carnality in many pastourelles outside the Galician-Portuguese corpus.

I Oí oj'eu ûa pastor cantar,	Today I heard a shepherdess singing,
du cavalgava per ûa ribeira,	as I rode by a river-bank.
e a pastor estava senlheira,	The shepherdess was alone—
e ascondi-me pola ascuitar	I hid to listen to her—
5 e dizia mui ben este cantar:	and she sang this song so well,
"So lo ramo verde frolido	"Under the blooming green branch,
vodas fazen a meu amigo	There's a wedding for my lover—
e choran olhos d'amor."	my eyes are weeping for love."

II E a pastor parecia mui ben	The shepherdess was very lovely—
10 e chorava e estava cantando	she wept and sang together.
e eu mui passo fui-mi achegando	Very softly I moved closer
pola oír e sol non falei ren,	to hear her, but I said nothing.
e dizia este cantar mui ben:	And she sang this song so well,
"Ai estorninho do avelanedo,	"Oh, starling of the hazel-grove,
15 cantades vós e moir' eu e pen':	you are singing while I'm dying of sorrow,
e d'amores ei mal."	and I suffer for love."

III E eu oí-a sospirar enton,	And then I heard her sigh—
e queixava-se estando con amores;	she was grieving with love.
e fazia guirlanda de flores	She made a garland of flowers
20 des i chorava mui de coraçon	and wept sore from her heart
e dizia este cantar enton:	as she sang this song:
"Que coita ei tan grande de sofrer:	"What great pain I must suffer,
amar amigu' e non ousar veer!	to love a lover and not dare see him!
e pousarei so l' avelanal."	I'll lay me down under the hazel-trees."

IV 25 Pois que a guirlanda fez a pastor,	When the shepherdess had made her garland,
foi-se cantando, indo-s' én manselinho,	singing, she went softly away.
e tornei-m' eu logo a meu camïo,	And I quickly returned to my path,
ca de a nojar non ouve sabor,	for I had no wish to trouble her.
e dizia este cantar ben a pastor:	And the shepherdess sang this song so well:
30 "Pela ribeira do rio	"By the bank of the river,
cantando ia la virgo	singing of love
d'amor:	went the maiden.
quen amores á,	Whoever's in love,
como dormirá,	how can they sleep,
35 ai bela frol?"	oh pretty flower?"

Meter: *Coblars singulars* (individually rhyming stanzas). The lineation of lines 30 ff. is uncertain.

Bailemos nós ja todas tres, ai amigas—*"Let us dance now, friends, all three"*

A joyful and spirited *bailada* or "dance song."

I Bailemos nós ja todas tres, ai amigas,	Let us dance now, friends, all three,
so aquestas avelaneiras frolidas,	beneath these hazel trees in bloom,
e quen for velida, como nós, velidas,	and if anyone is pretty, like us, pretty girls,
se amigo amar	if she truly loves her love,
5 so aquestas avelaneiras frolidas	beneath these hazel trees in bloom,
verrá bailar.	she'll come and dance.

II	Bailemos nós ja todas tres, ai irmanas,	Let us dance now, as sisters, all three,
	so aqueste ramo d'estas avelanas	beneath the branches of these hazel trees,
	e quen for louçana, como nós, louçanas	and if anyone is lovely, like us, lovely girls,
10	se amigo amar,	if she truly loves her love,
	so aqueste ramo d'estas avelanas	beneath the branches of these hazel trees,
	verrá bailar.	she'll come and dance.
III	Por Deus, ai amigas, mentr'al non fazemos,	For God's sake, friends, while we do nought else
	so aqueste ramo frolido bailemos	let's dance under these flowering branches,
15	e quen ben parecer, como nós parecemos,	and if anyone's good-looking—good-looking as we—
	se amigo amar,	if she truly loves her love,
	so aqueste ramo, so lo que nós bailemos	beneath these branches under which we dance
	verrá bailar.	she'll come and dance.

Provenance: Airas Nunez, probably from Galicia, was active during 1284–89 at the court of Sancho IV of Castile and Leon.
Meter: *Coblas singulars* of 4 lines with 2, separated, shorter refrain lines; parallelistic structure.

King Denis of Portugal

Ai flores, ai flores do verde pino—*"Oh flowers, oh flowers of the green pine"*

In this poem, the speaker's confidante is not her mother or her girl friends but the flowers of the pine tree, an externalization of her youthful self. The flowers tell her what she wants to hear.

I	"Ai flores, ai flores do verde pino,	"Oh flowers, oh flowers of the green pine,
	se sabedes novas do meu amigo?	have you news of my lover?
	Ai, Deus, e u é?	God! Where can he be?
II	Ai flores, ai flores do verde ramo,	Oh flowers, oh flowers of the green branch,
5	se sabedes novas do meu amado?	have you news of my beloved?
	Ai, Deus, e u é?	God! Where can he be?
III	Se sabedes novas do meu amigo,	Have you news of my lover,
	aquel que mentiu do que pôs comigo?	of him who was false to the pledge he gave me?
	Ai, Deus, e u é?	God! Where can he be?
IV 10	Se sabedes novas do meu amado,	Have you news of my beloved,
	aquel que mentiu do que mi á jurado?	of him who was false to the oath he swore me?
	Ai, Deus, e u é?"	God! Where can he be?"
V	["Vós me preguntades polo voss' amigo?	["You ask me about your lover,
	e eu ben vos digo que é san' e vivo."	and I tell you plainly he's alive and well."
15	"Ai, Deus, e u é?"]	"God! Where is he?"]
VI	"Vós me preguntades polo voss' amado?	"You ask me about your beloved:
	e eu ben vos digo que é viv' e sano."	I tell you plainly he's living and well."
	"Ai, Deus, e u é?"	"God! Where can he be?"
VII	"E eu ben vos digo que é san' e vivo	"I tell you plainly he's alive and well—
20	e seerá vosc' ant' o prazo saído."	he'll be with you before the deadline passes."
	"Ai, Deus, e u é?"	"God! Where can he be?"

VIII

"E eu ben vos digo que é viv' e sano
e seerá vosc' ant' o prazo passado."
"Ai, Deus, e u é?"

"I tell you plainly he's living and well—
he'll be with you before the deadline passes."
"God! Where can he be?"

Provenance: King Denis of Portugal lived during 1261–1325 and reigned from 1279.
Meter: Distichs with a shorter refrain line; *coblas alternas*; parallelistic structure and *leixa-pren*.

Johan Zorro

Cabelos, los meus cabelos—*"Flowing hair, my flowing hair"*

In this evocative little poem the girl's beautiful hair, which her mother bids her give to the king, becomes a symbol for herself and her virginity.

"Cabelos, los meus cabelos,
el-rei m'enviou por elos;
   madre, que lhis farei?"
   "Filha, dade-os a el-rei."

"Flowing hair, my flowing hair—
the king has sent for my lovely hair.
   Mother, what shall I do?"
   "Daughter, give the king his wish!"

5   "Garcetas, las mias garcetas,
el-rei m'enviou por elas;
   madre, que lhis farei?"
   "Filha, dade-as a el-rei."

"Curling hair, my curling hair—
The king has sent for my lovely hair.
   Mother, what shall I do?"
   "Daughter, give the king his wish!"

Provenance: Late thirteenth or early fourteenth century. Johan Zorro was probably Portuguese, from Lisbon; active at the court of King Denis of Portugal.
Meter: Two separately rhymed distichs with a refrain; parallelistic structure.

Pela ribeira do rio salido—*"By the bank of the swelling river"*

A girl confides in her mother that she has made love by the river. The word *trebelhei* has a sexual meaning, and the "swelling" or "brimming" river also conveys suggestions of the lovers and their desires.

I   Pela ribeira do rio salido
trebelhei, madre, con meu amigo:
   amor ei migo, que non ouvesse;
   fiz por amigo que non fezesse!

By the bank of the swelling river,
I was busy, mother, with my lover.
   I'm in love—if only I were not!
   What I've done for my lover—if only
      I had not!

II 5   Pela ribeira do rio levado
trebelhei, madre, con meu amado:
   amor ei migo que non ouvesse,
   fiz por amigo que non fezesse.

By the bank of the brimming river,
I was busy, mother, with my beloved.
   I'm in love—if only I were not!
   What I've done for my lover—if only
      I had not!

Meter: Two separately rhymed distichs with a 2-line refrain; parallelistic structure.

Castilian

The poems that follow are *villancicos*, a form composed for singing, and consisting of a short introductory stanza, the *estribillo*, which may then be recapitulated with variation in a *glosa* (gloss). The word *villancico* now means

"Christmas carol," earlier "village song" or "rustic song," suggesting a connection with peasant life and popular festivities. The Castilian *villancicos* are in many ways similar to the Galician-Portuguese *cantigas de amigo*, and very likely coexisted, unrecorded, with them. The *villancicos*, too, construct a youthful, artless femininity. From the late fifteenth century on *villancicos* are collected in manuscripts and printed books. Their popular provenance is reflected in the proliferation of variants. Typically, authors take a traditional *estribillo* and add a *glosa* of their own. Where multiple variants exist, it can be difficult to distinguish between different poems and variant versions of the same poem. For this reason, also, it is unrealistic to assign a precise date and provenance. Earlier scholars were attracted to these poems because of their popular and traditional background, but as preserved many have come to us from the hands of highly literate poets.

Most of the literature on the *cancionero* (songbook) collections containing the *villancicos* is in Spanish, but see John Cummins's anthology, *The Spanish Traditional Lyric* (1977). For readers of Spanish, the following are useful: Margit Frenk, "Fija ¿quiereste casar?" ["Daughter, do you want to get married?"], in *Nunca fue pena mayor*, ed. Ana Menéndez and Victoriano Roncero (1996); by the same author, "Símbolos naturales en las viejas canciones populares hispánicas" ["Nature symbols in the old popular Hispanic songs"], in *Lírica popular / lírica tradicional*, ed. Pedro Piñero (1998); Mariana Masera, "Tradición oral y escrita en el *Cancionero musical de Palacio*" ["Oral and Written Tradition in the *CmP*"], in *Cancionero Studies in Honour of Ian Macpherson*, ed. Alan Deyermond (1998).

Anonymous

Aunque soi morena—*"Although I'm dark"*

This poem seems to have its roots in popular proverbs. But it is also reminiscent of "Nigra sum sed formosa" ("I am black but comely") in the Song of Songs (1.5).

Aunque soi morena,	Although I'm dark
no soi de olbidar,	you shouldn't forget
que la tierra negra	that the black earth
pan blanco suele dar.	gives white bread.

Provenance: Preserved in a manuscript of 1620.
Meter: Four 6-syllable lines rhyming alternately.

Anonymous

Agora que soy niña—*"Now, while I'm young"*

This poem is a *malmonjada*, a lament of a reluctant nun—a genre that appears in other languages (cf. *Plangit nonna*), and has obvious affinities with the *mal maridada* (*chanson de malmariée*).

Agora que soy niña	Now, while I'm young,
quiero alegría,	I want to have fun.
que no se sirve Dios	It's no use to God
de mi mongía	my being a nun.

5 Agora que soy niña,	Now, while I'm young,
niña en cabello,	a young girl with silken hair,
me queréys meter monja	you want to make me a nun
en el monesterio:	in a convent.
que no se sirve Dios	It's no use to God
10 de mi mongía.	my being a nun.

Agora que soy niña	Now, while I'm young,
quiero alegría,	I want to have fun.
que no se sirve Dios	It's no use to God
de mi mongía.	my being a nun.

Provenance: Collected in the *Recopilación* of Juan Vásquez (1560).
Meter: Four-line *estribillo* framing a 6-line *glosa*.

Anonymous

Perdida traygo la color—*"I've lost my color"*

The *glosa* makes this a *romaria*, "pilgrimage song" like *Treides, ai mia madre*, earlier, and *So ell encina*, later. Here, the sudden effect of the three kisses that leave the young girl pining with love is a folkoristic, magical detail.

Perdida traygo la color:	I've lost my color;
todos me dizen que lo é de amor.	they all say it's because I'm in love.

Viniendo de la romería	Returning from pilgrimage,
encontré a mi buen amor;	I met my true love.
5 pidiérame tres besicos,	He asked me for three kisses.
luego perdí mi color.	Then I lost my color.
Dizen a mí que lo é de amor.	They say it's because I'm in love.

Perdida traygo la color:	I've lost my color;
Todos me dizen que lo é di amor.	they all say it's because I'm in love.

Provenance: Collected in Juan Vásquz, *Villancicos* (1551).
Meter: Two-line *estribillo* framing a 5-line *glosa*.

Anonymous

No pueden dormir mis ojos—*"My eyes can't sleep"*

Confiding in her mother, a girl confesses her longing and her sleepless night, culminating in a wish-fulfilling dream. Rose and rain become the external embodiment of her sexuality and her sadness.

No pueden dormir mis ojos,	My eyes can't sleep,
no pueden dormir.	they can't sleep.

Y soñava yo, mi madre,	I dreamed, mother,
dos oras antes del día,	two hours before dawn,
5 que me florecía la rrosa,	that the rose was in bloom—
el vino so ell agua frida.	he came in the cold rain.
No pueden dormir.	I can't sleep.

Provenance: Collected in the Cancionero musical de Palacio, early sixteenth century.
Meter: Two-line *estribillo* with a 5-line *glosa*.

Anonymous

Dentro en el vergel—*"Among the trees of the garden"*

Here, as in Mendinho's *Sedia m'eu*, earlier, the idea of dying for love is evoked with a peculiar intensity—and a sexual symbolism—through the seductive natural imagery and the incremental repetition.

Dentro en el vergel	Among the trees of the garden
moriré,	I'll die.
dentro en el rrosal	Among the roses
matarm'an.	I am to die.
5 Yo m'iva, mi madre,	I was going there, mother,
las rrosas coger,	to pick roses.
hallé mis amores	I met my lover
[dentro en el vergel.]	[among the trees of the garden.]
Dentro en el vergel	Among the trees of the garden
10 [moriré,]	[I'll die.]
dentro en el rrosal	Among the roses
matarm'an.	I am to die.

Provenance: Cancionero musical de Palacio, early sixteenth century.
Meter: Four-line *estribillo* framing a 4-line *glosa*.

Anonymous

So ell enzina, enzina—*"Under the oak-tree, oak-tree"*

A *romaria*. The speaker had not planned a meeting with her lover, but her protest that she went alone to be more devout is ironic—especially in the light of her final words. The sheltering oak-tree becomes a false-friend, an idea that is brought out more strongly if the refrain is reiterated throughout.

	So ell enzina, enzina,	Under the oak-tree, oak-tree,
	so ell enzina.	under the oak-tree!
I	Yo me iva, mi madre,	Mother, I was going
	a la romería.	on pilgrimage.
5	Por ir más devota,	To go more devoutly
	fuy sin compañía.	I was without companions.
	So ell enzina.	Under the oak-tree!
II	Por ir más devota,	To go more devoutly
	fuy sin compañía.	I was without companions.
10	Tomé otro camino,	I took another road;
	dexé el que tenía.	I left the one I was following.
	[So ell enzina.]	[Under the oak-tree!]
III	[Tomé otro camino,	[I took another road;
	dexé el que tenía.]	I left the one I was following.]
15	Halléme perdida	I found myself lost
	en una montiña.	in a mountain.
	[So ell enzina.]	[Under the oak-tree!]

V [Halléme perdida
en una montiña.]
0 Echéme a dormir
al pie d'ell enzina.
[So ell enzina.]

J [Echéme a dormir
al pie d'ell enzina,]
5 a la media noche,
recordé, mezquina.
[So ell enzina.]

JI [A la media noche,
recordé, mezquina,]
0 halléme en los braços
del que más quería.
[So ell enzina.]

JII [Halléme en los braços
del que más quería.]
5 Pesóme, cuytada,
desque amanecía.
[So ell enzina.]

JIII [Pesóme, cuytada,
desque amanecía.]
0 Porque ya goçaba
del que más quería.
[So ell enzina.]

X [Porque ya goçaba
del que más quería.]
5 ¡Muy bendita sía
la tal rromería!
[So ell enzina.]

[I found myself lost
in a mountain.]
I laid myself down to sleep
at the foot of the oak-tree.
[Under the oak-tree!]

[I laid myself down to sleep
at the foot of the oak-tree,]
in the middle of the night,
I awoke, poor me.
[Under the oak-tree!]

[In the middle of the night,
I awoke, poor me!]
I found myself in the arms
of the one I loved most.
[Under the oak-tree!]

[I found myself in the arms
of the one I loved most.]
I felt sad and distressed,
as the dawn was approaching.
[Under the oak-tree!]

[I felt sad and distressed,
as the dawn was approaching.]
For I was taking delight
in the one I loved most.
[Under the oak-tree!]

[For I was taking delight
in the one I loved most.]
Most blessed be
such a pilgrimage!
[Under the oak-tree!]

Provenance: Cancionero musical de Palacio, early sixteenth century.
Meter: Two-line *estribillo* with a *glosa* of nine 5-line stanzas.

Anonymous

Niña y viña—*"A girl and a vine"*

A proverbial *estribillo*. Rhyme linkage of girl and vine is reinforced by the word *viñadero*, "worker in a vineyard." It is he who will seduce her, an event symbolically foreshadowed by her going to cut roses.

Niña y viña,
peral y havar,
malo es de guardar.

Levantéme, ¡o, madre!,
5 mañanica frida,
fuy cortar la rosa,
la rosa florida.
Malo es de guardar.

A girl and a vine,
a pear tree and a bean-plant—
it's hard work to guard them!

I arose, my mother,
in the cold morning,
I went to cut roses,
red roses.
It's hard work to guard them!

Viñadero malo	A bad vine-tender
10 prenda me pedía,	asked me for a token.
dile yo un cordone,	I gave him a sash
de la mi camisa.	from my slip.
Malo es de guardar.	It's hard work to guard them!

Levantéme, ¡o, madre!,	I arose, my mother,
15 mañanica clara,	in the cold morning,
fui cortar la rosa,	I went to cut roses,
la rosa granada.	blooming roses.
Malo es de guardar.	It's hard work to guard them!

Viñadero malo	A bad vine-tender
20 prenda me demanda;	requested a token.
yo dile una cinta,	I gave him a belt,
mi cordón le daba.	my girdle I gave him.
Malo es de guardar.	It's hard work to guard them!

Provenance: Cancionero musical de la Colombina, end of the fifteenth century.
Meter: Three-line *estribillo* with a *glosa* of four 5-line stanzas.

Anonymous

Al alva venid, buen amigo—*"Come at dawn, good friend"*

Not an alba of dawn parting, but an *alborada* of dawn meeting. Haunting in its summons, urgently repeated with subtle variations, and in its musicality, with fluid liquids and nasals. This poem resembles the typical structure of the *cantiga de amigo*.

Al alva venid, buen amigo,	Come at dawn, good friend,
al alva venid.	come at dawn.
Amigo, el que yo más quería,	Friend, you whom I love best,
venid a la luz del día.	come at light of day.
5 Al alva venid, buen amigo,	Come at dawn, good friend,
al alva venid.	come at dawn.
Amigo, el que yo más amava,	Friend, you whom I cherish most,
venid a la luz del alva.	come at light of dawn.
Al alva venid, buen amigo,	Come at dawn, good friend,
10 al alva venid.	come at dawn.
Venid a la luz del día,	Come at light of day,
non trayáys compañía.	don't bring any company.
Al alva venid, buen amigo,	Come at dawn, good friend,
al alva venid.	come at dawn.
15 Venid a la luz del alva,	Come at light of dawn,
non traigáis gran compaña.	don't bring much company.
Al alva venid, buen amigo,	Come at dawn, good friend,
al alva venid.	come at dawn.

Provenance: Cancionero musical de Palacio, early sixteenth century.
Meter: Distichs with parallelism and *leixa-pren.*

Anonymous

Si la noche hace escura—*"If the night is dark"*

This version of a poem that exists in a number of forms conveys with particular intensity the sharp anguish of the speaker waiting for the lover who does not come.

Si la noche hace escura	If the night is dark
y tan corto es el camino,	and the road so short
¿cômo no venís, amigo?	why don't you come, beloved?
La media noche es pasada	Midnight is past
y el que me pena no viene:	and my tormentor doesn't come.
¡mi desdicha lo détiene,	In my unhappiness he stays away.
que nascí tan desdichada!	Oh, that I was born so unhappy!
Haceme vivir penada	He makes me live in suffering,
y múestraseme enemigo,	and acts like my enemy.
¿Como no venís, amigo?	Why don't you come, beloved?

Provenance: Cancionero de Upsala, dated 1556.
Meter: Three-line *estribillo* with a 6-line *glosa.*

CHAPTER 12
LATER MEDIEVAL ENGLAND

All the following lyrics are carols; that is, poems in a format originally created to accompany dancing, with separate sections for leader and chorus. The latter would have sung the "burden," which opens the poem and follows every stanza. Often woman's voice carols deal with the painful reality of sexual exploitation and subsequent abandonment. The light mode of dance-song downplays the potentially tragic theme, and many of the poems seem to reflect the knowing humor of a male circle—but the pathos remains. Only the earliest of the Middle English poems is translated here; the others are simply provided with glosses for unfamiliar words.

See the anthology *Middlle English Lyrics*, edited by Maxwell Luria and Richard Hoffman, in the Norton Critical Series (1974); also Thomas Duncan's *Middle English Lyrics* (1995). On songs of seduced girls, see Neil Cartlidge, "Alas I Go with Chylde," *English Studies* (1998): 395–414, and Judith Bennett, "Ventriloquisms" in *Medieval Woman's Song*, ed. Klinck and Rasmussen (2002).

Anonymous

Now springes the spray—*"Now springs the budding spray"*

A *chanson d'aventure* in which the narrator relates an encounter that befell him while he was "riding out." In this case he meets a girl cursing the lover who has abandoned her. Although her words are bitter—she wishes him dead, the poem's emphasis is on love as a common and pleasurable malady, the sweetness of the girl's song rather than its sentiments.

Now springes the spray,	Now springs the budding spray,
al for love iche am so seek	all for love I am so sick
that slepen I ne may.	that sleep I never may.
I Als I me rod this endre day	As I rode out the other day,
5 o mi pleyinge,	pleasure-taking,
seih I hwar a litel may	I saw where a little maid
bigan to singe:	began to sing:
"The clot him clinge!	"Let the earth to him cling!
Wai es him i love-longinge	Woe for one who in love-longing
10 sal libben ay."	must live always."
Now springes the spray,	Now springs the budding spray,
al for love iche am so seek	all for love I am so sick
that slepen I ne may.	that sleep I never may.

II 15	Son iche herde that mirye note, thider I drogh; I fonde hire in an herber swot under a bogh with joie inogh.	As soon as I heard that merry note, that way I drew; I found her in an arbor sweet, under a bough with so much joy.
20	Son I asked, "Thou mirye may hwi singes tou ay, Now springes the spray, al for love iche am so seek that slepen I ne may."	Promptly I asked, "You winning maid, why sing you always, Now springs the budding spray, all for love I am so sick that sleep I never may."
III 25	Than answerde that maiden swote midde wordes fewe: "My lemman me haves bihot of love trewe; he chaunges anewe.	Then answered that maiden sweet with words few: "My sweetheart's promise to me was love all true; he changes anew.
30	Yif I may, it shal him rewe, bi this day." Now springes the spray, al for love iche am so seek that slepen I ne may.	If I have the power, he shall rue, by this day." Now springs the budding spray, all for love I am so sick that sleep I never may.

Provenance: Late thirteenth or early fourteenth century. A memorandum in the manuscript dates the copying of this poem to the thirty-first year of Edward I's reign, that is, 1302–03. **Meter:** Seven-line stanzas rhyming ababbx; the final line (and penultimate line in stanza 2) is linked by rhyme to the 3-line burden.

Anonymous

Wolde God that hyt were so—"Would God that it were so"

Like *Now springes the spray*, this is a woman's love-complaint, but in the present example there is no narrative frame, and the tone is darker, as the speaker's grief and devotion are stressed. The stasis of the speaker and the mobility of the fickle lover are characteristic postures of woman's voice love poems. However, the pronouns have been changed in the manuscript so that the lyric can be spoken in the voice of a man, and the speaker thus metamorphoses into the typical male lover pining for a cruel lady. The poem would then draw on a quite different nexus of associations. Gender change is also seen in *Wære diu werlt alle mîn*, earlier.

	Wolde God that hyt were so as I coude wyshe bytwyxt us two.	
I 5	The man that I loved altherbest in al thys contre, est other west, to me he ys a strange gest; what wonder is't thow I be woo? Wolde God that hyt were so as I coude wyshe bytwyxt us two.	best of all guest
II 10	When me were levest that he schold dwelle, he wold noght sey onys farewell; he wold noght sey ones farewell wen tyme was come that he most go.	I would rather he should stay once

Wolde God that hyt were so
as I coude wyshe bytwyxt us two.

III 15 In places ofte when I hym mete,
I dar noght speke but forth I go;
with herte and eyes I hym grete,
so trewe of love I know no mo.   no more
Wolde God that hyt were so
20   as I coude wyshe bytwyxt us two.

IV   As he ys myn hert love,
my dyrward dyre, iblessed he be;   precious darling
I swere by God that ys above,
non hath my love but only he.
25   Wolde God that hyt were so
as I coude wyshe bytwyxt us two.

V   I am icomfortyd in euery syde,
the colures wexeth both fresh and newe;
when he ys come and wyl abyde,
30   I wott ful wel that he ys trewe.   I know
Wolde God that hyt were so
as I coude wyshe bytwyxt us two.

VI   I love hym trewely and no mo—   no more, no others
wolde God that he hyt knewe!
35   And ever I hope hyt shal be so;
then shal I chaunge for no new.
Wolde God that hyt were so
as I coude wyshe bytwyxt us two.

Provenance: Fifteenth century.
Meter: Quatrains rhyming abab; 2-line burden.

Anonymous

Rybbe ne rele ne spynne yc ne may—"I cannot scrape, wind, nor spin"

Both this and the following poem narrate the seduction of a servant girl on a public holiday by a certain "Jack," with vivid details of homely life, the girl's eagerness to enjoy herself, and her fear of her mistress. The sexual encounter is described in graphically physical terms. As in many poems of this type, illicit sex and its consequences are the object of a rough humor, which acknowledges, but refuses to explore, the girl's unhappy plight.

Rybbe ne rele ne spynne yc ne may   I cannot scrape, wind, nor spin (the flax)
for joye that it ys holyday.

I   Al this day ic han sought;   I have
spyndul ne werve ne vond Y nought;   I found neither spindle nor reel
5   to myche blisse ic am brout
ayen this hyghe holyday.   because of this high holiday
Rybbe ne rele ne spynne yc ne may
for joye that it ys holyday.

II	Al unswope ys oure vlet,	unswept / floor
10	and oure fyre ys vnbet;	unmade
	oure rushen ben unrepe yet	our rushes are still uncut
	ayen this hy halyday.	
	Rybbe ne rele ne spynne yc ne may	
	for joye that it ys holyday.	
III 15	Yc moste feshun worton in;	I have to bring vegetables in
	predele my kerchef undur my chyn;	fasten
	leve Jakke, lend me a pyn	dear
	to predele me this holiday.	
	Rybbe ne rele ne spynne yc ne may	
20	for joye that it ys holyday.	
IV	Now yt draweth to the none,	noon
	and al my cherrus ben undone;	chores
	Y moste a lyte solas mye schone	polish my shoes a little
	to make hem dowge this holiday.	be suitable
25	Rybbe ne rele ne spynne yc ne may	
	for joye that it ys holyday.	
V	Y moste mylkyn in this payl;	
	out me bred al this shayl;	spread out all this pan
	yet is the dow undur my nayl	the dough is still under my nails
30	as ic knad this holyday.	kneaded
	Rybbe ne rele ne spynne yc ne may	
	for joye that it ys holyday.	
VI	Jakke wol brynge me onward in my wey,	
	wyth me desyre for to pleye;	play
35	of my dame stant me non eye	I'm not afraid of my mistress
	an never a god haliday.	on any good holiday
	Rybbe ne rele ne spynne yc ne may	
	for joye that it ys holyday.	
VII	Jacke wol pay for my scot	contribution
40	a Sonday atte the ale-shot;	ale-levy
	Jacke wol souse wel my wrot	wet my snout well
	every god haliday.	
	Rybbe ne rele ne spynne yc ne may	
	for joye that it ys holyday.	
VIII 45	Sone he wolle take me be the hond,	
	and he wolle legge me on the lond,	put me on the ground
	that al my buttockus ben of sond,	sand
	upon this hye holyday.	
	Rybbe ne rele ne spynne yc ne may	
50	for joye that it ys holyday.	
IX	In he pult, and out he drow,	thrust
	and ever yc lay on hym y-low:	lay beneath him
	"By Godus deth, thou dest me wow	you cause me grief
55	upon this hey holyday!"	
	Rybbe ne rele ne spynne yc ne may	
	for joye that it ys holyday.	
X	Sone my wombe began te swelle	
	as gret as a belle;	great

60 durst Y nat my dame telle
    wat me betydde this holyday.   what happened to me
      Rybbe ne rele ne spynne yc ne may
      for joye that it ys holyday.

Provenance: Mid-fifteenth century.
Meter: Four-line stanzas rhyming aaax; the fourth line is linked by end-word and rhyme to the 2-line burden.

Anonymous

Alas, alas, the wyle!—*"Alas, alas, the time"*

At a dance on Midsummer Day (i.e., June 24, the Nativity of Saint John the Baptist) the speaker catches the attention of "Jack," who invites her to his home. In this poem, unlike the previous one, the speaker says she had a thoroughly good time. But the upshot is similarly disturbing.

    Alas, alas, the wyle!   time, occasion
    Thout Y on no gyle,   I suspected no deceit
    so have Y god chaunce.   as (I hope) to have good fortune
    Alas, alas, the wyle
5   that ever Y coude daunce!

I   Ladd Y the daunce a Myssomur Day;
    Y made smale trippus, soth for to say.   little steps / truth
    Jak, oure haly-watur clerk, com be the way,
    and he lokede me upon; he thout that Y was
      gay,   attractive
10 thout yc on no gyle.
      Alas, alas, the wyle!
      Thout Y on no gyle,
      so have Y god chaunce.
      Alas, alas, the wyle
15   that ever Y coude daunce!

II   Jak, oure haly-watur clerk, the yonge
      strippelyng,
    for the chesoun of me he com to the ryng,   because of me / dancing circle
    and he trippede on my to and made a
      twynkelyng;   winked
    ever he cam ner; he sparet for no thynge.   came closer
20 Thout Y on no gyle.
      Alas, alas, the wyle!
      Thout Y on no gyle,
      so have Y god chaunce.
      Alas, alas, the wyle
25   that ever Y coude daunce!

III Jak, ic wot, preyede in my fayre face;   I know / peered
    he thout me ful werly, so have Y god grace;   attractive
    as we turndun oure daunce in a narw place,
    Jak bed me the mouth; a cussynge ther was.   offered / kissing
30 Thout Y on no gyle.
      Alas, alas, the wyle!
      Thout Y on no gyle,
      so have Y god chaunce.

Alas, alas, the wyle
35   that ever Y coude daunce!

IV   Jak tho began to roune in myn ere: *then / whisper*
     "Loke that thou be privey, and graunte that   *discreet*
        thou the bere   *promise to wear*
     a peyre wyt glovus ic ha to thyn were."   *white gloves*
     "Gramercy, Jacke!" that was myn answere.   *thank you*
40   Thoute yc on no gyle.
        Alas, alas, the wyle!
        Thout Y on no gyle,
        so have Y god chaunce.
        Alas, alas, the wyle
45   that ever Y coude daunce!

V   Sone aftur evensong Jak me mette:
     "Com hom aftur thy glovus that yc the
        byhette."   *promised*
     Wan ic to his chambre com, doun he me sette;   *when*
     from hym mytte Y nat go wan we were mette.   *could (might)*
50   Thout Y on no gyle.
        Alas, alas, the wyle!
        Thout Y on no gyle,
        so have Y god chaunce.
        Alas, alas, the wyle
55   that ever Y coude daunce!

VI   Shetus and chalonus, ic wot, a were yspredde;   *sheets and blankets / I know*
     forsothe tho Jak and yc wenten to bedde;   *truly / then*
     he prikede and he pransede; nolde he   *would not*
        never lynne;   *cease*
     yt was the murgust nyt that ever Y cam ynne.   *merriest night*
60   Thout Y on no gyle.
        Alas, alas, the wyle!
        Thout Y on no gyle,
        so have Y god chaunce.
        Alas, alas, the wyle
65   that ever Y coude daunce!

VII Wan Jak had don, tho he rong the bell;
     al nyght ther he made me to dwelle;
     oft Y trewe we haddun yserved the ragged   *I believe*
        devel of helle;
     of othur smale burdus kep Y nout to telle.   *matters / I do not care*
70   Thout Y on no gyle.
        Alas, alas, the wyle!
        Thout Y on no gyle,
        so have Y god chaunce.
        Alas, alas, the wyle
75   that ever Y coude daunce!

VIII The other day at prime Y come hom, as ic   *early morning / I think*
        wene;
     met Y my dame, coppud and kene: *bad-tempered / harsh*
     "Sey thou stronge strumpet, ware hastu bene?   *where have you been*
     Thy trippyng and thy dauncyng, wel it wol
        be sene."
80   Thout Y on no gyle.

Alas, alas, the wyle!
Thout Y on no gyle,
so have Y god chaunce.
Alas, alas, the wyle
85   that ever Y coude daunce!

IX   Ever bi on and by on my dame reched me clot;   gave me a blow
ever Y ber it privey wyle that Y mout,   kept it secret / could
tyl my gurdul aros, my wombe wax out;
evel yspunne yern, ever it wole out.   ill-spun yarn will always come apart
90   Thout Y on no gyle.
Alas, alas, the wyle!
Thout Y on no gyle,
so have Y god chaunce.
Alas, alas, the wyle
95   that ever Y coude daunce!

Provenance: Fifteenth century.
Meter: Stanzas of 4 monorhymed lines plus refrain line, the latter linked by repetition and rhyme to the 5-line burden.

Anonymous

A, dere God, what I am fayn—*"Ah, dear God, how worthless I am"*

The speaker is not explicitly defined here as a servant girl, but her gullibility is contrasted with the cleverness of the clerk who seduces her. Still, there is a certain resourceful defiance in her plan to represent her unfortunate accident as a consequence of going on pilgrimage, which, she hopes, will excuse it.

A, dere God, what I am fayn,   How worthless I am
for I am madyn now gane.   I am no longer a maiden

I   This enther day I mete a clerke,   other
and he was wyly in hys werke;   cunning / strategy
5   he prayd me with hym to herke,
and hys counsell all for to layne.   hide
A, dere God, what I am fayn,
for I am madyn now gane.

II   I trow he coud of gramery;   I'm sure he knew magic
10   I shall now a good skyll wy: (tell) a good reason why
for what I hade siccurly,   surely
to warne hys wyll had I no mayn.   refuse / strength
A, dere God, what I am fayn,
for I am madyn now gane.

III 15 Whan he and me browt un us the shete,   put the sheet over us
of all hys wyll I hym lete;   permitted
now wyll not my gyrdyll met;
a, dere God, what shal I sayn?
A, dere God, what I am fayn,
20   for I am madyn now gane.

IV   I shall sey to man and page
that I have bene of pylgrymage;

now wyll I not lete for no wage
with me a clerk for to pleyn.
25   A, dere God, what I am fayn,
    for I am madyn now gane.

Provenance: Fifteenth century.
Meter: Four-line stanzas rhyming aaax; the final line is linked by rhyme to the 2-line burden.

Anonymous

Were it undo that is ydo—*"Were it undone that is done"*

This song is less graphic and more plaintive than some of the other carols. The
speaker is abandoned and probably pregnant, but the details are left unexplained.

Were it undo that is ydo	undone / done
I wold be war.	careful

I   Y lovede a child of this cuntre,
    and so Y wende he had do me;   thought
5   now myself the sothe Y see,
    that he is far.
        Were it undo that is ydo
        I wold be war.

II   He seyde to me he wolde be trewe
10   and chaunge me for none othur newe;
    now Y sykke and am pale of hewe,   sigh
    for he is far.
        Were it undo that is ydo
        I wold be war.

III 15 He seide his sawus he wolde fulfulle;   promises
    therfor Y lat him have al his wille;
    now Y sykke and mourne stille,
    for he is fare.
        Were it undo that is ydo
20   I wold be war.

Provenance: Fifteenth century.
Meter: Four-line stanzas rhyming aaax; the final line is linked by rhyme to the 2-line burden.

Anonymous

I have forsworne hit whil I live—*"I have forsworn it while I live"*

Again, the speaker has been taken advantage of on a festive occasion, here, by
the parish priest, as indicated by his title "Sir" John. The apparently cheerful
"-ey" refrain suggests his callousness—and her bitterness.

I have forsworne hit whil I live,	
to wake the well-ey	keep the wake by the well

I   The last tyme I the wel woke,
    Ser John caght me with a croke;   crock, pitcher

5	he made me to swere be bel and boke	book
	I shuld not tell-ey.	
	I have forsworne hit whil I live,	
	to wake the well-ey	

II 10	Yet he did me a wel wors turne:	
	he leyde my hed agayn the burne;	stream
	he gafe my maydenhed a spurne	tore my cloak
	and rofe my bell-ey.	[with a sexual innuendo]
	I have forsworne hit whil I live,	
15	to wake the well-ey	

III	Sir John came to oure hous to play	
	fro evensong tyme till light of the day;	
	we made as mery as flowres in May;	
	I was begyled-ay.	deceived
20	I have forsworne hit whil I live,	
	to wake the well-ey	

IV	Sir John he came to our hous;	
	he made hit wondur copious;	full of gifts
	he seyd that I was gracious	
25	to beyre a childe-ey.	
	I have forsworne hit whil I live,	
	to wake the well-ey	

V	I go with childe, wel I wot;	I know
	I shrew the fadur that hit gate,	curse / conceived
30	withouten he fynde hit mylke and pap	unless / soft food
	a long while-ey.	
	I have forsworne hit whil I live,	
	to wake the well-ey	

Provenance: Fifteenth century. Although the author is unknown, his first name may be recorded in the signature following the poem: "Bryan hys my name iet."
Meter: Four-line stanzas rhyming aaax; the final line is linked by rhyme to the 2-line burden.

Anonymous

Kyrie, so kyrie—*"Kyrie, kyrie"*

Here the guilty clerk is "Jolly Jankin." Possibly the woman's name is Alison, and the refrain a pun. The poem contrasts the conventional words of the Latin mass with her personal feelings and her sharp fear for her future.

"Kyrie, so kyrie,"
Jankyn syngyt merie,
with "aleyson."

I	As I went on Yol Day in our prosessyon,	
5	knew I Joly Jankyn be his mery ton.	voice
	Kyrieleyson.	"Lord have mercy"
	"Kyrie, so kyrie,"	
	Jankyn syngyt merie,	
	with "aleyson."	

II 10	Jankyn began the offys on the Yol day,	
	and yet me thynkyt it dos me good, so merie	it seemed to me
	gan he say	began to
	kyrieleyson.	
	"Kyrie, so kyrie,"	
	Jankyn syngyt merie,	
15	with "aleyson."	

III	Jankyn red þe pystyl ful fayr and ful wel,	epistle
	and yet me thynkyt it dos me good, as evere	
	have I sel.	blessing, good fortune
	Kyrieleyson.	
	"Kyrie, so kyrie,"	
20	Jankyn syngyt merie,	
	with "aleyson."	

IV	Jankyn at the Sanctus crackit a merie note,	"Holy, holy, holy"
	and yet me thynkyt it dos me good—I payid	
	for his cote.	
	Kyrieleyson	
25	"Kyrie, so kyrie,"	
	Jankyn syngyt merie,	
	with "aleyson."	

V	Jankyn crackit notes an hunderid on a knot,	
	and yet he hackyt hem smaller than wortes	vegetables for the pot
	to the pot.	
30	Kyrieleyson.	
	"Kyrie, so kyrie,"	
	Jankyn syngyt merie,	
	with "aleyson."	

VI	Jankyn at the Agnus beryt the pax-brede;	"Lamb of God" / tray
35	he twynkelid, but sayd nowt, and on myn	winked
	fot he trede.	
	Kyrieleyson.	
	"Kyrie, so kyrie,"	
	Jankyn syngyt merie,	
	with "aleyson."	

VII 40	Benedicamus Domino, Cryst for shame me	"Blessings be to God"
	shylde.	
	Deo gracias therto—alas, I go with chylde!	"Thanks be to God"
	Kyrieleyson.	
	"Kyrie, so kyrie,"	
	Jankyn syngyt merie,	
45	with "aleyson."	

Provenance: Mid-fifteenth century.
Meter: Stanzas of rhyming couplets, plus refrain word, echoing the final word of the 3-line burden.

Anonymous

Hey noyney!—*"Hey nonny!"*

Again the seducer is a womanizing priest called Sir John. In this poem the speaker seems quite satisfied with the situation, and the dark prospect of pregnancy and an illicit child is left out of the picture.

Hey noyney!
I wyll love our Ser John and I love eny.   if I love anyone

I   O Lord, so swet Ser John dothe kys,
      at every tyme when he wolde pley;
5   of hymselfe so plesant he ys,
      I have no powre to say hym nay.
        Hey noyney!
        I wyll love our Ser John and I love eny.

II   Ser John loves me and I love hym;
10   the more I love hym the more I maye.
      He says, "Swet hart, cum kys me trym"—   nicely
      I have no powre to say hym nay.
        Hey noyney!
        I wyll love our Ser John and I love eny.

III 15 Ser John to me is proferyng
      for hys plesure ryght well to pay,
      and in my box he puttes hys offryng—
      I have no powre to say hym nay.
        Hey noyney!
20   I wyll love our Ser John and I love eny.

IV   Ser John ys taken in my mouse-trappe:
      fayne wold I have hem bothe nyght and day.   gladly
      He gropith so nyslye about my lape,
      I have no pore to say hym nay.
25   Hey noyney!
        I wyll love our Ser John and I love eny.

V   Ser John gevyth me reluys rynges,   shining
      with praty plesure for to assay—   pleasing
      furres of the fynest with other thynges:
30   I have no powre to say hym nay.
        Hey noyney!
        I wyll love our Ser John and I love eny.

Provenance: Late fifteenth or early sixteenth century.
Meter: Quatrains rhyming abab, the last line being a refrain; 2-line burden.

Anonymous

I pray yow, cum kyss me—*"I pray you, come kiss me"*

A dialogue in which the man begs for a kiss and the girl continues to refuse.
Stanzas 5 and 10 imply that he has more in mind than kissing.

"I pray yow, cum kyss me,
  my lytle prety Mopse,
I pray yow, com kyss me."

I   "Alas, good man, most yow be kyst?
5   Ye shall not now, ye may me trust;
      wherefore go where as ye best lust,   desire
      for, iwyss, ye shall not kyss me."   certainly

        "I pray yow, cum kyss me,
          my lytle prety Mopse,
10   I pray yow, com kyss me.

II   Iwyss, swet hart, yf that ye
        had askyd a gretur thyng of me,
        so unkynd to yow I wold not have be;
        wherefore, I pray yow, com kyss me.
15   I pray yow, cum kyss me,
          my lytle prety Mopse,
          I pray yow, com kyss me."

III   "I thynke very well that ye ar kynd
        whereas ye love and set your mynd,
20   but all your wordes be but as wynd,
        wherefore nowe ye shall not kyss me."
          "I pray yow, cum kyss me,
          my lytle prety Mopse,
          I pray yow, com kyss me.

IV 25 I do but talke, ye may me trust,
        but ye take everythyng at the worst."
        "Wherefore I say, as I sayd furst,
        iwyss, ye shall not kyss me."
          "I pray yow, cum kyss me,
30   my lytle prety Mopse,
          I pray yow, com kyss me.

V   I pray yow, let me kyss yow.
        If that I shall not kyss yow,   opening in your kerchief
        let me loke, let me kyss your karchos nocke;   [with a sexual innuendo]
35   I pray yow, let me kyss yowe.
          I pray yow, cum kyss me,
          my lytle prety Mopse,
          I pray yow, com kyss me."

VI   "All so I say as I furst have sayd,
40   and ye wyll not therewith be dysmayd;
        yet wyth that onsar ye shall be payd: answer
        iwyss, ye shall not kyss me."
          "I pray yow, cum kyss me,
          my lytle prety Mopse,
45   I pray yow, com kyss me.

VII   Now I se well that kyssys ar dere,   expensive
        and, yf I shold labur al the hole yere,
        I thynke I shold be never the nere;   would never get any closer
        wherefore I pray yow, cum kyss me.
50   I pray yow, cum kyss me,
          my lytle prety Mopse,
          I pray yow, com kyss me."

VIII "Never the nere, ye may be shewre,
        for ye shall not so sone bryng me yn ure   bring me to the point
55   to consent unto yore nyse plesure,   wanton
        nor, iwyss, ye shall not kyss me."   certainly

"I pray yow, cum kyss me,
my lytle prety Mopse,
I pray yow, com kyss me.

IX 60 I pray yow, com and kyss me,
my lytle prety Mopse,
and yf that ye wyll not kyss me,
I pray yow, let me kyss you.
I pray yow, cum kyss me,
65   my lytle prety Mopse,
I pray yow, com kyss me."

X   "Well, for a kyss I wyll not styck,
so that ye wyll do nothyng but lyck,
but, and ye begyn on me for to pryck,
70 iwyss, ye shall not kyss me."
"I pray yow, cum kyss me,
my lytle prety Mopse,
I pray yow, com kyss me.

XI   Now I se well that ye ar kynd;
75 wherefore ye shall cum know my mynd,
and ever yore owne ye shall me fynd
at all tymys redy to kyss yow.
I pray yow, cum kyss me,
my lytle prety Mopse,
80 I pray yow, com kyss me."

Provenance: Ca. 1500.
Meter: Four-line stanzas rhyming aaax; the final line is linked by repetition and rhyme to the 3-line burden. Lines 35 and 78 rhyme on "yow" instead of "me."

Textual Notes

These notes are intended to indicate the sources for the poems and passages included in this anthology, and the divergences between the major editions as they affect the present texts and translations. Unusual features of language are commented on very briefly. Where the translation is particularly free, the literal version is supplied.

1 Ancient Greece

Most of the manuscripts of ancient works are medieval, but early fragments have been found preserved on papyrus, especially at Oxyrhynchus in Egypt. The papyri are particularly important for some of the Greek texts.

Alcman 26 (Alcman 3, Page)

Manuscripts
Papyrus Oxyrhynchus 2387, fragments 1 and 3; first century B.C.–first century A.D.

Selected Editions
Page, *Poetae Melici Graeci*.
Calame, *Alcman*.
Campbell, *Greek Lyric*, vol. 2 (with translation).

Text as in Calame, in the main identical to Page. The tiny preserved fragments in the missing sections are ignored here. I have adopted Page's ἴδοιμ' ("I would see," 79) and ἱκέτις ("suppliant," 81). Both Page and Calame omit the θ of βαθύφρονα (82) as illegible.

Sappho 1, 16, 31, 47, 102, 105c, 111, 130, 140

Manuscripts and Sources
Poem 1 quoted by Dionysius of Halicarnassus, first century B.C. (*De compositione verborum* 23); the only poem of Sappho's that is preserved complete. Also preserved fragmentarily in Papyrus Oxyrhynchus 2288, second century A.D.

Frag. 16: Papyrus Oxyrhynchus 1231, fragment 1, second century A.D.

Frag. 31 quoted by pseudo-Longinus, first century A.D. (*De sublimitate* 10.1–3). Also preserved very fragmentarily in a papyrus commentary, third century A.D.

Frag. 47 quoted by Maximus of Tyre 18.9.1, second century A.D.

Frag. 105c quoted by Demetrius Phalereus, fourth century B.C., in his *On Style* (*Elocutio* 106). The tentative attribution to Sappho is modern.

Frags. 102, 111, 130, 140 quoted by Hephaestion, second century A.D., in his *Handbook on Meters* (*Enchiridion* 7.7 [130], 10.4 [140]), 10.5 [102], and *On Poems* (περὶ ποιημάτων 7.1 [111]).

Selected Editions
   Lobel-Page, *Poetarum Lesbiorum Fragmenta.*
   Voigt, *Sappho et Alcaeus.*
   Campbell, *Greek Lyric*, vol. 1 (with translation).

Text as in Voigt. I adopt Lobel-Page's ἀλλ’ ἄκαν ("but in silence," 31.9) for Voigt's ἀλλὰ †καμ†. It is possible that Frag. 16 ends at line 20 and that what follows is another poem.

Aristophanes, Ecclesiazusae

Manuscripts
   Ravenna, Biblioteca Classense, 429, mid-tenth century (R).
   Florence, Biblioteca Mediceo-Laurenziana, Laurentianus 31.15, ca. 1325 (Γ).
   Perugia, Biblioteca Comunale, Perusinus H56, early fifteenth century (Λ).

The oldest and most important manuscript is R, which contains all the extant plays of Aristophanes.

Selected Editions
   Ussher.
   Parker (text and meter of lines 952–68).
   Sommerstein (with translation).
   Henderson, *Aristophanes*, vol. 4 (with translation).

Text as in Ussher. Text and lineation of this passage vary among editions.

Euripides

The plays of Euripides survive in numerous manuscripts, and, very fragmentarily, in some papyri. For *Medea* and *The Trojan Women*, the principal manuscripts are the following:
   Paris, Bibl. Nat., Parisinus gr. 2712, thirteenth century (A).
   Paris, Bibl. Nat., Parisinus gr. 2713, twelfth or thirteenth century (B).
   Rome, Biblioteca Vaticana, Vaticanus gr. 909, late thirteenth century (V).
   Florence, Biblioteca Mediceo-Laurenziana, Laurentianus 32.2, late thirteenth century (L).
   Rome, Biblioteca Vaticana, Palatinus gr. 287, early fourteenth century (P).
   London, British Library, Harley 5743, very late fifteenth century (Q).

Medea

Manuscripts
   ABVLP and others.

Selected Editions
   Page, *Euripides: Medea.*
   Diggle, *Euripidis Fabulae*, vol. 1.
   Kovacs, *Euripides*, vol. 2 (with translation).

Text as in Kovacs, identical to Page and Diggle, except for ζεύγλῃσι, line 479 (Page). Line 468, θεοῖς τε κἀμοὶ παντί τ’ ἀνθρώπων γένει, is bracketed as spurious by all three.

The Trojan Women

Manuscripts
   VPQ and others.

Selected Editions
Lee.
Diggle, *Euripidis Fabulae*, vol. 1.
Barlow (with translation).
Kovacs, *Euripides*, vol. 4 (with translation).

Theocritus 18, The Epithalamion for Helen

Manuscripts
For *Idyll* 18, the principal manuscripts are the following:
Milan, Biblioteca Ambrosiana, Ambrosianus 390 (G. 32 sup), late thirteenth century (A).
Rome, Biblioteca Vaticana, Vaticanus gr. 1825, fourteenth century (U).
Florence, Biblioteca Mediceo-Laurenziana, Laurentianus 32.16, A.D. 1280 (S).
Rome, Biblioteca Vaticana, Vaticanus gr. 1311, fifteenth century (X), lines 51–end only.
Paris, Bibl. Nat., Parisinus gr. 2832, fourteenth century (Tr).

Selected Editions
Edmonds (with translation).
Gow (with translation).

Text as in Gow. See Gow 1.xlvii on his selection of these mss.

The Locrian Song

Source
Quoted in Athenaeus, *Philosophers at Dinner* (*Deipnosophistae* 15.697b–c), ca. A.D. 200.

Selected Editions
Gulick (with translation).
Page, *Poetae Melici Graeci*.

Text as in Page. In a footnote, Gulick comments briefly on the passage in Clearchus that mentions Locrian songs (Gulick 6.449).

2   Ancient Rome

Catullus 64

Manuscripts
The following are the three principal manuscripts of Catullus, all ca. 1375:
Oxford, Bodleian Library, Canon. cl. lat. 30, "Oxoniensis" (0).
Paris, Bibl. Nat., lat. 14137, formerly at St.-Germain-des Prés, "Sangermanensis" (G).
Rome, Biblioteca Vaticana, Ott. lat. 1829, "Romanus" (R).

O is a copy of the lost Verona Codex (V), probably late twelfth century. G and R were both copied at one remove from V.

Selected Editions
Mynors, *C. Valerii Catulli Carmina*.
Quinn.
Goold (with translation).
Thomson.

Text as in Quinn, in the main identical to Mynors's Oxford Classical Texts edition, except for the following lines:

148 *metuere* Mynors / *meminere* Quinn.
174 *Cretam* Mynors / *Creta* Quinn.
184 *colitur sola insula* Mynors / *litus, sola insula* Quinn.

Virgil, Aeneid

Manuscripts
Notable among the many are several very early manuscripts written in capital letters. For the passages from Book 4 included here, the manuscripts from this early group are:

Rome, Biblioteca Vaticana, lat. 3225, "Fulvianus," late fourth century (F); here 306–11 only.
Florence, Biblioteca Mediceo-Laurenziana, Laurentianus 39.1, "Mediceus," fifth century (M).
Rome, Biblioteca Vaticana, Palatinus 1631, fifth or sixth century (P).

Selected Editions
Pease.
Mynors.
Fairclough (with translation).

Text as in Mynors's Oxford Classical Texts edition.

Sulpicia

Manuscripts
All complete manuscripts of Tibullus, including the Sulpicia poems, go back to a lost manuscript of which a copy is preserved:

Milan, Biblioteca Ambrosiana, Ambrosianus R.26 sup., ca. A.D. 1375 (A).

Among other sources, readings from the early *fragmentum Cuiacianum* (F), collated in the sixteenth century and now lost.

Selected Editions
Smith.
Postgate.
Cornish, Postgate, and MacKail, rev. Goold (with translation).

Text as in Cornish, Postgate, and MacKail, rev. Goold. I have adopted Smith's *quamvis non sinis esse meo* (3.14.8) and *opinanti . . . forte* (3.15.4) instead of Goold's *quam vis non sinit* and *opinata . . . sorte*, resp., and Smith's and Postgate's *dolori est* (3.16.5) instead of Goold's *doloris*. Many editors understand *cedam ignoto . . . toro* (3.16.6), lit. "yield to an unknown marriage-bed," to mean something like "give place to an ignominious partner," that is, the prostitute referred to in lines 3–4.

Ovid, Heroides *10, 15*

Manuscripts
For *Heroides* 10, the principal manuscripts are the following four. Excerpts from *Heroides* 15 are found between 14 and 16 in the twelfth century *Florilegium Gallicum*. Otherwise, the poem is absent from the older manuscripts; of those below, it only appears in F, where it is separated from the rest of the *Heroides*:

Frankfurt, Universitätsbibliothek Ms. Barth. 110, late twelfth / early thirteenth century (F).

Wolfenbüttel, Herzog August Bibliothek, Guelferbytanus Extrav. 260, twelfth
century (G).
Paris, Bibl. Nat., Parisinus lat. 8242 ("Puteaneus"), ninth century (P).
Vienna, Österreichische Nationalbibliothek, ser. nov. 107, late eleventh / early
twelfth century (W); here, *Heroides* 10.14–end only.

Selected Editions
Showerman.
Knox.

Text as in Showerman. I have adopted Knox's *rupta* ("torn," 10.16) instead of Showerman's
rapta, "snatched." Some editors, including Knox, print *vilis, mihi crede, Gyrinno* ("nothing,
believe me, Gyrinno," 15.17), since Gyrinno is attested as one of Sappho's lovers, and Cydro
is not. In 15.19, F reads *non*, "not," the later mss *hic*, "here"—"a transparent attempt to
deny Sappho's homosexuality" (Knox, Commentary). 15.134: literally, "I can't stay dry."

3   Ireland

Créde's Lament for Cáel

Manuscripts
The following are the manuscripts of the *Acallam na Senórach*:
Oxford, Bodleian Library, Laud 610, late fifteenth or early sixteenth century.
Library of the Duke of Devonshire, the "Book of Lismore," ca. 1400.
Oxford, Bodleian Library, Rawlinson B 487, sixteenth century.
Killiney, Franciscan Library, A IV, fifteenth or sixteenth century.

Edition
Murphy (with translation).

Text and translation reprinted from Murphy and from Dooley-Roe, resp. I have chosen
the slightly freer translation by Dooley and Roe as being closer in spirit to my own trans-
lations of the other poems in this anthology. Murphy uses the Book of Lismore as his base
text. Dooley-Roe's translation is based on the readings of the main manuscripts, that is,
the first three above.

4   Anglo-Saxon England

Wulf and Eadwacer, The Wife's Lament

Manuscript
Exeter Cathedral, Chapter Library 3501, the "Exeter Book," late tenth century,
fols. 100v–101r (*Wulf*) and 115rv (*Wife*).

Selected Editions
Hamer (with translation).
Klinck.
Muir.

Text as in Klinck.

Wulf and Eadwacer

The femininity of the speaker is established by the inflections -*u* and -*e* in *reotugu* ("weep-
ing," 10) and *seoce* ("sick," 14). Many of the words are ambiguous or obscure: *lac* (1),

either "gift" or "sacrifice"; *apecgan* (2,7), "take in"—either "accept" or "consume, destroy"; *dogode* (9), "dogged" (?), often emended to *hogode*, "thought about"; *bogum* (11), probably "fore-limbs" in this context, that is, arms; ms earne (16), usually emended to *eargne*, "cowardly," or *earmne*, "wretched," as here. In keeping with the designation of the speaker's lover as Wolf, the language is colored by "beastly" words and motifs. The poem has also been taken as a lament for a son and as an animal story.

The Wife's Lament

The femininity of the speaker is established by the *-re* inflections in *geomorre* ("sad," 1), *minre sylfre* ("of my self," 2). Much of what follows could have been spoken by a man about his lord, but a personal relationship is indicated by *unc* ("us two," 12, 22), *uncer* ("our two," 25), *wit* ("we two," 13, 21). A specifically sexual envy emerges in the lines about lovers keeping their bed together (33–34) in contrast with the speaker's solitude. Early scholars thought this was a male exile's lament, like the Old English *Wanderer* and *Seafarer*.

5   Scandinavia or Iceland

Guðrúnarkviða in fyrsta

Manuscript
Reykjavik, Armagnaean Institute; formerly Copenhagen, Royal Library, Gl. Kgl. Sml. 2365 4to, the "Codex Regius," Iceland, ca.1270.

Edition
Neckel-Kuhn.

Text as in Neckel-Kuhn, except that *i* yod is rendered by *j, k* replaces *c* and *q*. In stanza 18 some editors assume an opening line "Þá kvað þat Guðrún, Gjúka dóttir." The closing prose passage begins "Gunnar . . . ," presumably an error for "Guthrun."

6   Early Medieval Spain

Arabic and Mozarabic

For the sake of simplicity, in the transliteration of Arabic words the macrons marking long vowels and the subscript dots distinguishing certain consonants (varieties of d, h, s, t, z) are omitted in this book. Arabic letters often rendered with the use of diacritics are here represented as follows: th (tha'), j (jim), kh (kha'), dh (dhal), ' ('ayn), sh (shin), ' (hamza).

Wallada (Arabic)

Sources
Wallada's poems are found in three collections: the *Dhakira* of Ibn Bassam (twelfth century), the *Nuzha* of al-Suyuti (late fifteenth century), and the *Nafh at-tib* of al-Maqqari (late sixteenth or early seventeenth century). The poems included here are located as follows:
Asluhu li-l-ma'ali: Dhakhira 1.429–30; Maqqari 4.205; *Nuzha* 77,79.
Idha janna l-zalamu: Dhakhira 1.430; Maqqari 4.206; *Nuzha* 80.
A-la hal la-na min ba'di: Maqqari 4.206–7; *Nuzha* 80–81.
Law kunta tunsifu: Dhakhira 1.431–32; Maqqari 4.205; *Nuzha* 77,78.

Texts transliterated by Teresa Garulo from the editions of Ihsan 'Abbas (for Ibn Bassam and al-Maqqari) and al-Munajjid (for al-Suyuti).

Kharjas (Mozarabic)

The manuscripts that contain muwashshahas with Romance kharjas were copied by Muslim and Jewish scribes, and are preserved in manuscripts that are often very late. Also, most of these manuscripts were compiled outside Spain, and the copyists did not understand Romance. Thus, the texts of the kharjas, written in Arabic or Hebrew characters with little or no vowel notation, are often uncertain. The Arabic muwashshahas are principally gathered in two collections, both originally compiled in the fourteenth century:

The 'Uddat al-jalis of Ibn Bushra; unique ms. in the library of the late Georges Colin, sixteenth century or later.

The Jaysh al tawshih of Ibn al-Khatib; Tunis, the Zaytuna Mosque, 4583, eighteenth century (the two other mss. of this collection are of less importance).

The Hebrew muwashshahas are preserved in codices, and in fragments from the Genizah ("storage room") of the Fostat Synagogue in Cairo (on the significance of the Genizah fragments see Benabu and Yahalom). The following are the relevant manuscripts for the kharjas included here:

Oxford 1971 (OPP, Add. 4, 81), thirteenth century.

Oxford 1970 (Pococke 74), seventeenth century.

Jerusalem, Schocken Library, 37 (derived directly or indirectly from Oxford 1971), seventeenth century.

Cambridge, University Library, T.-S. Collection, Miscellany 35 (a Genizah fragment), twelfth century.

Selected Editions
García Gómez.
Solá-Solé.

Texts as in Solá-Solé. The kharjas are cited here both by their García Gómez and their Solá-Solé numbers. García Gómez uses Roman numerals for the kharjas in Arabic muwashshahas, Arabic numerals for the ones in Hebrew muwashshahas.

Ibn Labbun and al-Khabbaz al-Mursi, Ya mamma, mio al-habibi (GGxxi ba, S-S7ab)

Manuscripts
7a; Colin (without authorial attributions); Zaytuna et al.
7b: Zaytuna et al.

Jones is critical of Solá-Solé's text, and comments that it is difficult to achieve satisfactory sense and meter for the second and fourth hemistichs (Jones 151–56 and 159–60).

Ibn 'Ezra, al-Saraqusti al-Jazzar, and Ibn Baqi, Adamey filiolo alieno (GG41 and xxviii ba; S-S 14cab)

Manuscripts
S-S14c (Ibn 'Ezra): Oxford 1972, no. 253.
S-S14ab: Zaytuna et al.

S-S14ab reads alino and is metrically different.

Al-Kumayt al-Garbi, No she kedadh *(GGxv, S-S18)*

Manuscript
    Colin.

Solá-Solé suggests that the lines originally consisted of only the first 11 syllables, the final word being inessential to the sense. Both Solá-Solé's and García Gómez's versions are criticized by Jones, who notes that they make the kharja inconsistent with "sleep filling your eyes" in the muwashshaha (Jones 121). The accompanying muwashshaha is also preserved with a different kharja (S-S17).

Yehuda Halevi, Ibn Ruhaym, and Ibn Baqi, Non me tanqesh, ya, habibi *(GG8 and xxii ba; S-S29cba)*

Manuscripts
    S-S29c: Oxford 1971; Schocken 37.
    S-S29b: Colin; Zaytuna et al.
    S-S29a: Colin.

Translation uncertain. The variants among the three versions are mostly small, but 29b Zaytuna and 29a have *mordesh,* "bite" instead of *tanqesh,* "touch" (see Jones 173–74; Solá-Solé indicates *tanqesh* for 29a). Ibn Baqi's muwashshaha (29a) has the girl lying naked with her lover. Solá-Solé notes differences of pronunciation, including vowel elisions, in Yehuda Halevi's text (29c) as against the other two; hence the smaller number of syllables.

Yehuda Halevi, Garid bosh, ay yermanellash *(GG4, S-S33)*

Manuscripts
    Oxford 1971; Oxford 1970; Schocken 37.

Solá-Solé notes that the proportion of Romance words is extremely high, only *al-habib* being Arabic.

Yehuda Halevi, Ya rabb, komo bibreyo *(GG6, S-S34)*

Manuscripts
    Cambridge, T.-S. 35; Oxford 1971; Oxford 1970; Schocken 37.

The final word of the first line is problematic. Solá-Solé supposes an Arabic form *al-khallaq* (Hebrew *al-kallaq*), rendered by Solá-Solé as "violent, impetuous," but by Stern (*Chansons mozarabes* 6–7), as "seducer." Other editors have suggested various different interpretations.

Anonymous and Yehuda Halevi, Komo si filiolo alieno *(GGxviii and 7; S-S37ab)*

Manuscripts
    S-S37a (in Arabic muwashshaha): Colin.
    S-S37b (Halevi): Oxford 1970; Oxford 1971; Schocken 37.

S-S37a reads *alino.* S-S37b omits the opening words *Komo si.* This kharja is entirely in Romance.

Ibn al-Sayrafi, Bokella al-'iqdi *(GGxxxv, S-S43)*

Manuscripts
Zaytuna et al.

Mamma, ayy habibi *(GGxiv, S-S51)*

Manuscript
Colin.

Amanu, ya habibi *(GGxxiii, S-S53)*

Manuscript
Colin.

7 France

The lyrics of the Occitan troubadours and the Old French trouvères are preserved in a number of songbooks or *chansonniers*: Italian, Catalan, and French. Separate *sigla* are assigned to the manuscripts of the southern troubadours and the northern trouvères; however, some southern poems are included in northern collections. AHIK below contain miniatures of the trobairitz; H miniatures of the trobairitz only, suggesting a particular interest in them. The Northern French manuscripts usually have musical notation; the others usually do not.

Poems by the troubadours and trobairitz are identified by their number in the Pillet-Carstens *Bibliographie der Troubadours*, those of the trouvères by their number in the Raynaud-Spanke and Linker bibliographies of OF lyrics. The later, Middle French, poems included here are contained in single-author collections; these mss. are identified separately within the notes that follow.

The following are the relevant troubadour manuscripts:
Rome, Biblioteca Vaticana, lat. 5232, Italy, thirteenth century (A).
Paris, Bibl. Nat., fr. 1592, Provence, thirteenth century (B).
Paris, Bibl. Nat., fr. 856, Narbonne, Languedoc, fourteenth century (C).
Modena, Biblioteca Estense, α R.4.4, Italy, thirteenth century (D).
Milan, Biblioteca Ambrosiana, R71 sup., Italy, fourteenth century (G); music.
Rome, Biblioteca Vaticana, lat. 3207, Italy, thirteenth century (H).
Paris, Bibl. Nat., fr. 854, Italy, thirteenth century (I).
Paris, Bibl. Nat., fr. 12473, Italy, thirteenth century (K).
Rome, Biblioteca Vaticana, lat. 3206, Italy, fourteenth century (L).
Paris, Bibl. Nat., fr. 12474, Italy, fourteenth century (M).
New York, Pierpont Morgan Library 819, Italy, fourteenth century (N).
Florence, Biblioteca Riccardiana 2909, Italy, early fourteenth century (Q).
Paris, Bibl. Nat., fr. 22543, Toulouse, Languedoc, fourteenth century (R); music.
Barcelona, Biblioteca de Cataluña, 146, Catalonia, late fourteenth century (Sg).
Paris, Bibl. Nat., fr. 15211, Italy, fifteenth century (T).
Paris, Bibl. Nat., fr. 844, Northern France, thirteenth century (W); music.
Paris, Bibl. Nat., fr. 20050, Northern France, thirteenth century (X); music.
Florence, Biblioteca Riccardiana 2814, sixteenth century copy of lost thirteenth century Provençal ms (a).
Modena, Biblioteca Estense, Campori γ N.8.4; 11, 12, 13; continuation of a (a¹).
Rome, Biblioteca Vaticana, Barberiniani 4087, sixteenth century copy of a lost Provençal ms (b).
Modena, Biblioteca Estense, α R.4.4, Appendix to D; late sixteenth century copy of K (d).

The following are the relevant trouvère manuscripts, from Northern France:

Oxford, Bodleian Library, Douce 308, first half of the fourteenth century (I).

Paris, Bibl. de l'Arsenal 5198, thirteenth century (K); music.

Manuscrit du Roi (M = troubadour manuscript W, above).

Paris, Bibl. Nat., fr. 845 (N); music.

Paris, Bibl Nat., fr. 847, thirteenth century (P); music.

Chansonnier of St.-Germain-des-Prés, Lorraine, late thirteenth century (U = troubadour manuscript X, above).

Paris, Bibl. Nat., fr. 24406, thirteenth to fourteenth century (V); music.

Paris, Bibl. Nat. fr. 25566, late thirteenth century (W); music.

Paris, Bibl. Nat., n.a. fr. 1050, thirteenth century (X); music.

Marcabru, A la fontana *(PC293.1),* L'autrier *(PC293.30)*

Manuscripts

> *A la fontana:* C173.
>
> *L'autrier:* A33, C176–77, I120, K106, N266–67, R5, T205–06, a 310–11, d307–08.

Selected Editions

> Déjeanne.
>
> Paden, *The Medieval Pastourelle* (with translation).
>
> Rosenberg, Switten, and Le Vot (with translation).
>
> Gaunt, Harvey, and Paterson (with translation).

Texts as in Gaunt (*A la fontana* and *L'autrier* edited by Harvey and Gaunt, resp.). In *A la fontana* the manuscript has *l'erb era*, line 2; *equezentendes*, line 13. Gaunt's text of *L'autrier* follows a[1] with some corrections. In the title line 1, I adopt the more familiar *autrier* instead of Gaunt's *l'autrer*. There is a good deal of variation in spelling and vocabulary between mss. Gaunt notes that *atropellada* (48), "gathering together," a word recorded only here, plays on *tropel* in the sense of "flock of sheep," alluding to the girl's profession. Other editors print *genz anciana* (84), "the ancients," following CR, and suggesting an allusion to the Aristotelian Golden Mean.

Comtessa de Dia, Ab ioi et ab ioven *(PC46.1),* A chantar m'er *(PC46.2),* Estat ai *(PC46.4)*

Manuscripts

> *Ab ioi:* A167, B104, D85, H49, I141, K126, T197, a232.
>
> *A chantar:* A168, B104, C371, D85, G114, I141, K127, L120, M204, N229, R22, W204, a231, b12.
>
> *Estat ai:* A168, D85, I141, K137.

Selected Editions

> Rieger.
>
> Bruckner et al. (with translation).
>
> Rosenberg, Switten, and Le Vot (with translation).

Text as in Bruckner. *Ab ioi* and *A chantar* based on B, *Estat ai* on A. The first stanza only of *A chantar* is included in W, where it is accompanied by musical notation, the only trobairitz song for which music is preserved. In *Ab ioi* 29 I have adopted *que m'aia* as in Rieger and Rosenberg, instead of Bruckner's negative *non aia*; in *Ab ioi* 33 *Floris*, the reading of DIKT, as in Rieger and Rosenberg, instead of *Amics* as in ABa and Bruckner. The final lines of *Estat ai* have sometimes been understood as denying the lover full consummation. But "do all I'd wish" is not the same as "do *only* what I'd wish." See Rieger 623–25.

Raimbaut d'Aurenga and a Lady, Amics, en gran cosirier *(PC389.6)*

Manuscripts
C199, D90, M139.

Selected Editions
Pattison (with translation).
Rieger.
Bruckner et al. (with translation).

Text as in Bruckner et al., based on M.; Pattison and Rieger base their texts on C. The differences between C and M are mainly orthographic, but occasionally affect the sense. I have adopted *dans* ("harm," 30), from C, following Rieger, instead of M's *ditz,* "saying." C reads *vostr'* and *vos* (24, 27), making the slanderers the enemies of the lady rather than of both lovers. *Ospital* ("Hospital," 35) may be an allusion to "Raimbaut's predilection for the Hospitalers" (Pattison 158). *Serena* (51) elsewhere is a songbird, but apparently a hunting bird here.

Castelloza, Mout avetz faich lonc estatge *(PC109.3)*

Manuscripts
A169, I125, K111, N228, d311.

Selected Editions
Paden, "Castelloza" (with translation).
Rieger.
Bruckner et al. (with translation).
Rosenberg, Switten, and Le Vot (with translation).

Text as in Bruckner and Rieger, based on A. Paden's text is based on N, which differs significantly from A. The lacuna in 47–48, left blank by Bruckner, is here filled from N, as by Rieger.

En un vergier sotz fuella d'albespi *(PC141.113)*

Manuscript
C383.

Selected Editions
Bartsch, *Chrestomathie provençale.*
Bruckner et al.

Text as in Bruckner et al.

Quant lo gilos er fora *(PC461.201)*

Manuscript
Q5.

Selected Editions
Appel.
Mölk.

Text as in Mölk.

Quan vei los praz verdesir *(PC461.206)*

Manuscript
W198.

Selected Editions
Bartsch.
Mölk.
Rieger.

Text re-Occitanized as in Rieger, in the main following Bartsch. Mölk assumes an Occitan origin, but keeps the northern manuscript forms and is more conservative in his emendations: in particular, *mal agrea*, "is unpleasing" (Bartsch *m'a lograda*; ms. malegrea, 4); *et ves*, "torment (myself)" (Bartsch *e pes*; ms. et veill, 10).

A l'entrade del tens clar *(PC461.12)*

Manuscripts
X82.

Selected Editions
Bartsch.
Appel.
Hill and Bergin.

Text as in Appel and Hill-Bergin. Bartsch restores Occitan forms, but the manuscript may be Occitanized French rather than the reverse. Accompanied by musical notation in ms.

Richard de Semilly, L'autrier tout seus chevauchoie mon chemin *(RS 1362, L224.6)*

Manuscripts
K176, N84, P172, V48, X125.

Selected Editions
Paden, *Medieval Pastourelle* (with translation).
Johnson.

Text as in Paden, based on K. Accompanied by musical notation in all the mss.

Maroie de Diergnau, Mout m'abelist quant je voi revenir *(RS1451, L178.1)*

Manuscripts
M181, T169.

Selected Editions
Coldwell.
Doss-Quinby et al. (with translation).

Text as in Doss-Quinby; ed. Wendy Pfeffer, who notes that this single stanza "is followed by a blank space large enough to accommodate four more stanzas" (116). Accompanied by musical notation in mss.

Bele Yolanz en chambre koie *(RS1710, L222)*

Manuscript
U70.

Edition
Zink.

Text as in Zink.

Quant vient en mai, que l'on dit as lons jors *(RS2037, L265.1485)*

Manuscript
U69–70.

Selected Editions
Zink.
Rosenberg, Switten, and Le Vot (with translation).

Text as in Rosenberg; as in Zink except for one or two orthographical modifications. Lorraine forms: *meis* (*mes*), *lo* (*le*). A line may be missing near the end, but it is also possible the final stanza is shorter.

Jherusalem, grant damage me fais *(RS191, L265.939)*

Manuscript
M180.

Selected Editions
Bédier and Aubry.
Rosenberg, Switten, and Le Vot (with translation).
Doss-Quinby et al. (with translation).

Text as in Doss-Quinby, in the main identical to Rosenberg. The latter prints *aïst* (15). The three editions understand the ambiguous line 18 as "has more than one day's journey," but "only one" seems to me to fit the context better. This is not one of the songs accompanied by musical notation in M.

Adam de la Halle, Fi, maris, de vostre amour
(L45, van den Boogaard no. 74)

Manuscripts
W33; Rome, Vatican Regina lat. 1543, no. 746.

Selected Editions
van den Bogaard.
van der Werf.
Badel.

Text as in van den Boogaard.

Au cuer les ai, les jolis malz *(RS386, L265.154)*

Manuscript
I198–99.

Selected Editions
   Bartsch, *Romances et pastourelles françaises.*
   Bec, *Lyrique française.*
   Rosenberg and Tischler.
   Doss-Quinby et al. (with translation).

Text as in Doss-Quinby following Rosenberg-Tischler. Stanza 1: lit., "When the boor goes to market, / he doesn't go to bargain, / but to watch his wife / so no one seduces her." Stanza 3: lit., "Boor, do you expect to have everything, / both a pretty wife and lots of money?" The following are Lorraine forms: *lai* (*la*), *nuns* (*nus*), *amins* (*amis*), *vait* (*va*), *marchiet* (*marchie*), *ocidrait* (*ocidra*), *departirait* (*departira*).

Por coi me bait mes maris *(RS1564, L265.1346)*

Manuscript
   I197.

Selected Editions
   Bec, *Lyrique française.*
   Rosenberg and Tischler.
   Rosenberg, Switten, and Le Vot (with translation).
   Doss-Quinby et al. (with translation).

Text as in Doss-Quinby following Rosenberg-Tischler; identical to Rosenberg-Switten-Le Vot except for *riens* (2), *soulette* (4), in the latter. The following are Lorraine forms: *bait* (*bat*), *laisette* (*lassette*), *acolleir* (*acoller*), *dureir* (*durer*), *amin* (*ami*), *lou* (*le*).

Entre moi et mon amin *(RS1029, L265.665)*

Manuscript
   I207.

Selected Editions
   Bartsch, *Romances et pastourelles françaises.*
   Rosenberg and Tischler.
   Rosenberg, Switten, and Le Vot (with translation).
   Doss-Quinby et al. (with translation).

Text as in Doss-Quinby following Rosenberg-Tischler. The following are Lorraine forms: *amin* (*ami*), *boix* (*bois*), *baixait* (*baisait*), *vocexiens* (*voulussions*), *dixant* (*disant*), *lai* (*la*), *mairdi* (*mardi*), *juwant* (*jouant*); and some distinctive verb endings.

Guillaume de Machaut, Celle qui nuit et jour desire *(Le Livre du Voir Dit 727–39)*

Manuscripts
The principal manuscripts for the *Voir Dit* are three collections of the works of Machaut:
   Paris, Bibl. Nat. fr. 1584, fols. 221–306, ca. 1370 (A).
   Paris, Bibl. Nat. fr. 9221, fols. 171–210, 1390s (E).
   Paris, Bibl. Nat. fr. 22545, fols. 137–98, 1390s (F).

E bears the signature of Jean, Duc de Berry.

Selected Editions
Paris.
Leech-Wilkinson and Palmer.
Imbs.

Text as in Leech-Wilkinson, based on A. *Celle qui nuit et jour desire* appears on fol. 227r. Leech-Wilkinson largely retains the ms. presentation as regards punctuation and orthography. Line 739 is absent in E; Paris omits. Imbs's edition based on F. This poem is included in Letter 3; Letter 5 in Paris's arrangement.

Eustache Deschamps, Il me semble, a mon avis

Manuscript
Paris, Bibl. Nat. fr. 840, fols. 173–74, first quarter of fifteenth century.

Selected Editions
Saint-Hilaire and Raynaud.
Boudet and Millet.

Text as in Boudet-Millet.

Christine de Pizan, Seulete sui *(Cent Balades 11);* Doulce chose . . . mariage *(Autres Balades 26)*

Manuscripts
Paris, Bibl. Nat. fr. 835, ca. 1410, the "Manuscrit du Duc [de Berry]" (A1).
London, British Library, Harley 4431, shortly after A1, the "Manuscrit de la Reine [Isabeau de Bavière]" (A2).

Selected Editions
Roy.
Varty.

Text as in Varty, based on A2. Roy's edition of the complete works is based on A1 and follows the arrangement of the ms., grouping the poems by collections; his "Autres Balades" is ms. "balades de divers propos." Some editors print *messiée* in *Seulete sui* 12: "nothing so displeases me."

8   Medieval Europe: Latin and Macaronic

Plangit nonna

Manuscript
Rome, Biblioteca Vaticana, Vaticanus lat. 3251, fol. 178v, twelfth century.

Edition
Dronke, *Medieval Latin* 357–60.

Text as in Dronke. The manuscript is damaged and many letters are no longer legible. I adopt Dronke's restorations. Line 57 is very defective: ms. dormi ue mecum s . . . is.

Carmina Cantabrigiensia *14A, 40, 49*

Manuscript
Cambridge, University Library Gg. 5.35, copied at Canterbury ca. 1050, fols. 436r1, 441r1, 441v2, resp.

Selected Editions
Strecker.
Dronke, *Medieval Latin* 275–76 (CC 14A), 274 (CC 49).
Ziolkowski (with translation).

Text as in Ziolkowski, following Dronke. CC 14A is copied between stanzas 3b and 4a of CC 14, the story of the snow child. Most scholars regard it as a separate poem. The text of CC 49 is severely damaged.

Carmina Burana *126, 149, 185*

Manuscript
Bayerische Staatsbibliothek, clm 4660, fols. 52v and 72rv, resp., from the monastery of Benediktbeuern in Bavaria, but probably produced in southern Tyrol, ca. 1230 (M).

Selected Editions
Hilka and Schumann.
Blodgett and Swanson (translation only; for use with Hilka and Schumann).

Text as in Hilka and Schumann. In *CB* 126 the following stanza precedes the text:

Tempus instat floridum,
cantus crescit avium,
tellus dat solacium.
Eya!
qualia
sunt amoris gaudia!

("The time of flowers is at hand; the song of the birds increases; the earth gives solace. Oh, the delights of love!") In *CB* 185, H and S suggest that stanza 4 should perhaps be placed after stanza 6.

9   Germany

The most famous manuscript of medieval German lyrics is the large and handsomely illuminated Great Heidelberg, or Manesse, Codex. Sources for the medieval German lyrics included here are the following:

Heidelberg, Universitätsbibliothek, cod. pal. germ. 357, Alsace, ca. 1275, the Kleine Heidelberger Liederhandschrift (A).

Stuttgart, Württembergische Landesbibliothek, HB XIII poetae germanici 1, Constance, early fourteenth century, the Weingarten Manuscript (B).

Heidelberg, Universitätsbibliothek, cod. pal. germ. 848, Zurich, first half of the fourteenth century, the Grosse Heidelberger Liederhandschrift or Manesse Codex (C).

Munich, Universitätsbibliothek, 2 cod. 731, Würzburg, 1345–54, the Würzburg Manuscript (E).

Munich, Bayerische Staatsbibliothek, cgm 19, mid-thirteenth century, the *Parzival* Manuscript (G).

The *Carmina Burana* Manuscript (M); see above.

Munich, Bayerische Staatsbibliothek, clm 19411, late twelfth century, the Tegernsee Manuscript (T).

Berlin, Staatsbibliothek Preussischer Kulturbesitz, germ. fol. 779, Nuremberg?, second half of fifteenth century, a Neidhart collection (c).

Poems from A, B, C, and E are located by strophe number, not folio. The poems included here are cited by their traditional *Minnesangs Frühling* numbers, as well as by the new *MF* numbers assigned by Moser and Tervooren. Poems in the *Carmina Burana* cited by the *CB* number. Wolfram von Eschenbach and Walther von der Vogelweide cited by the Lachmann numbers, Otto von Botenlauben by the von Kraus number, Neidhart by the Hauptmann-Wiessner number.

Selected Editions

Moser and Tervooren (those poems that are cited by M-T numbers).

Kasten, *Frauenlieder* (all poems except *CB* 174A [*Chume, chume, geselle min*]).

Müller (*MF* 3.1, 3.7, 37.4; Walther L39.1; Neidhart HW3.22; Otto *KLD* 41).

Kasten, *Deutsche Lyrik* (*MF* 3.1, 3.7, 3.17, 6.5, 8.33, 37.4, 197.37, 217.14; Wolfram L4.8; Walther L39.1).

Other selected editions are indicated separately, beneath the relevant poems.

Texts as in Moser-Tervooren unless otherwise indicated.

Dû bist mîn *(MF 3.1, M-T 1.8)*

Manuscript

T, fol. 114v.

Contained in a Latin love-letter from a woman. The letter is printed in *MF* 3.2:318–20; German translation pages 521–23; page facsimile *MF* 2:169.

Waere diu werlt *(CB 145A, MF 3.7, M-T 1.9.1)*

Manuscript

M, fol. 60r.

Text as in M-T, except that I adopt the corrector's final n's in *mînen armen*. In the ms. chunich ("king") is crossed out and diu chuᵉnegin ("the queen") written above. M-T treats *Waere diu werlt* as the first half of a 2-stanza poem, the second half, *Taugen minne, diu ist guot* ("Secret love, that is good") on fol. 69v, like *Waere diu werlt* following a Latin poem *(CB 175)* in the ms. Kasten does not regard the two as connected; see *Deutsche Lyrik 577*.

Chume, chume, geselle min *(CB 174A)*

Manuscript

M, fol. 69v.

Selected Editions

Hilka and Schumann.

Vollmann.

Gérard.

not in Kasten.

Text as in Hilka-Schumann. Line 7: lit. "come and heal me." Gérard treats this poem as part of the preceding one, *Veni, veni, venias* ("Come, come, may you come"), *CB* 174: three Latin stanzas in a man's voice followed by these two in German.

Mich dunket niht sô guotes *(MF 3.17, M-T 1.10)*

Manuscripts
38 A.
14 C.

Text based on C. Attributed to Niune in A, to Alram von Gresten in C. Line 2 follows A.
C: diu minne minnesam.

Mir hât ein ritter *(MF 6.5, M-T 1.12)*

Manuscripts
46 A.

Attributed to Niune in the ms.

Der von Kürenberg, Ich zôch mir einem valken *(MF 8.33, 9.5; M-T 2.2.6)*

Manuscript
8–9 C.

The falcon is widely taken to be the lover. But see Kasten, who notes that a male speaker and other kinds of symbolism have been posited ("Poetologie" 15–16).

Dietmar von Aist, Ez stuont ein vrouwe alleine *(MF 37.4, M-T 8.4)*

Manuscript
12 C.

The ms. attribution to Dietmar has been disputed.

Hartmann von Aue, Diz waeren wunneclîche tage *(MF 217.14, M-T 22.16)*

Manuscript
55–57 C.

Reinmar der Alte, War kan iuwer schoener lîp *(MF 197.37, M-T 21.50)*

Manuscripts
236–41 C.

Zuo niuwen vröuden *(CB 143A, MF 203.10, M-T 21.59)*

360–61 E.
M, fol. 59rv (first stanza only).

Text based on E. The ms. attribution to Reinmar is disputed.

Wolfram von Eschenbach, Sîne klâwen *(L4.8, M-T 24.2)*

Manuscript
G, fol. 75v.

Moser-Tervooren slightly normalize the text. Earlier editors of *MF* do not include Wolfram. *Sîne klâwen*, along with another lyric, appears without authorial attribution at the end of the ms. In I.8 some editors print *în bî naht verliez*, following the ms.; others omit *bî naht* to correct the meter. In IV.6, many editors omit *der*.

Walther von der Vogelweide, Under der linden *(L39.11, Cormeau no. 16)*

Manuscripts
    42–45 B.
    128–31 C.

Selected Editions
    (Lachmann,) Cormeau et al.
    Kasten, *Frauenlieder*.
    Schweikle.

Text as in Kasten following C; identical to Cormeau, except for II.7 *Kuster mich* (Cormeau), and III.1 where I adopt *hat*, as in C and Cormeau, instead of Kasten's *het* (from B). II.5 *hêre frowe*, lit. "noble lady"; I understand this as an interjection addressed to the Virgin. Some scholars take these words as a reference to the speaker's self indicating that she is a high-born lady, that is, not the peasant girl typical of the pastourelle genre.

Otto von Botenlauben, Waere Kristes lôn niht alsô süeze *(KLD 41.12)*

Manuscript
    17–18 C.

Selected Editions
    Kasten, *Frauenlieder*.
    Kraus-Kornrumpf, *Liederdichter* (*KLD*).

Text as in Kraus-Kornrumpf.

Neidhart, Der meie der ist rîche *(HW3.22)*

Manuscripts
    222–26 C (stanzas I-V only).
    c, no. 55 (stanzas I-VII).

Selected Editions
    Kasten, *Frauenlieder*.
    Wiessner.

Text as in Wiessner, based on c, which diverges significantly from C in III.1–2, 4; IV.4. In V.4, *Riuwental* (Reuental), "Vale of Rue," may be a real or an allegorical place.

10   Italy

The poems included here are found either in *canzonieri*, songbooks, or as fillers in the Memoriali Bolognesi, the collection of legal contracts drawn up in Bologna. The *canzonieri* were copied in Northern Italy, but include material originally composed in the Sicilian dialect. The following are the relevant manuscripts:

Rome, Biblioteca Vaticana, lat. 3793, Florence, late thirteenth century (V; formerly A)
Florence, Biblioteca Nazionale di Firenze, Banco Rari 217, formerly Palatino
   418, Florence, late thirteenth century (P; formerly C)
Bologna, Archivio di Stato, Memoriali, 322 volumes dating 1265–1436.

In the following notes, minor emendations are not commented on. The Sicilian-dialect
texts are modified by Panvini to correct meter, rhyme, or sense.

King Frederick II of Sicily, Dolze meo drude

Manuscript
V, fol. 13rv, no. 48.

Selected Editions
Panvini.
Jensen.
Mölk.

Text as in Panvini. *Gioia* for ms. noia, "tiresomeness" (8); *la Toscana* for ms. la dolze
Toscana (15); *amore mi tene* for ms. amore che mi tene (25); *memoranza* for ms.
namoranza, "amorousness" (37).

Rinaldo d'Aquino, Ormai quando flore

Manuscript
P, fol. 27r, no. 46.

Selected Editions
Panvini.
Mölk.

Text as in Panvini. Lines 26–27 could also be understood as "that, in brief, the
love . . . ." *Che* (27) is an editorial insertion. *Mi sicura* for ms. mincora (36). The ending ora
emended to Sicilian *-ura* in stanza IV. *Senza rumore* (45), lit., "without noise."

Compiangomi, laimento

Manuscript
V, fol. 54v, no. 170.

Selected Editions
Panvini.
Mölk.

Text as in Panvini. *Dolze aulente* (4), lit., "sweet and sweet-smelling"; *afare* for ms.
affanno (26).

Tapina in me

Manuscript
V, fol. 158v, no. 797.

Selected Editions
  Contini.
  Panvini.
  Mölk.

Text as in Panvini.

La Compiuta Donzella, A la stagion

Manuscript
  V, fol. 129v, no. 510.

Selected Editions
  Contini.
  Mölk.

Text as in Contini.

Mamma, lo temp' è venuto

Manuscript
  Memoriali bolognesi 47, fol. 1v.

Selected Editions
  Contini.
  Orlando.
  Mölk.

Text as in Orlando. Identical to Contini except for the latter's ç for z in *plaçuto* (refrain), *plaçe* (5), etc.; x for s in *duxo* (34), *vixin* and *camixa* (56); also *pacto* (9), *c'aibi* (20), *ài* (42), *hom* (44), ò (48), *tutta nuda* (57). I follow Contini and Mölk in line 11: *te se* (Orlando *se te*).

Pàrtite, amore, adeo

Manuscript
  Memoriali bolognese 64, fol. 152v.

Selected Editions
  Orlando.
  Mölk.

Text as in Orlando.

11   Spain and Portugal

Galician-Portuguese

The *cantigas de amigo* are preserved principally in three codices, of which the Cancioneiro da Ajuda is the oldest. In addition, six of the seven poems of Martin Codax are preserved on a single leaf, the Sharrer Fragment (D), with musical notation. The following are the relevant manuscripts for the poems included here (sigla as in Brea):

  Lisbon, Cancioneiro da Biblioteca Nacional, cod. 10991, Italy, late fifteenth or early sixteenth century (B).

Rome, Cancioneiro da Biblioteca Vaticana, lat. 4803, Italy, late fifteenth or early sixteenth century (V).
New York, Pierpont Morgan Library 979, the Pergaminho Vindel, Portugal?, late thirteenth century (N).

Selected Editions
Nunes.
Jensen (with translation).
Brea.

Text as in Jensen, in the main identical to Nunes's edition of the *cantiga de amigo* corpus. Where Nunes differs, his version is noted in the following.

Martin Codax, Ondas do mar *(Nunes no. 491)*, Ai Deus *(Nunes no. 494)*

Manuscripts
Ondas do mar: B1278, V884, N1.
Ai Deus: B1281, V887, N4.

In *Ondas do mar*, Nunes prints *gram cuidado* (11); *coidado* (N) is the Galician variant (Jensen 512). Brea's edition comments that the arrangement in N suggests a narrative sequence; in such a sequence *Ai Deus* would precede *Ondas do mar*. See Brea 609, n. 213.

Nuno Fernandes Torneol, Levad', amigo *(Nunes no. 75)*, Vi eu, mia madr' *(Nunes no. 79)*

Manuscripts
B641, V242.

In *Levad', amigo*, Nunes emends to *manhãas* (1,4), and prints *diziam* (7), *enmentavam* (16), *banhanan* (23). He adds an eighth stanza to *Vi eu, mia madr', andar*; there is "no support in the transmitted evidence" for this reconstruction (Jensen 533).

Martin de Ginzo, Treides, ai mia madr', en romaria *(Nunes no. 485)*

Manuscripts
B1272, V878.

Nunes: *chamam* (2).

Pero Meogo, Digades, filha, mia filha velida *(Nunes no. 419)*

Manuscripts
B1192, V796.

Mendinho, Sedia-m'eu na ermida de San Simion *(Nunes no. 252)*

Manuscripts
B852, V438.

Nunes: *eu atendend'* (refrain).

Airas Nunez, Oí oj'eu *(Nunes no. 256),* Bailemos nós ja;
(Nunes 258)

Manuscripts
   Oí oj' eu: B868–70, V454.
   Bailemos nós ja: B879, V462.

In *Oí oj'eu,* Nunes supplies i: *estava i senlheira* (3), prints *rem, bem* (12, 13),*ũa guirlanda* (19), and emends to *caminho* (27); he arranges lines 30 ff. as three, rather than six, lines. Jensen regards the song snatches at the end of each stanza as fragments of real, probably popular, *cantigas de amigo* (Jensen lxx). In *Bailemos nós ja,* Nunes emends to *-ãa(s)* (7, 8, 9, 11). His emendation *so lo que bailemos* ("under which we dance," 17) is adopted by Jensen. Some editors retain ms. *sol que bailemos* ("provided that we dance").

King Denis of Portugal, Ai flores, ai flores do verde pino
(Nunes no. 19)

Manuscripts
   B568, V171.

Nunes: *pĩo* (1), *são* (14, 17, 19, 22). Since the pine is not a flowering tree, it has been suggested that *pino* may be a misinterpretation of Occitan *albespin,* "hawthorn." See Jensen 445. Lines 8 and 11 are inverted in V. The fifth stanza, missing in both mss., is restored on the basis of the parallelistic structure.

Johan Zorro, Cabelos *(Nunes no. 385),* Pela ribeira *(Nunes no. 389)*

Manuscripts
   Cabelos: B1154, V756.
   Pela ribeira: B1150, V753.

Jensen notes, "The basic value of *trebelhar* is . . . 'jugar, folgar' ['to play,' 'to have sex'],'' and that this is unusually explicit for a *cantiga de amigo* (Jensen 501).

Castilian

These Castilian lyrics are preserved in manuscripts and early printed books dating from the fifteenth century and later, especially in the *cancioneros,* or song collections. The following are the relevant collections for the poems included here:
   Seville, Biblioteca Colombina 7-1-28, Cancionero musical de la Colombina, end of the fifteenth century.
   Madrid, Biblioteca del Palacio Real 1335, Cancionero musical de Palacio, early sixteenth century.
   Madrid, Biblioteca Nacional de Madrid (BNM):
      2621, mid-sixteenth century.
      3915, dated 1620.
      5593, mid-sixteenth century.
   Luis de Milán, *Libro de música de vihuela de mano* (Valencia, 1536).
   Juan Fernández de Heredia, *Obras* (Valencia, 1562).
   Diego Pisador, *Libro de música de vihuela* (Salamanca, 1552).
   Juan Vásquez, *Recopilación de sonetos y villancicos* (Seville, 1560).
   ——, *Villancicos i canciones* (Osuna, 1551).
   Villancicos de diversos autores (*Cancionero de Upsala*) (Venice, 1556).

Except where otherwise indicated, the texts of these poems follow Frenk's edition. Differences between this and the other editions cited are mainly orthographical, but occasionally affect the sense. Editors also sometimes differ on the treatment of possible repetitions.

Aunque soi morena *(Frenk no. 140)*

Manuscript
   BNM 3915, fol. 320v.

Selected Editions
   Frenk.
   Alín.

Alín: *soy, olvidar.*

Agora que soy niña *(Frenk no. 207)*

Source
   Juan Vásquez, *Recopilación* 2, no. 12.

Selected Editions
   Alonso-Blecua.
   Frenk.
   Alín.

Alonso-Blecua, Alín: *monjía* (4, etc.), *queréis* (7). A somewhat similar 6-line poem, *No quiero ser monja, no,* "I don't want to be a nun, no!" is found in the Cancionero musical de Palacio, fol. 6r; see Alonso-Blecua, Perez Priego, Alín. Frenk prints only the opening distich of this one (Frenk no. 210).

Perdida traygo la color *(Frenk no. 273A)*

Source
   Juan Vásquez, *Villancicos,* no. 12.

Selected Editions
   Alonso-Blecua.
   Frenk.
   Alín.

Alonso-Blecua, Alín: *traigo, dicen, he* (refrain); Alín: *diicen* (7). A similar poem, *Perdida teñyo la color* (Frenk no. 273B) is preserved in Luis de Milán, *Libro de música,* fol. [93]v; this is the main version in Alín, with *Perdida traigo la color* included as a variant.

No pueden dormir mis ojos *(Frenk no. 302C)*

Manuscript
   Cancionero musical de Palacio.

Selected Editions
   Alonso-Blecua.
   Frenk.
   Alín.

I adopt the emendation *el vino,* "he came" (6), suggested in Frenk's notes and printed in Alonso-Blecua's and Alín's texts, for ms. el lyino. Alonso-Blecua, Alín: *soñaba, rosa.*

Dentro en el vergel *(Frenk no. 308B)*

Manuscript
  Cancionero musical de Palacio, fol. 247r.

Selected Editions
  Frenk.
  Perez Priego.
  Alín.

Frenk reconstructs lines 8 and 10, not in the ms. Alonso-Blecua and Alín print without these lines. Alonso-Blecua, Alín: *rosal, rosas.* Alonso-Blecua: *matarm' han; m' iba.* Alín: *matarme han; me iba.*

So ell enzina, enzina *(Frenk no. 313)*

Manuscript
  Cancionero musical de Palacio, fol. 13r.

Selected Editions
  Alonso-Blecua.
  Frenk.
  Perez Priego.
  Alín.

Ms. del que yo más quería (31). Frenk's reconstructions of repeated lines do not appear in Alonso-Blecua's or Perez Priego's texts. Alonso-Blecua, Alín: *encina, iba, fuí, dejé, brazos, cuitada, gozaba, romería.* Alín: *el* (refrain).

Niña y viña *(Frenk no. 314C)*

Manuscript
  Cancionero musical de la Colombina, fol. 72v.

Selected Editions
  Alonso-Blecua.
  Frenk.
  Perez Priego.
  Alín.

In the other three editions, stanza 4 precedes stanza 3. I adopt *de la mi camisa* (12), as suggested in Frenk's notes and printed in Perez Priego's and Alín's texts (Frenk prints *dile mi camisa*, "I gave him my slip"). I arrange the *estribillo* in 3 lines, as in Alín. Alonso-Blecua, Alín: *habar* (refrain), *oh* (4,9). Alonso-Blecua: *fuí a cortar* (6). Line 5 could be *mañanita*, as in Perez Priego and Alín. Alonso-Blecua: *dile yo mi cinta*, "I gave him my belt" (12, my text). Editors variously reconstruct lines 21–23, beginning "I gave him." Alonso-Blecua: "dile yo un cordone, / dile yo una banda" (" . . . a sash . . . a band"); Perez Priego, Alín: "yo dile una cinta / de la mi delgada" (" . . . a belt from my [dress of] fine cloth").

Al alva venid, buen amigo *(Frenk no. 452)*

Manuscript
  Cancionero musical de Palacio, fol. 5r.

Selected Editions
  Alonso-Blecua.
  Frenk.
  Perez Priego.
  Alín.

Alonso-Blecua, Perez Priego, Alín: *alba*. This poem is variously arranged by editors. Alonso-Blecua, Alín: 5 distichs only, no repeated refrain. Perez Priego: 6 distichs. In distich 2 he prints *venid al alba del dia*; his distich 4 is identical to distich 2, my text.

Si la noche hace escura *(Frenk no. 573)*

Manuscript
  Cancionero de Upsala, fol. 7v.

Selected Editions
  Alonso-Blecua.
  Frenk.
  Perez-Priego.
  Alín.

Text as in Alín similiarly Alonso-Blecua and Perez Priego. Frenk prints a shorter version as in Fernández de Heredia, *Obras*, fol. 87v; also in BNM 2621, fol. 91v; BNM 5593, fol. 82v. Alonso-Blecua also prints another version, following Diego Pisador's *Libro música de vihuela*, fol. 9, which has a different *glosa* (see Alonso-Blecua nos. 30 and 39). Alín remarks that the song had a wide diffusion (Alín 107, n.).

12   Later Medieval England

These poems are preserved, usually in one manuscript only, in collections of songs dating from ca. 1300 to ca. 1500. Most of these lyrics are anonymous. They are catalogued by title in the *Index of Middle English Verse* (*IMEV*). Poems included here are cited by *IMEV* number and by the number in Greene's edition.

Selected Editions
  Brown (*IMEV* 360).
  Robbins (all poems except *IMEV* 360).
  Luria and Hoffman (all poems).
  Greene (all poems).
  Duncan (*IMEV* 360, 377).

Texts of all poems based on Greene. Thorn (þ) is here represented by th, yogh (ȝ) by gh, or eliminated where silent; th is represented by t where required by the pronunciation; sch by ch or sh; other letter sequences are occasionally modified in the direction of modern spelling.

Now springes the spray *(IMEV 360, Greene no. 450)*

Manuscript
  London, Lincoln's Inn, Hale 135, fol. 137v.

The poem may be based on an Old French original *L'autrier defors Picarni*. See Bartsch, *Romanzen und Pastourellen*, no. 2.

Wolde God that hyt were so *(IMEV 3418, Greene no. 451)*

Manuscript
   Cambridge University Add. 5943 (formerly Lord Howard de Walden MS), fol. 178v, fifteenth century.

Robbins notes that "the appropriate feminine pronouns [*sche* and *hyre*] have been interlined in another hand." Greene comments: "The changing in MS of the gender of the pronouns throughout a medieval love-lyric is rare, if not unique to this text" (Notes). On this gender-switching see also Klinck "Poetic Markers of Gender." The repetition of line 10/11 may be an error; Greene suggests "he maketh haste to go me fro" (Notes).

Rybbe ne rele ne spynne yc ne may
(IMEV 225, Greene no. 452)

Manuscript
   Cambridge, Gonville and Caius College 383, page 41, fifteenth century.

The language of this poem is difficult. I follow Greene, but see Cartlidge 403, n. 22, for some significant criticisms of Greene's text. Robbins prints *wybbe* ("to weave") in the burden; *wond* ("wound," 2); *þredele* ("thread," that is, fasten, 16,18); *þrot* ("throat, 41). I have changed *ch* (ms. and Greene) to *t* (rather than *th*) to indicate the pronunciation of ms. vlech, unbech, yech (9–11), and ale-shoch, wroch (40–41). The poem shows some Southern dialect forms: ms. vond ("found," 4), vlech ("floor," 9), yut ("yet," 29), murgust ("merriest," 59).

Alas, alas the wyle *(IMEV 1849, Greene no. 453)*

Manuscript
   Gonville and Caius 383, page 41.

I adopt Y ("I") as in Brown and others, which makes better sense than Greene's "that *he* was gay" ("that *he* was attractive," 9). Greene understands "rong the bell" (66) as "achieve[d] orgasm." "[Y]served the ragged devel of helle" (68) presumably means "had sex."

A, dere God, what I am fayn
(IMEV 3594, Greene no. 454)

Manuscript
   Cambridge, St. John's College, S. 54, fol. 2v, fifteenth century.

For the sake of the rhyme, I adopt Brown's emendations *layne* ("hide," 6), *mayn* ("strength," 12), and (infinitive) *sayn, pleyn* (18, 24), instead of Greene's *lerne* ("learn," ms. lene), *may, say, pley*. Robbins emends ms. qage (23) to *rage*, that is, ardor, Greene to *quage* (meaning "wage"?). Cartlidge understands this poem very differently, interpreting *fayn* ("vain") in the refrain as "glad," and *gane* ("gone") as "again" (Cartlidge 395–97).

Were it undo that is ydo *(IMEV 1330, Greene no. 455)*

Manuscript
   Gonville and Caius 383, page 210.

I have forsworn hit whil I live *(IMEV 3409, Greene no. 456)*

Manuscript
Cambridge University Library, Ff. 5.48, fol. 114v, fifteenth century.

Greene comments: "Sir John is probably the village priest, or at any rate a cleric." Brown prints *kell-ey* (13) and glosses *kell* "maidenhead."

Kyrie, so kyrie *(IMEV 377, Greene no. 457)*

Manuscript
London, British Library, Sloane 2593, fol. 34r, fifteenth century.

Greene explains "pax-brede" as "the disc of silver or gilt with a handle and a sacred symbol used in giving the 'kiss of peace' to the congregation" (Notes).

Hey, noyney *(IMEV 2494, Greene no. 456.1)*

Manuscript
San Marino, Ca., Huntington EL 1160 (formerly Ellesmere MS), fol. 11r., ca. 1500.

I pray yow, cum kyss me *(IMEV 150, Greene no. 443)*

Manuscript
Canterbury Cathedral, Christ Church Letters 2.173, ca. 1500.

The author may have been a monk at Christ Church monastery. A damaged colophon in the ms. reads "Finys quod wulstane p . . . one" ("The end of what Wulstan P . . . [wrote?]"). Greene very tentatively suggests that the author might be identified with a Will Preston who died in 1457. Brown understands *karchos nocke* as "cleft in the buttocks." See his Glossary.

WORKS CITED

Acallam na Senórach. See Dooley and Roe; Murphy.

Akehurst, F.R.P. and Judith M. Davis, eds. *A Handbook of the Troubadours*. Berkeley and Los Angeles: University of California Press, 1995.

Alcman. See Calame; Campbell; Page.

Alín, José María, ed. *Cancionero traditional*. Madrid: Castalia, 1991.

Al-Maqqari. *Nafh at-tib min gusn al-Andalus ar-ratib*. 8 vols. Ed. Ihsan 'Abbas. Beirut: Dar Sadir, 1968.

Alonso, D. and J.M. Blecua, eds. *Antología de la poesía española de tipo tradicional*. Madrid: Gredos, 1956.

Al-Suyuti. *Nuzhat al-julasa' fi ash'ar an-nisa'*. Ed. Salah ad-Din al-Munajjid. Beirut: Dar al-kitab al-jadid, 1978.

Anderson, Sarah M., ed., with Karen Swenson. *Cold Counsel: Women in Old Norse Literature and Mythology*. New York: Routledge, 2002.

Appel, Carl. *Provenzalische Chrestomathie*. 2nd ed. Leipzig: Reisland, 1902.

Aristophanes. See Henderson; Parker; Sommerstein; Ussher.

Ashley, Kathleen. "Voice and Audience: The Emotional World of the *cantigas de amigo*." Plummer 35–45.

Astell, Ann W. *The Song of Songs in the Middle Ages*. Ithaca: Cornell University Press, 1990.

Auerbach, Erich. Review of Theodor Frings, *Minnesinger und Troubadours. Romance Philology* 4 (1950–51): 65–67.

Badel, Pierre-Yves, ed. and trans. *Adam de la Halle, Oeuvres complètes*. Paris: Librairie Générale Française, 1995.

Barlow, Shirley A. *Euripides: Trojan Women*. Warminster: Aris & Phillips, 1986.

Bartsch, Karl. *Romances et pastourelles françaises des XIIe et XIIe siècles: Altfranzösische Romanzen und Pastourellen*. Leipzig, 1870. Repr. Darmstadt: Wissenschaftliche Buchgesellschaft, 1967.

——. *Chrestomathie provençale, (Xe – XVe siècles)*. Entièrement refondue par Eduard Koschwitz, 6th ed. Marburg: Elwert, 1904. Repr. Geneva: Slatkine, 1973.

Bec, Pierre. "Quelques réflexions sur la poésie lyrique médiévale. Problèmes et essai de caracterisation." *Mélanges offerts à Rita Lejeune*. Gembloux: Duculot, 1969. 2: 1309–29 (paginated continuously).

——. *La lyrique française au Moyen Âge, XIIe-XIIIe siècles*. 2 vols. Paris: Picard, 1977–78.

——. "*Trobairitz* et chansons de femme. Contribution à la connaissance du lyrisme féminin au Moyen Âge." *Cahiers de Civilisation Médiévale* 22 (1979): 235–62.

——. *Chants d'amour des femmes-troubadours: Trobairitz et "chansons de femme."* Paris: Stock, 1995.

Bédier, Joseph and Pierre Aubry, eds. *Les chansons de croisade*. Paris: Champion, 1909. Repr. Geneva: Slatkine, 1974.

Belanoff, Patricia. "Women's Songs, Women's Language: *Wulf and Eadwacer* and *The Wife's Lament*." *New Readings on Women in Old English Literature*. Ed. Helen Damico and Alexandra Hennessey Olsen. Bloomington: Indiana University Press, 1990. 193–203.

Belanoff, Patricia. "*Ides . . . geomrode giddum*: The Old English Female Lament." Klinck and Rasmussen 29–46 and 214–18.

Benabu, Isaac and Joseph Yahalom. "The Importance of the Genizah Manuscripts for the Establishment of the Text of the Hispano-Romance *Kharjas* in Hebrew Characters." *Romance Philology* 40 (1986): 139–58.

Bennett, Judith M. "Ventriloquisms: When Maidens Speak in English Songs, c. 1300–1550." Klinck and Rasmussen 187–204 and 253–59.

Blodgett, E.D. and R.A. Swanson, trans. *Love Songs of the Carmina Burana*. New York: Garland, 1987.

Blumenfeld-Kosinski, Renata, ed., with Kevin Brownlee, trans. *The Selected Writings of Christine de Pizan*. Norton Critical Edition. New York: Norton, 1997.

Boudet, Jean-Patrice and Hélène Millet, eds. *Eustache Deschamps en son temps*. Paris: Sorbonne, 1997.

Bowers, Jane and Judith Tick, eds. *Women Making Music: The Western Art Tradition, 1150–1950*. Urbana: University of Illinois Press, 1986.

Boynton, Susan. "Women's Performance of the Lyric Before 1500." Klinck and Rasmussen 47–65 and 219–23.

Bragg, Lois. *The Lyric Speakers of Old English Poetry*. Rutherford: Fairleigh Dickinson University Press, 1991.

Bray, Dorothy Ann. "A Woman's Loss and Lamentation: Heledd's Song and *The Wife's Lament*." *Neophilologus* 79 (1995): 147–54.

Brea, Mercedes, ed. *Lírica profana galego-portuguesa. Corpus completo das cantigas medievais, con estudio biográfico, análise retórica e bibliografía específica*. 2 vols., paginated continuously. Santiago de Compostela: Centro de Investigacións Lingüísticas e Literarias Ramón Piñero, 1996.

Brown, Carleton, ed. *English Lyrics of the XIIIth Century*. Oxford: Clarendon, 1932.

——and Rossell Hope Robbins. *The Index of Middle English Verse*. New York: Columbia University Press, 1943.

Brownlee, Kevin. *Poetic Identity in Guillaume de Machaut*. Madison: University of Wisconsin Press, 1984.

Bruckner, Matilda Tomaryn. "Fictions of the Female Voice." *Speculum* 67 (1992): 865–91. Repr. with minor modifications Klinck and Rasmussen 127–51 and 239–45.

——, Laurie Shepard, and Sarah White, eds. and trans. *Songs of the Women Troubadours*. New York: Garland, 1995, 2000.

Burns, E. Jane. "Sewing Like a Girl: Working Women in the *chansons de toile*." Klinck and Rasmussen 99–126 and 232–39.

——, Sarah Kay, Roberta L. Krueger, and Helen Solterer. "Feminism and the Discipline of Old French Studies: Une Belle Disjointure." *Medievalism and the Modernist Temper*. Ed. R. Howard Block and Stephen G. Nichols. Baltimore: Johns Hopkins University Press, 1996. 225–66.

Cairns, Francis. *Virgil's Augustan Epic*. Cambridge: Cambridge University Press, 1989.

Calame, Claude. *Choruses of Young Women in Ancient Greece*. Trans. D. Collins and J. Orion. Lanham, Md.: Rowman & Littlefield, 1997. With updated bibliography, from *Les choeurs de jeunes filles en Grèce archaïque* (Rome: Università di Urbino, 1977).

Campbell, David, ed. and trans. *Greek Lyric*. 5 vols. Loeb. Cambridge, Mass.: Harvard University Press, 1982–93.

Carson, Anne, ed. and trans. *If Not, Winter: Fragments of Sappho*. New York: Knopf, 2002.

Cartlidge, Neil. " 'Alas, I Go with Chylde.' Representations of Extra-Marital Pregnancy in Middle English Lyric." *English Studies* 79 (1998): 395–414.

Cerquiglini-Toulet. See Imbs.

Cheyette, Fredric and Margaret Switten. "Women in Troubadour Song: Of the Comtessa and the Vilana." *Women and Music: A Journal of Gender and Culture* 2 (1998): 24–46.

Christine de Pizan. See Roy; Varty.

Clauss, James J. and Sarah Iles Johnston, eds. *Medea: Essays on Medea in Myth, Literature, Philosophy, and Art*. Princeton, Princeton University Press, 1997.

Cohen, Judith. "*Ca no soe joglaresa*: Women and Music in Medieval Spain's Three Cultures." Klinck and Rasmussen 66–80 and 223–28.

Coldwell, Maria V. "*Jougleresses* and *Trobairitz*: Secular Musicians in Medieval France." *Women Making Music: The Western Art Tradition*. Ed. Jane Bowers and Judith Tick. Urbana: University of Illinois Press, 1986. 39–61.

Compton, Linda Fish. *Andalusian Lyrical Poetry and Old Spanish Love Songs*. New York: New York University Press, 1976.

Contini, Gianfranco. *Poeti del Duecento*. 2 vols. La Letteratura italiana storia e testi 2. Milan: Ricciardi, 1960.

Cormeau, Christoph, ed. *Walther von der Vogelweide: Leich, Lieder, Sangsprüche*. 14th ed. Revision of editions by Karl Lachmann et al. With contributions by Thomas Bein and Horst Brunner. Berlin: de Gruyter, 1996.

Cornish, Francis Warre et al., eds. and trans. *Catullus, Tibullus, and Pervigilium Veneris*. Catullus trans. F.W. Cornish; Tibullus trans. J.P. Postgate; *Pervig. Ven.* trans. J.W. MacKail. 2nd ed., rev. G.P. Goold. Loeb. Cambridge, Mass.: Harvard University Press, 1988.

Corral, Esther. "Feminine Voices in the Galician-Portuguese *cantigas de amigo*." Trans. Judith Cohen with Anne L. Klinck. Klinck and Rasmussen 81–98 and 228–32.

Croally, N.T. *Euripidean Polemic: The Trojan Women and the Function of Tragedy*. Cambridge: Cambridge University Press, 1994.

Cummins, John. *The Spanish Traditional Lyric*. Oxford: Pergamon, 1977.

de Clercq, Charles, ed. *Concilia Galliae, A.511–A.695*. Corpus Christianorum Series Latina 148a. Turnhout: Brepols, 1964.

Déjeanne, J.M.L. *Poésies complètes du troubadour Marcabru*. Toulouse: Privat, 1909. Repr. New York: Johnson, 1971.

Deschamps, Eustache. See Boudet and Millet; Saint-Hilaire and Raynaud.

Desmond, Marilynn. "When Dido Reads Virgil: Gender and Intertextuality in Ovid's *Heroides* 7." *Helios* 20 (1993): 56–68.

——. *Reading Dido: Gender, Textuality, and the Medieval Aeneid*. Minneapolis: University of Minnesota Press, 1994.

Deyermond, Alan. "Lust in Babel: Bilingual Man-Woman Dialogues in the Medieval Lyric." *Nunca fue pena mayor: Estudios de literatura española en homenaje a Brian Dutton*. Ed. Ana Menéndez Collera and Victoriano Roncero López. Cuenca: Universidad de Castilla-La Mancha, 1996. 199–221.

Dhakhira. See Ibn Bassam.

Diggle, James, ed. *Euripidis Fabulae*. 3 vols. Oxford Classical Texts. Oxford: Clarendon, 1981 (2), 1984 (1), 1994 (3).

Dooley, Ann and Harry Roe, eds. and trans. *Tales of the Elders of Ireland (Acallam na Senórach)*. Oxford: Oxford University Press, 1999.

Doss-Quinby, Eglal, Joan Tasker Grimbert, Wendy Pfeffer, and Elizabeth Aubrey, eds. *Songs of the Women Trouvères*. New Haven: Yale University Press, 2001.

Dronke, Peter. *The Medieval Lyric*. 1968. 3rd ed. Woodbridge: Brewer, 1996.

——. *Medieval Latin and the Rise of European Love-Lyric*. 2nd ed. 2 vols. Oxford: Clarendon, 1968.

Dronke, Ursula, ed. *The Poetic Edda, Vol. 1: Heroic Poems*. Oxford: Clarendon, 1969.

Duncan, Thomas, ed. *Medieval English Lyrics, 1200–1400*. London: Penguin, 1995.

Earnshaw, Doris. *The Female Voice in Medieval Romance Lyric*. New York: Lang, 1988.

Edmonds, J.M., ed. and trans. *The Greek Bucolic Poets*. Loeb. Cambridge, Mass.: Harvard University Press, 1912, 1928.

Euripides. See Diggle; Kovacs; Page.

Fairclough, H.R., ed. *Virgil*. Rev. ed. 2 vols. Loeb. Cambridge, Mass.: Harvard University Press, 1935.

Faral, Edmond. "Les chansons de toile ou chansons d'histoire." *Romania* 69 (1946–47): 453–59.

Ferrante, Joan. *Woman as Image in Medieval Literature, from the Twelfth Century to Dante.* New York: Columbia University Press, 1975.

——. "Male Fantasy and Female Reality in Courtly Literature." *Women's Studies* 11 (1984): 67–97.

——. "Notes Towards the Study of a Female Rhetoric in the Trobairitz." Paden, *Voice of the Trobairitz* 63–72.

Fowler, Barbara Hughes. *Songs of a Friend: Love Lyrics of Medieval Portugal.* Chapel Hill: University of North Carolina Press, 1996.

Frenk, Margit. *Corpus de la lírica antigua popular hispánica (siglos xv a xvii).* Madrid: Castalia, 1987.

——. "Fija, ¿quiéreste casar?" ["Daughter, do you want to get married"]. Menéndez Collera and Roncero López 259–74.

——. "Símbolos naturales en las viejas canciones populares hispánicas." Piñero Ramírez 159–82.

Frings, Theodor. *Minnesinger und Troubadours.* Berlin: Akademie, 1949.

Gaissner, Julia Haig. "Threads in the Labyrinth: Competing Views and Voices in Catullus 64." *American Journal of Philology* 116 (1995): 579–616.

Galmés de Fuentes, Álvaro. "Las jarchas mozárabes y la tradición lírica románica." Piñero Ramírez 27–53.

García Gómez, Emilio. *Las jarchas romances de la serie árabe en su marco.* 3rd ed. Madrid: Alianzo, 1990.

Garulo, Teresa. *Dīwān de las poetisas de al-Andalus.* Madrid: Hiperión, 1986.

Gaunt, Simon. *Gender and Genre in Medieval French Literature.* Cambridge: Cambridge University Press, 1995.

——, Ruth Harvey, and Linda Paterson, eds. *Marcabru: A Critical Edition.* Cambridge: Brewer, 2000.

—— and Sarah Kay, eds. *The Troubadours: An Introduction.* Cambridge: Cambridge University Press, 1999.

Gérard, Marcel, ed. and trans. *Les chansons d'amour des Carmina Burana.* Luxembourg: Saint-Paul, 1990.

Gibbs, Marion E. and Sidney M. Johnson. *Medieval German Literature.* New York: Garland, 1997. Repr. Routledge, 2000.

Goold, G.P., ed. and trans., *Catullus.* 2nd ed. London: Duckworth, 1989.

Gordon, Pam. "The Lover's Voice in *Heroides* 15: Or, Why is Sappho a Man?" Hallett and Skinner 274–91.

Gow, A.S.F., ed. and trans. *Theocritus.* 2nd ed. 2 vols. Cambridge: Cambridge University Press, 1952.

Greene, Richard Leighton, ed. *The Early English Carols.* 1935. 2nd ed. Oxford: Clarendon, 1977.

Grimbert, Joan. See Doss-Quinby.

Gulick, Charles Burton, ed. and trans. *Athenaeus: The Deipnosophists.* 7 vols. Loeb. Cambridge, Mass.: Harvard University Press, 1927–41.

Hallett, Judith. "Women's Voices and Catullus' Poetry." *Classical World* 95 (2002): 421–24.

—— and Marilyn B. Skinner, eds. *Roman Sexualities.* Princeton: Princeton University Press, 1997.

Hamer, Richard, ed. and trans. *A Choice of Anglo-Saxon Verse.* London: Faber, 1970.

Hartmann, Wilfried, ed. *Die Konzilien der karolingischen Teilreich 843–59.* Monumenta Germaniae Historica, Concilia 3. Hannover: Hahn, 1984.

Hatto, Arthur T., ed. *Eos: An Inquiry into the Theme of Lovers' Meetings and Partings at Dawn in Poetry.* The Hague: Mouton, 1965.

Heale, Elizabeth. "Women and the Courtly Love Lyric: The Devonshire Ms (BL Additional 17492)." *Modern Language Review* 90 (1995): 297–313.

Heger, Klaus. *Die bisher veröffentlichten Harğas und ihre Deutungen.* Tübingen: Niemeyer, 1960.

Henderson, Jeffrey, ed. and trans. *Aristophanes.* 4 vols. Loeb. Cambridge, Mass.: Harvard University Press, 2002.

Hilka, Alfons and Otto Schumann, eds. *Carmina Burana 1.2. Die Liebeslieder.* Heidelberg: Winter, 1941.

Hill, R.T. and T.G. Bergin, eds. *Anthology of Provençal Troubadours.* New Haven: Yale University Press, 1973.

Hitchcock, Richard. "The Girls from Cádiz and the Kharjas." *Journal of Hispanic Philology* 15 (1991): 103–16.

Holst-Warhaft, Gail. *Dangerous Voices: Women's Laments and Greek Literature.* London: Routledge, 1992.

Holzberg, Niklas. "Four Poets and a Poetess or a Portrait of the Poet as a Young Man? Thoughts on Book 3 of the *Corpus Tibullianum.*" *Classical Journal* 94 (1999): 169–91.

Huchet, Jean-Charles. "Les femmes troubadours ou la voix critique." *Littérature* 51 (1983): 59–90.

Ibn Bassam. *Al-Dhakhira fi mahasin ahl al-Jazira.* Ed. Ihsan 'Abbas. Beirut: Dar al-Thaqafa, 1979.

Ibn Sana' al-Mulk. See Compton; Heger.

†Imbs, Paul and Jacqueline Cerquiglini-Toulet. *Guillaume de Machaut, Le Livre du Voir-Dit.* Ed. and trans. Imbs; introduction and revision Cerquiglini-Toulet. Livre de Poche, Lettres gothiques. Paris: Librairie Générale Française, 1999.

Index of Middle English Verse. See Brown.

Ingalls, Wayne B. "Ritual Performance as Training for Daughters in Archaic Greece." *Phoenix* 54 (2000): 1–20.

Jackson, William E. *Reinmar's Women: A Study of the Woman's Song of Reinmar der Alte.* Amsterdam: Benjamins, 1981.

Jeanroy, Alfred. *Les origines de la poésie lyrique en France au Moyen Âge.* 1889. 4th ed. Paris: Champion, 1965.

Jensen, Frede. *The Earliest Portuguese Lyrics.* Odense: Odense University Press, 1978.

——, ed. and trans. *The Poetry of the Sicilian School.* New York: Garland, 1986.

——. *Medieval Galician-Portuguese Poetry: An Anthology.* New York: Garland, 1992.

——. *Tuscan Poetry of the Duecento: An Anthology.* New York: Garland, 1994.

Jochens, Jenny. *Old Norse Images of Women.* Philadelphia: University of Pennsylvania Press, 1996.

Johnson, Susan M., ed. *The Lyrics of Richard de Semilli: A Critical Edition and Musical Transcription.* Medieval & Renaissance Texts and Studies 81. Binghamton: Center for Medieval and Early Renaissance Studies SUNY, 1992.

Jones, Alan. *Romance Kharjas in Andalusian Arabic Muwaššaḥ Poetry: A Palaeographical Analysis.* London: Ithaca, 1988.

——and Richard Hitchcock, eds. *Studies on the Muwaššaḥ and the Kharja.* Reading: Ithaca, 1991.

Kasten, Ingrid. "The Conception of Female Roles in the Woman's Song of Reinmar and the Comtessa de Dia." Trans. Ann Marie Rasmussen. Klinck and Rasmussen 152–67 and 246–49. From "Weibliches Rollenverständnis in den Frauenliedern Reinmars und der Comtessa de Dia." *Germanisch-romanische Monatsschrift* 37 (1987): 131–46.

——, ed. and trans. *Frauenlieder des Mittelalters.* Stuttgart: Reclam, 1990.

——, ed. and Margherita Kuhn, trans. *Deutsche Lyrik des frühen und hohen Mittelalters.* Frankfurt: Deutscher Klassiker Verlag, 1995.

Kay, Sarah. "Derivation, Derived Rhyme, and the Trobairitz." Paden, *Voice of the Trobairitz* 157–82.

Keith, Alison. "*Tandem venit amor*: A Roman Woman Speaks of Love." Hallett and Skinner 295–310.

Kelley, Mary Jane. "Virgins Misconceived: Poetic Voice in the Mozarabic *Kharjas.*" *La Corónica* 19.2 (1991): 1–23.

Klinck, Anne L. *The Old English Elegies: A Critical Edition and Genre Study*. Montreal and Kingston: McGill-Queen's University Press, 1992. Repr. with updated bibliography 2001.

——. "The Oldest Folk Poetry? Medieval Woman's Song as 'Popular' Lyric." *From Arabye to Engelond: Medieval Studies in Honour of Mahmoud Manzalaoui on His 75th Birthday*. Ed. A.E. Christa Canitz and Gernot R. Wieland. Ottawa: University of Ottawa Press, 1999. 229–52.

——. "Sappho and Her Daughters: Some Parallels Between Ancient and Medieval Woman's Song." Klinck and Rasmussen 15–28 and 209–14.

——. "Poetic Markers of Gender in Medieval 'Woman's Song': Was Anonymous a Woman?" *Neophilologus* 87 (2003): 339–59.

——and Ann Marie Rasmussen, eds. *Medieval Woman's Song: Cross-Cultural Approaches*. Philadelphia: University of Pennsylvania Press, 2002.

Knox, Peter E., ed. *Ovid: Heroides: Select Epistles*. Cambridge: Cambridge University Press, 1995.

Koch, John and John Carey. *The Celtic Heroic Age*. Andover, Mass.: Celtic Studies Publications, 2000.

Kornrumpf. See Kraus.

Kovacs, David, ed. and trans. *Euripides*. 6 vols. Loeb. Cambridge, Mass.: Harvard University Press, 1995–2003.

Kraus, Carl von. *Deutsche Liederdichter des 13. Jahrhunderts*. 2nd ed. 2 vols. 1: Text, continued Gisela Kornrumpf. 2: Commentary, corrected Hugo Kuhn, rev. G. Kornrumpf. Tübingen: Niemeyer, 1978.

Lachmann, Karl, ed. *Die Gedichte Walthers von der Vogelweide*. See Cormeau.

——et al., eds. *Des Minnesangs Frühling*. See Moser and Tervooren.

Larrington, Carolyne, trans. *The Poetic Edda*. Oxford: Oxford University Press, 1996.

Lee, K.H., ed. *Euripides: Troades*. London: Macmillan, 1976.

Leech-Wilkinson, Daniel, ed. and R. Barton Palmer, trans. *Guillaume de Machaut, Le Livre dou Voir Dit (The Book of the True Poem)*. New York: Garland, 1998.

Linker, Robert White. *A Bibliography of Old French Lyrics*. Romance Monographs Inc. 31. University Miss.: Romance Monographs, 1979.

Lobel, Edgar and Denys Page, eds. *Poetarum Lesbiorum Fragmenta*. Oxford: Clarendon, 1955.

Luria, Maxwell S. and Richard L. Hoffman, eds. *Medieval Lyrics*. New York: Norton, 1974.

Machaut, Guillaume de. See Imbs; Leech-Wilkinson; Paris.

MacLachlan, Bonnie. "Love, War and the Goddess in Fifth-Century Locri." *The Ancient World* 26 (1995): 203–23.

Maqqari. See al-Maqqari.

Marnette, Sophie. "L'expression féminine dans la poésie lyrique occitane." *Romance Philology* 11 (1997): 170–93.

Masera, Mariana. "Tradición, oral y escrita en el *Cancionero musical de Palacio*: el símbolo del cabello como atributo erótico de la belleza feminina." *Cancionero Studies in Honour of Ian Macpherson*. Ed. Alan Deyermond. London: Department of Hispanic Studies, Queen Mary and Westfield College, 1998. 151–71.

McCone, Kim. *Pagan Past and Christian Present in Early Irish Literature*. Maynooth: Maynooth Monographs 3, 1990.

McDermott, Emily A. *Euripides' Medea: The Incarnation of Disorder*. University Park: Pennsylvania State University Press, 1989.

Menéndez Collera, Ana and Victoriano Roncero López, eds. *Nunca fue pena mayor: Estudios de Literatura española en homenaje a Brian Dutton*. Cuenca: Ediciones de la Universidad de Castilla-La Mancha, 1996.

Menéndez Pidal, Ramón. "Cantos románicos andalusíes: Continuadores de una lírica latina vulgar." *Boletin de la Real Academía Española* 31 (1951): 187–270.

Minnesangs Frühling. See Moser and Tervooren.

Mölk, Ulrich, ed. *Romanische Frauenlieder*. Klassische Texte des romanischen Mittelalters in zweisprachigen Ausgaben 28. Munich: Fink, 1989.

——. " 'Frauenlieder' des Duecento im Gewande der Ballade." *Gestaltung-Umgestaltung: Beiträge zur Geschichte der romanischen Literaturen. Festschrift zum sechzigsten Geburtstag von Margot Kruse*. Ed. Bernhard König and Jutta Lietz. Tübingen: Narr, 1990. 245–54.

Moser, Hugo and Helmut Tervooren, eds. *Des Minnesangs Frühling*. 3 vols. Stuttgart: Hirzel, 1977–88. 1: Texte (1988). 2: Editionsprinzipien, Melodien, Handschriften, Erläuterungen (1977). 3.1: Untersuchungen von C. von Kraus (1939, repr. 1981). 3.2: Anmerkungen von K. Lachmann, M. Haupt, Fr. Vogt, C. von Kraus (1950, repr. 1981). Vol. 1, 38th ed. Vols. 2 and 3, 36th ed.

Monroe, James T. *Hispano-Arabic Poetry: A Student Anthology*. Berkeley: University of California Press, 1974.

Morgner, Irmtraud. *The Life and Adventures of Trobadora Beatrice as Chronicled by Her Minstrel Laura*. Trans. Jeanette Clausen. Lincoln: University of Nebraska Press, 2000. From *Leben und Abenteuer der Trobadora Beatriz nach Zeugnissen ihrer Spielfrau Laura*. Darmstadt: Luchterhand, 1976.

Muir, Bernard J., ed. *The Exeter Anthology of Old English Poetry*. 1994. 2nd ed. 2 vols. Exeter: University of Exeter Press, 2000.

Müller, Ulrich, ed. and trans., with Gerlinde Weiss. *Deutsche Gedichte des Mittelalters*. Stuttgart: Reclam, 1993.

Murphy, Gerard, ed. and trans. *Early Irish Lyrics*. Oxford: Clarendon, 1956. Reissued with Foreword by Tomás Ó Cathasaigh. Dublin: Four Courts, 1998.

Mynors, R.A.B., ed. *G. Valerii Catulli Carmina*. Oxford Classical Texts. Oxford: Clarendon, 1958.

——, ed. *P. Vergili Maronis Opera*. Oxford Classical Texts. Oxford: Clarendon, 1969.

Nagy, Joseph. *The Wisdom of the Outlaw*. Berkeley: University of California Press, 1985.

Neckel, Gustav, ed. *Die Lieder des Codex regius nebst verwandten Denkmälern*. 2 vols. Rev. H. Kuhn. Text: 5th ed., Heidelberg: Winter, 1983. Glossary: 3rd ed., 1968.

Nugent, S. Georgia. "The Women of the *Aeneid*: Vanishing Bodies, Lingering Voices." Perkell 251–70.

Nunes, José Joaquim, ed. *Cantigas d'Amigo dos Trovadores Galego-Portugueses*. 3 vols. Coimbra,1928; repr. New York: Kraus, 1971.

Nuzha. See al-Suyuti.

Ó Hógáin, Dáithi. *Fionn Mac Cumhall: Images of a Gaelic Hero*. Dublin: Gill and Macmillan, 1988.

Orlando, S. *Rime dei Memoriali Bolognesi 1279–1300*. Turin: Einandi, 1981.

Otto von Boten lauben. See Kraus.

Paden, William D., ed. "The Poems of the *Trobairitz* Na Castelloza." *Romance Philology* 35 (1981): 158–82.

——, ed. *The Medieval Pastourelle*. 2 vols. New York: Garland, 1987.

——, ed. *The Voice of the Trobairitz*. Philadelphia: University of Philadelphia Press, 1989.

Page, Christopher. *Voices and Instruments of the Middle Ages*. London: Dent, 1987.

Page, Denys L., ed. *Euripides: Medea*. Oxford: Clarendon, 1938, 1961.

——, ed. *Poetae Melici Graeci*. Oxford: Clarendon, 1962.

Palmer, R. Barton, ed. *Chaucer's French Contemporaries: The Poetry/Politics of Self and Tradition*. New York: AMS, 1999 (1992).

Pantelia, Maria. "Theocritus at Sparta." *Hermes* 123 (1995): 76–81.

Panvini, Bruno. *Le Rime della scuola siciliana*. 2 vols. Florence: Olschki, 1962–64.

Paris, Gaston. "Études sur les romans de la Table Ronde: *Lancelot du Lac*." *Romania* 12 (1883): 459–534.

——. "*Les* origines de la poésie lyrique en France." Review of Alfred Jeanroy, *Origines de la poésie lyrique. Journal des savants*, 1891: 674–88 and 729–42; 1892: 155–64 and 407–30. Repr. G. Paris, *Mélanges de littérature française au Moyen Âge*, ed. Mario Roques. Paris: Champion, 1912. 539–615.

Paris, Paulin, ed. *Le Livre du Voir-Dit de Guillaume de Machaut*. Paris: Société des Bibliophiles François, 1875.

Parker, Holt N. "Sulpicia, the *Auctor de Sulpicia*, and the Authorship of 3.9 and 3.11 of the *Corpus Tibullianum*." *Helios* 21 (1994): 39–61.

Parker, L.P.E. *The Songs of Aristophanes*. Oxford: Clarendon, 1997.

Pattison, Walter T. *The Life and Works of the Troubadour Raimbaut d'Orange*. Minneapolis: University of Minnesota Press, 1952.

Pavlock, Barbara. *Eros, Epic, and Imitation*. Ithaca: Cornell University Press, 1990.

Pease, Arthur Stanley, ed. *Publi Vergili Maronis Aeneidos Liber Quartus*. Cambridge, Mass.: Harvard University Press, 1935, 1963.

Perez Priego, Miguel Angel, ed. *Poesía feminina en los cancioneros*. Madrid: Castalia, 1989.

Perkell, Christine, ed. *Reading Vergil's Aeneid: An Interpretive Guide*. Oklahoma: University of Oklahoma Press, 1999.

Pertz, Georg Heinrich, ed. "Karoli magni capitularia." Monumenta Germaniae Historica, Leges 1. Hannover: Societas Aperiendis Fontibus Rerum Germanicarum, 1835. 32–194.

Pillet, Alfred and Henry Carstens. "Bibliographie der Troubadours." *Schriften der Königsberger gelehrten Gesellschaft, Sonderreihe 3*. Halle, 1933; repr. New York: Burt Franklin, 1968.

Piñero Ramírez, Pedro M., ed. *Lírica popular / lírica tradicional: Lecciones en homenaje a Don Emilio García Gómez*. Seville: Universidad de Sevilla, 1998.

Plummer, John F., ed. *Vox Feminae: Studies in Medieval Woman's Song*. Kalamazoo: Medieval Institute Publications, 1981.

Postgate, John Percival. *Tibulli aliorumque carminum libri tres*. 2nd ed. Oxford Classical Texts. Oxford: Clarendon, 1915.

Powell, Anton. *Euripides, Women and Sexuality*. London: Routledge, 1990.

Quinn, Kenneth, ed. *Catullus. The Poems*. London: MacMillan, 1970.

Rasmussen, Ann Marie. "Representing Woman's Desire: Walther's Woman's Stanza in 'Ich hoere in sô vil tugende jehen' (L43,9), 'Under der linden' (L39,11), and 'Frô Welt' (L100,24)." *Women as Protagonists and Poets in the German Middle Ages*. Ed. Albrecht Classen. Göppingen: Kummerle, 1991. 69–85.

——. *Mothers and Daughters in Medieval German Literature*. Syracuse: Syracuse University Press, 1997.

——. "Reason and the Female Voice in Walther von der Vogelweide's Poetry." Klinck and Rasmussen 168–86 and 249–53.

Raynaud. See Spanke.

Reynolds, Margaret. *The Sappho Companion*. London: Vintage, 2001.

Rieger, Angelica, ed. *Trobairitz: Der Beitrag der Frau in der altokzitanischen höfischen Lyrik: Edition des Gesamtkorpus*. Tübingen: Niemeyer, 1991.

Robbins, Rossell Hope, ed. *Secular Lyrics of the XIVth and XVth Centuries*. 2nd ed. Oxford: Clarendon, 1955.

Rosenberg, Samuel, Margaret Switten, and Gérard Le Vot, eds. *Songs of the Troubadours and Trouvères: An Anthology of Poems and Melodies*. New York: Garland, 1998.

——, and Hans Tischler, eds. *Chanter m'estuet: Songs of the Trouvères*. Bloomington: Indiana University Press, 1981.

Roy, Maurice, ed. *Oeuvres poétiques de Christine de Pisan*. 3 vols. Paris: Firmin-Didot, 1886–96. Vol. 1.

Saint-Hilaire, A. Queux de and Gaston Raynaud, eds. *Oeuvres complètes de Eustache Deschamps*. 11 vols. Paris: Firmin-Didot, 1878–1903. Vol. 4 (1884).

Sankovitch, Tilde. "The *Trobairitz*." Gaunt and Kay 113–26.

Sayce, Olive. *The Medieval German Lyric 1150–1300*. Oxford: Clarendon, 1982.

Schotter, Anne Howland. "Woman's Song in Medieval Latin." Plummer 19–33.

Schweikle, Günther. *Walther von der Vogelweide: Liedlyrik. Werke 2*. Stuttgart: Reclam, 1998.

Showerman, Grant, ed. and trans. *Ovid: Heroides and Amores*. Loeb. Cambridge, Mass.: Harvard University Press, 1921.

Sigal, Gale. *Erotic Dawn-Songs of the Middle Ages*. Gainesville: University Press of Florida, 1996.

Skoie, Mathilde. *Reading Sulpicia*. Oxford: Oxford University Press, 2002.

Smith, Kirby Flower, ed. *Elegies of Albius Tibullus*. 1913. Repr. New York: Arno, 1979.

Solá-Solé, Josep M, ed. *Corpus de poesía mozarabe*. Barcelona: Hispam, 1973.

———, ed. and trans. *Las jarchas romances y sus moaxajas*. Madrid: Taurus, 1990.

Spanke, Hans. *G. Raynauds Bibliographie des altfranzösischen Liedes*. Leiden: Brill, 1955.

Spitzer, Leo. "The Mozarabic Lyric and Theodor Frings' Theories." *Comparative Literature* 4 (1952): 1–22.

Stern, Samuel. "Les vers finaux en espagnol dans les muwassahas hispano-hébraïques." *Al-Andalus* 13 (1948): 299–346.

———. *Les chansons mozarabes*. Palermo: Manfredi, 1953. Repr. Oxford: Cassirer, 1964.

Strecker, Karl, ed. *Die Cambridger Lieder / Carmina Cantabrigiensia*. Monumenta Germaniae Historica Scriptores 40. Berlin: Weidmann, 1926.

Sulpicia. See Cornish et al.; Postgate; Smith.

Switten, Margaret et al. *Teaching Medieval Lyric with Modern Technology*. CD-Rom. Mount Holyoke College, 2001.

Taaffe, Lauren K. *Aristophanes and Women*. London: Routledge, 1993.

Taylor, Jane H.M. "Mimesis Meets Artifice: Two Lyrics by Christine de Pizan." *Christine de Pizan 2000: Studies in Christine de Pizan in Honour of Angus J. Kennedy*. Ed. John Campbell and Nadia Margolis. Amsterdam: Rodopi, 2000. 115–22.

Theocritus. See Edmonds; Gow.

Thomson, D.E.S., ed. *Catullus*. Toronto: University of Toronto Press, 1997.

Ussher, R.G., ed. *Aristophanes: Ecclesiazusae*. Oxford: Oxford University Press, 1973.

van den Boogaard, Nico H.J., ed. *Rondeaux et refrains. Du XIIe siècle au début du XIVe*. Paris: Klincksieck, 1969.

van der Werf, Hendrik. *The Chansons of the Troubadours and Trouvères*. Utrecht: Oosthoek, 1972.

Varty, Kenneth, ed. *Christine de Pisan's Ballades, Rondeaux, and Virelais: An Anthology*. Leicester: Leicester University Press, 1965.

Verducci, Florence. *Ovid's Toyshop of the Heart: Epistulae Heroidum*. Princeton: Princeton University Press, 1985.

Voigt, Eva-Maria, ed. *Sappho et Alcaeus*. Amsterdam: Polak and van Gennep, 1971.

Vollmann, Benedikt Konrad, ed. and trans. *Carmina Burana*. Frankfurt: Deutscher Klassiker Verlag, 1987.

Walther von der Vogelweide. See Cormeau; Schweikle.

Whetnall, Jane. "Lírica Feminina in the Early Manuscript Cancioneros." *What's Past is Prologue: A Collection of Essays in Honour of L.J. Woodward*. Ed. Salvador Bacarisse et al. Edinburgh: Scottish Academic Press, 1984. 138–50 and 171–75.

Wiessner, Edmund, ed. *Die Lieder Neidharts*. Continued Hanns Fischer. From the 1858 edition of Moritz Haupt, rev. E. Wiessner, 1923. 4th ed., rev. Paul Sappler. Tübingen: Niemeyer, 1984.

Wilhelm, James J. *Lyrics of the Middle Ages: An Anthology*. New York: Garland, 1990.

Williamson, Margaret. *Sappho's Immortal Daughters*. Cambridge, Mass.: Harvard University Press, 1995.

Zink, Michel. *Les chansons de toile*. Paris: Champion, 1977.

Ziolkowski, Jan M., ed. and trans. *The Cambridge Songs (Carmina Cantabrigiensia)*. New York: Garland, 1994. Repr. Tempe, Arizona: Medieval & Renaissance Texts and Studies, 1998.

Zumthor, Paul. *Essai de poétique médiéval*. Paris: Seuil, 1972.

INDEX

The listings cover primary and secondary authors and works, technical terms, and also major concepts, themes, and motifs. Medieval authors are referred to by first name unless better known by last. Except where there is a well-known title, poems are cited by first line. Modern works of criticism and scholarship are cited by author or editor, not by title. Translations are included for headwords in languages that may be unfamiliar. This Index was compiled with the assistance of Allison Comeau.